Puzzles of Reference

CONTEMPORARY INTRODUCTIONS TO
PHILOSOPHY OF LANGUAGE

Herman Cappelen and Josh Dever

Context and Communication

Puzzles of Reference

Further titles in preparation

CONTEMPORARY INTRODUCTIONS TO
PHILOSOPHY OF LANGUAGE

Puzzles of Reference

Herman Cappelen and Josh Dever

OXFORD
UNIVERSITY PRESS

OXFORD

UNIVERSITY PRESS

Great Clarendon Street, Oxford, OX2 6DP,
United Kingdom

Oxford University Press is a department of the University of Oxford.
It furthers the University's objective of excellence in research, scholarship,
and education by publishing worldwide. Oxford is a registered trade mark of
Oxford University Press in the UK and in certain other countries

© Herman Cappelen and Josh Dever 2018

The moral rights of the authors have been asserted

First Edition published in 2018
Impression: 1

Published in the United States of America by Oxford University Press
198 Madison Avenue, New York, NY 10016, United States of America

British Library Cataloguing in Publication Data
Data available

Library of Congress Control Number: 2017963139

ISBN 978-0-19-879983-2 (hbk.)
      978-0-19-879984-9 (pbk.)

Printed and bound by
CPI Group (UK) Ltd, Croydon, CR0 4YY

CONTEMPORARY INTRODUCTIONS TO
PHILOSOPHY OF LANGUAGE

Puzzles of Reference

Herman Cappelen and Josh Dever

OXFORD
UNIVERSITY PRESS

OXFORD
UNIVERSITY PRESS

Great Clarendon Street, Oxford, OX2 6DP,
United Kingdom

Oxford University Press is a department of the University of Oxford.
It furthers the University's objective of excellence in research, scholarship,
and education by publishing worldwide. Oxford is a registered trade mark of
Oxford University Press in the UK and in certain other countries

First Edition published in 2018
Impression: 1

Published in the United States of America by Oxford University Press
198 Madison Avenue, New York, NY 10016, United States of America

British Library Cataloguing in Publication Data
Data available

Library of Congress Control Number: 2017963139

ISBN 978-0-19-879983-2 (hbk.)
      978-0-19-879984-9 (pbk.)

Printed and bound by
CPI Group (UK) Ltd, Croydon, CR0 4YY

Contents

Detailed Contents

Preface

One of the great breakthroughs in twentieth-century philosophy happened in the early 1970s. Work by Saul Kripke, Ruth Barcan Marcus, Hilary Putnam, and Tyler Burge changed the way we think about language, communication, and thought, as well as the connections between these three areas. The views developed by these authors have had immense influence on all areas of philosophy and on philosophy of language in particular. This book takes this body of work as a starting point and looks at what has happened in the roughly forty years since. To make things simple, we use as our baseline the view Kripke outlines in his *Naming and Necessity* (1980), and then consider a number of puzzles that arise if you endorse his view. We sketch various solutions to those puzzles. In working through these puzzles, the reader will be introduced to some of the important work done on reference during the last forty years.

The 'some' part of the previous sentence is important. This book is *not* meant to be a comprehensive guide to work on reference. The amount of work done by philosophers and linguists on this topic is immense. To cover it all, we would have had to write an extremely long and unwieldy book. So we don't aspire to comprehensiveness. Instead, we have picked some *topics*, *views*, and *arguments* that we think are *important, interesting*, and *instructive*. Our hope is that a reader who has understood and engaged with this selection of material will be in a good position to start engaging with much of the work we don't cover in this book.

The book is written to be accessible to someone with no prior knowledge of the material.[1] It can be used as part of a philosophy of language course or as part of a general introduction to philosophy.

We initially set out hoping to write a single book that could serve as an introduction to philosophy of language. We gave up. We now think that goal is too ambitious for any one book. There is simply too much interesting work that has been done in this field over the last 100 years

---

[1] That said, we recommend that it be read in conjunction with Kripke's *Naming and Necessity*.

to cover it all (or even most of it) in a single book. A book that tried to do that would inevitably be so superficial that it would fail to convey to the readers how rich, complex, and important these topics are. To do justice to the field, we have set out to write a series of introductions to philosophy of language, each one covering an important topic, and each one of which would be a way into the field as a whole. These books aim to provide systematic introductions to important questions, data, theories, and arguments. Those looking for a history of the discipline should look elsewhere.

1

Introduction to Kripkeanism and the Rejection of Fregeanism

Killing Bill is no small undertaking. You need to figure out who Bill is, and where Bill is. Then you have to get yourself close enough to Bill to do some killing—within gunshot range, if you're planning to shoot him, or within arm's reach, if you prefer hand-to-hand combat. Then you have to have a very special set of skills, that let you carry out the actual killing. If you were a magician, you could kill Bill with a word from a distance, without concern for distance or difficulty, without knowing or caring where Bill was at the time. But we aren't magicians, so killing involves planning, coordination, and effort.

It's just as well that killing is hard in this way, but it's not just killing that poses these difficulties. If you want to administer CPR to Bill, you again need to know who Bill is, and get yourself where he is, and have the right skills. If you can't tell Bill from Adam, you're not going to have any luck administering CPR to Bill. Similarly if Bill is in Athens and you are in Oslo. And if you don't know how to administer CPR, then even if Bill is right in front of you, your efforts will fail. This is the same for many of our ways of interacting with objects. If you want to shake Bill's hand, or beat Bill at chess, or tie Bill's shoelaces, you need to find Bill, get yourself where he is, and deploy the right causal capacities.

But referring is different. If you want to refer to Bill, it doesn't matter where he is. Whether Bill is in Athens or Oslo, underground or on the moon, or in a far distant galaxy, he can be referred to with a word. It doesn't matter whether Bill is alive or dead, around now or in the distant past or distant future. Even if you couldn't pick Bill out of a crowd, you can still effortlessly refer to him. And it is indeed effortless—no special training or skills are needed to refer to Bill; no one tries but fails. With reference, we *are* the magicians. The word 'Bill' is a magic spell that lets us do this one specific thing to Bill (refer to him) without fail and without regard to causal obstacles.

Philosophers of language have been very interested in how this trick is turned. Here are two important models they have developed for how it is done:

- **The Causal-Communicative Model:** Suppose long ago Bill's enemy Alex put Bill on the edge of a cliff and tied a rope around his waist. From then on everywhere Alex went, he unraveled the rope behind him. Any time Alex met anyone, when he talked about Bill to someone who didn't know Bill, he tied a new rope onto his rope, and gave it to the person he met. They, in turn, unwound the new rope behind them, and added new connected ropes when they spoke about Bill to people who hadn't heard of him. You've come into possession of a rope, connected through a series of other ropes to Alex's rope, and if you give it a tug. Bill will be yanked off the cliff and will fall to his death. You don't need to get near Bill or keep track of where he is—the practice of passing on ropes has automatically connected you to a system that lets you effortlessly affect Bill from a distance.

  On this model, the stock of names in language is in some respects like a collection of 'ropes' we have all been accumulating throughout our lives. They are of course not real ropes, but there's an important analogy: the 'rope' is first tied to someone (the referent of the name) when someone else gives them that name ('baptizes' them with it, in Kripke's terminology). New connected 'ropes' are added when speakers pass the name on to new language users.

  Of course, there are no actual ropes involved—talk of 'ropes' is a metaphor. What we have is a *causal chain* of name uses that can be traced from us back to the original bearer of the name. We can think of the causal chain of uses as a linking of invisible ropes. If a person uses a name, they got it from someone. And that person got it from someone, and so on, until we come to a baptism. There's thus a chain of users that maintains a causal connection between any link in the chain and the person the chain winds up at. You are causally connected to Bill because you are a link in the chain ending with Bill, and that's how you manage to refer to Bill using 'Bill'. If a name refers to whatever is at the origin of the causal chain, then we have an explanation for how we can effortlessly and 'magically' refer to it.

• **The Descriptive Model:** Suppose you want to kill Bill but don't know where he is. Fortunately, you do have on hand a specially designed virus fatal to all humans. So now there's an easy way to kill Bill: release the virus and wait. You don't know where Bill is, but you know that he's in the target audience for the designer virus, so eventually it will kill him. You don't need to keep specific track of Bill, because you have a method targeted at a whole *kind*, and you know Bill is of that kind.

Of course, this is a rather indiscriminate way of killing Bill—it's rather hard on all the non-Bill humans. But suppose you know that Bill is a redhead, and you have another designer virus that targets specifically redheads. You can use that virus to kill Bill, and with less collateral damage. The more you know about Bill, the more specifically you can target him (so long as you've got a sufficient stock of viruses, or have some genetic engineering skills yourself). In the limiting case, suppose you know of some feature Bill has that *no one else* has. Perhaps Bill is the only redheaded San Francisco Giants fan who owns a penguin. So release your 'death to all redheaded penguin-owning Giants fans' virus, and Bill, wherever he is, dies.

According to this model, your stock of names works like a collection of 'viruses' you have accumulated or built. Of course, there are no actual viruses involved—that's a metaphor. The idea is that we 'target' an individual for reference by knowing enough about them to pick a feature that they and *only* they have. We then use the descriptive resources of the language to build that feature—these are our viruses. If we want to refer to Aristotle, we use the fact that Aristotle is the unique last great philosopher of antiquity, and then take the words 'last great philosopher of antiquity' that express that feature, and introduce a name 'Aristotle' that also expresses that feature.

1.1 The Descriptive Model

To understand the role of language in connecting us to things in the world, we need to understand how particular bits of language come to be about particular things. Consideration of examples like 'the largest country in South America' suggests a certain model of the word-to-world connection:

The Descriptive Model: An expression connects to a thing in the world by *describing* that thing. 'The largest country in South America', for example, is about Brazil because the expression specifies a feature (being the largest country in a specific continent), and then comes to be about whatever object has that feature.

The Descriptive Model offers an appealing picture, because it gives a simple and natural explanation for how the word-to-world connection can allow language to connect us to objects distant in space and time, without our knowing much about those objects. We can, on this picture, pick out Brazil with language even if it is half a world away, because we can pick out *whatever* has the feature *largest country in South America*, and Brazil in fact has that feature.

But if we endorse the Descriptive Model, we have to say something about how the name 'Brazil' picks out what it does, as well as how the phrase 'the largest country in South America' does. 'Brazil', unlike 'the largest country in South America', doesn't obviously come with a way of describing an object. But the standard line on incorporating names into the Descriptive Model, deriving from the work of the German mathematician and philosopher Gottlob Frege, says that there is a non-obvious description. A *Fregean* theory of names takes each name to be associated with a property (or a cluster of properties) giving the meaning of the name. The associated properties aren't *manifestly presented* by the form of the language, as they are in a phrase like 'the largest country in South America'. Rather, the associated properties are conventionally linked to the name, and the association is something that speakers must learn when learning the name. But once the properties are associated, we can now run the Descriptive Model. Suppose 'Brazil' is linked to the properties:

- largest country in South America;
- location of the world's largest Carnival celebration;
- country that has won the most World Cup titles in soccer.

Then since the country Brazil in fact has those properties, the name 'Brazil' picks out that country.

1.2 *Naming and Necessity*

For much of the twentieth century, the Fregean theory of names was the dominant philosophical view. However, this application of the Descriptive Model to the meaning of names came under extensive and devastating criticism in Saul Kripke's seminal book *Naming and Necessity*. *Naming and Necessity*, a transcript of three lectures Kripke gave at Princeton in 1970 and later published in 1980, is one of the most influential works of twentieth-century philosophy. It revolutionized the philosophy of language and philosophy more generally. Our central goal in this book is to examine where the discussion of *reference* has gone in the post-Kripkean philosophical literature—how various work has responded to Kripke, elaborated on Kripke, or proposed alternatives to Kripke. We recommend that readers read *Naming and Necessity* before reading this book, but in this chapter we will lay out some central points Kripke makes in those lectures, focusing on those points that will play a central role in our subsequent discussions.

Three elements of *Naming and Necessity* are important in what follows:

i. Kripke divorces names (and natural kind terms) from the Descriptive Model, proposing a new account that distinguishes between the way names (such as 'Bill') stand for their bearers and the way descriptive terms (such as 'the president') stand for the object that the description fits.
ii. Kripke couples his positive account of reference with extensive criticisms of the Fregean incorporation of names into the Descriptive Model. Many philosophers take Kripke's criticisms to refute the Fregean view of names.
iii. Finally, Kripke provides reasons for thinking that the theory of reference is philosophically rich and important, showing its wide-reaching implications for many areas of philosophy.

In what follows, we present each of these elements in turn.

1.3 The Causal-Communicative Model

The core of the positive theory in *Naming and Necessity* is that names refer non-descriptively. Names pick out things in the world. But they don't describe those things; they simply refer to them. (Note that in saying this we are using 'refer' in a slightly technical way—just what we mean will get clearer along the way.) Of course, the rejection of the Descriptive Model for names isn't yet a positive view. If names don't pick things out descriptively, we need some other account of how it is that names refer to what they refer to. Why does 'Brazil' refer to Brazil, if it doesn't do so by being associated with some features that Brazil has?

Kripke's answer is that names refer by virtue of *causal-communicative chains* as on the rope metaphor at the start of the chapter. The central idea is simple, pre-theoretically plausible, and easy to understand. Kripke says:

Someone, let's say, a baby, is born; his parents call him by a certain name. They talk about him to their friends. Other people meet him. Through various sorts of talk the name is spread from link to link as if by a chain. A speaker who is on the far end of this chain, who has heard about, say Richard Feynman, in the market place or elsewhere, may be referring to Richard Feynman even though he can't remember from whom he first heard of Feynman or from whom he ever heard of Feynman. He knows that Feynman is a famous physicist. A certain passage of communication reaching ultimately to the man himself does reach the speaker. He then is referring to Feynman even though he can't identify him uniquely.   (Kripke 1980: 91)

Kripke gives another, slightly more elaborate version of this picture:

A rough statement of a theory might be the following: An initial 'baptism' takes place. Here the object may be named by ostension [. . .]. When the name is 'passed from link to link', the receiver of the name must, I think, intend when he learns it to use it with the same reference as the man from whom he heard it. If I hear the name 'Napoleon' and decide it would be a nice name for my pet aardvark, I do not satisfy this condition.   (Kripke 1980: 96)

Kripke's answer to the question of how names refer has three components:

i. There is first an event by which a term is introduced as the name of an object. This can happen by a baptism (call this baby 'Nora') or by a description (call the church to be built on this spot 'Notre Dame').

ii. Then names are spread around a linguistic community—passed from one person to another. First just a few people know about the use of 'Nora', then others hear the word 'Nora' used in that way, and they can then pass it along, as if in a chain.

iii. Finally, there is the overall account of how a particular use of a name refers: it refers to the person at the beginning of the chain that the speaker is a part of. So you can refer to Plato using the word 'Plato' because you're part of a chain of communication that reaches back to the man.

On this view, what we refer to by a name is determined in part by our speech community and in part by its linguistic history. It is not determined by the speaker in isolation from her community and its linguistic history. In that sense Kripke's theory is *anti-individualistic*—reference determination is a communal process and not within the control of individual speakers.

1.4 Names and Quantified Noun Phrases

Kripke's Causal-Communicative Model of names doesn't require a complete rejection of the Descriptive Model, but just a limitation of its scope. On Kripke's view, there are many linguistic expressions whose connection to the world *is* correctly characterized by the Descriptive Model. The paradigm Descriptive Model expressions are *quantified noun phrases*, such as:

Every philosopher in Texas
Some philosopher in Texas   is happy.
No philosopher in Texas
The philosopher in Texas

In each of these sentences, the property expressed by the noun phrase *philosopher in Texas* connects the language to a certain portion of the world—namely, everything having that property. The quantificational terms 'every'/'some'/'no'/'the' then place a requirement on how many things in that portion of the world are happy. Kripke agrees that quantified noun phrases fall under the Descriptive Model—he just rejects the view that names should be assimilated to quantified noun phrases in the way that the Fregean view does.

Consider some ways in which the behavior of names, as characterized by Kripke's Causal-Communicative Model, differs from the behavior of quantified noun phrases, as characterized by the Descriptive Model.

1.4.1 Transparent Characterization

Quantified noun phrases: When a speaker picks out Brazil using the expression 'the largest country in South America', it is transparent to the speaker that the object they are picking out has the property of being the largest country in South America. To say that it is transparent to the speaker is to say that the speaker is always in a position to know that *the largest country in South America is the largest country in South America*. That bit of knowledge is available a priori: it can be known without any evidence, and the speaker doesn't need to do any checking of the world (consulting an atlas, measuring Brazil) to learn it.[1]

Names: When a speaker picks out Brazil with 'Brazil', it is *not* transparent to the speaker that the object they are picking out has the property of being the largest country in South America. In fact, *no* property of Brazil is guaranteed to be transparent to the speaker when they pick out Brazil with the name 'Brazil'. This fact, on Kripke's view, is part of what makes names so useful. Sometimes we want to refer to something while knowing little or nothing about it. If someone has heard the name 'Barack Obama', but somehow doesn't know that Obama was the president in 2012, he is still in a position to pick out Obama using the name 'Barack Obama', but wouldn't know to pick him out using the phrase 'the president'.

1.4.2 Referential Stability

Quantified noun phrases: Objects change their properties over time. In 2012, Barack Obama was the president, but in 2018, he was not. So 'the president' is an unstable device for picking out Obama: it worked in 2012, but in 2018 it no longer worked. This instability is characteristic of quantified noun phrases governed by the Descriptive Model. Since these phrases pick objects out by property-matching, when objects' properties change, so do the property-matching facts. That's a good feature sometimes (when we want to keep picking out whoever is president, without worrying about who it is at any given time), but a bad feature other times (when we want to track the same individual, but can't keep track of that individual's changing features).

Names: Names, on Kripke's account, are stable referential devices. Because they aren't governed by the Descriptive Model, they don't pick out objects by way of their features. So when Obama shifts from being

---

[1] Distracting subtlety: there might not be a largest country in South America. South America could be divided into equal-sized countries, or (like Antarctica) not be divided into countries at all. Had things been this way, 'the largest country in South America is the largest country in South America' wouldn't have been true. So some worldly evidence is needed to know this claim. To make things genuinely a priori, we should use something more like 'if there is a largest country in South America, then the largest country in South America is the largest country in South America'. Notice that 'if there is a largest country in South America, then Brazil is the largest country in South America' is not trivial in the same way.

president to not being president, nothing changes about the ability of the name 'Barack Obama' to pick him out. Names, on this view, are useful just where quantified noun phrases are not—they are perfect when we want to keep track of some individual without keeping track of that individual's changing features.

1.4.3 Emptiness and Superfluity

Quantified noun phrases: *Largest country in South America* is, conveniently, the kind of property that's guaranteed to be had by one and only one object at a time. So 'the largest country in South America' is guaranteed to pick out a unique object (as long as South America exists). But not every property is like this. Some properties, like *being a unicorn*, aren't had by anything, while other properties, like *being a philosopher*, are had by many objects. As a result, on the Descriptive Model, picking out a single object fits naturally into a continuum from picking out no objects to picking out many objects. With the right choice of quantifier, we can make claims that exploit properties of all these types:

1. There have been no female US presidents (*female US president* is a property had by no objects).

2. The senior senator from Wyoming introduced the bill (*senior senator from Wyoming* is a property had by one object).

3. Every baseball player practices frequently (*baseball player* is a property had by many objects).

Names: If names are not governed by the Descriptive Model, then we can't use variation in the associated property to get cases of names referring to nothing or to many things. So the Causal-Communicative Model doesn't give any obvious or natural account of names of those sorts. The Causal-Communicative Model is friendly to a view on which each name corresponds to one thing (the thing at the origin of the causal-communicative chain). Arguably, that is the right thing to say about names (although see the chapters on predicativism (Chapter 7) and plural reference (Chapter 8) for superfluity, and the chapter on fictional names (Chapter 3) for emptiness).

1.4.4 Rigidity

Quantified noun phrases: The properties used in determining what a quantified noun phrase picks out can interact with other parts of the sentence.[2] For example, these properties can interact with tense and specifications of time. For someone speaking in 2012, the phrase 'the president' normally picks out Barack Obama. Consider an utterance in 2012 of:

4.   The president is a Cubs fan.

It is Barack Obama who must be a Cubs fan for this utterance to be true (not George Bush or George Washington). Contrast this with a tensed claim like:

5.   In 1972, the president went to China.

Here, 'the president' doesn't pick out Barack Obama (the *current* (at the time of utterance) possessor of the property), but rather picks out Richard Nixon (a *former* possessor of the property). We get the same effect with specifications of alternative possibilities:

6.   If Mitt Romney had won the 2012 presidential election, the president would have been a Republican.

Again, in these sentences 'the president' doesn't pick out Barack Obama (the *actual* (at the time of utterance) possessor of the property), but rather picks out Mitt Romney (the *possible* possessor of the property).[3] Quantified noun phrases are thus, in the terminology introduced by Kripke, not temporally or modally rigid, because they do not persist in picking out the same objects when used in sentences that are about other times and other possibilities.

Names: On the Causal-Communicative Model, since the referent of a name is fixed by the actual facts of the origin of the causal-communicative chain, it doesn't matter where the name occurs in a sentence. Even in temporally or modally shifting contexts, names continue to refer in the same way. They are both temporally and modally rigid. Thus the

---

[2] See Chapter 4 of Cappelen and Dever (2016) for an introduction to rigidity.

[3] Distracting subtlety: 'In 1972, the president went to China' can in fact also be used to make a claim about Barack Obama. The sentence is ambiguous between a reading on which it's about *the president in 1972* and a reading on which it's about *the current president* (and what he was doing in his pre-presidential days). The first disambiguation is much more natural, but the second is also available. Similarly, for 'If Mitt Romney had won the 2012 presidential election, the president would have been a Republican'—this sentence can somewhat unnaturally be used to say that if Romney had won, Obama would have joined the Republicans. Importantly, names (unlike descriptions) don't produce these ambiguities.

Causal-Communicative Model predicts that 'Barack Obama' continues to refer to Barack Obama in the following (false) utterances:[4]

7.   In 1972, Barack Obama went to China.

8.   If Mitt Romney had won the 2012 presidential election, Barack Obama would have been a Republican.

Terms which are both temporally and modally rigid are often called *rigid designators*, so called because they pick out (or designate) the same thing at different times and worlds.

Kripke's view, then, differs from the simple Descriptive Model in not offering a *unified* account of the word-to-world connection. Kripke's view treats *descriptive specification*, of the sort used by quantified noun phrases, as a fundamentally different linguistic phenomenon from *reference*, of the sort used by names. Because Kripke's view allows two different forms of word-to-world connection, it suggests the following question:

The Boundary Question: Which linguistic expressions connect to the world descriptively, and which connect referentially via causal-communicative chains? There are various expressions that pick out objects, such as pronouns (*she, we*), dates (*December 7, 1941*), family names (*the Kennedys*), plural nouns (*tigers*), abstract nouns (*redness*), and many others, that are neither quantified noun phrases nor proper names. A full continuation of the Kripkean project requires determining where, among these many expressions, the boundary between description and reference lies.

This question will be important throughout, for example when we consider fictional names in Chapter 3 and predicativism in Chapter 7.

1.5 The Refutation of Fregeanism

On the Fregean view of names, names are governed by the Descriptive Model, and act like quantified noun phrases. On the Kripkean view, names are fundamentally different from quantified noun phrases, in the ways discussed above. One source of the lasting influence of *Naming and Necessity* is Kripke's powerful arguments against the Fregean view. The heart of these arguments is the presentation of a number of cases that

---

[4] Made in 2012 or at any other time.

make it clear that names *do not* behave in the same way that quantified noun phrases do. Consider three cases:

i. **Descriptive Underdetermination Cases:** Suppose Alex knows very little about Murray Gell-Mann, other than that he is a physicist. Nevertheless, Alex can refer to Gell-Mann using the name 'Gell-Mann'. But no property that Alex could associate with the name 'Gell-Mann' would be sufficient to allow the name to pick out Gell-Mann via the Descriptive Model. Thus the Fregean theory of names, which says that names are governed by the Descriptive Method, must be wrong. With some creativity, we can produce similar cases in which *no one* knows enough about the referent of a name to pick it out descriptively.

ii. **Misidentification Cases:** Suppose that Alex *thinks* she knows a great deal about Kurt Gödel, but many of her beliefs are incorrect. She thinks that Gödel proved the incompleteness of arithmetic, but in fact he did not. An unknown logician Schmidt did, and Gödel stole the work from him. Her association of the property *proved the incompleteness of arithmetic* with the name 'Gödel' does not, as the Fregean model predicts, make it the case that 'Gödel' refers to Schmidt. Moreover, Alex can conceive of this possibility, and so even if the Gödel–Schmidt story isn't true, she can't know a priori that Gödel proved the incompleteness of arithmetic.

iii. **Modal Cases:** Suppose Aristotle is the last great philosopher of antiquity, and Alex knows this. Even in such a case, the Fregean theory doesn't capture the behavior of names. That's because, as Kripke's view predicts and the Fregean view does not, names are *rigid*. Alex can truthfully say:

9.   If Aristotle had gone into medicine instead of philosophy, Plato would have been the last great philosopher of antiquity.

But she cannot truthfully say:

10.   If Aristotle had gone into medicine instead of philosophy, Plato would have been Aristotle.

Kripke's considerations have persuaded many philosophers that the Fregean view of names is incorrect. However, ways of resisting the Kripkean arguments continue to be explored, and a number of important new objections to Kripke's positive Causal-Communicative Model have been advanced. Another question about reference that has been prominent in the post-Kripkean literature is thus:

The Kripke-versus-Frege Question: Which account of names is correct: Kripke's or Frege's? Can the Fregean remain within the Descriptive Model while still accounting for the rigidity of names and the possibility of underdescription and misidentification cases? Does the Kripkean account prove vulnerable to counter-attacks from Fregeans?

Again, this question will be of importance in several places in what follows, notably in Chapters 2 and 3.

1.6 Kripke on Descriptive Names

Despite his endorsement of the Causal-Communicative Model, Kripke agrees that there are names in which descriptive properties play an important role. He discusses two such cases in *Naming and Necessity*:

Jack the Ripper: 'Another case, if you want to call this a name, might be when the police in London use the name "Jack" or "Jack the Ripper" to refer to the man, whoever he is, who committed all these murders (or at least most of them). Then they are giving the reference of the name by a description.'   (1980: 79–80)

Neptune: 'An even better case of determining the reference of a name by description, as opposed to ostension, is the discovery of the planet Neptune. Neptune was hypothesized *as* the planet which caused such and such discrepancies in the orbits of certain other planets. If Leverrier indeed gave the name "Neptune" to the planet before it was ever seen, then he fixed the reference of "Neptune" by means of the description just mentioned. At that time he was unable to see the planet even through a telescope.'   (1980: 79, footnote 33)

Kripke's thought is that the names 'Jack the Ripper' and 'Neptune' weren't introduced by first *encountering* an object and *naming* it, and then passing the name along. Rather, there was an unknown object that we wanted to talk about but hadn't encountered (the person committing various murders in London; the planet causing various irregularities in the orbit of Uranus), and we introduced a name for that object by using a *description* which is associated with that object.

But even in these cases Kripke rejects the Fregean use of the Descriptive Model. Importantly, these descriptively introduced names are still rigid. Jack the Ripper may be the person (whoever he is) who committed the murders, but Jack didn't *have* to commit the murders. (It would be absurd, for example, for him to defend himself in court by saying he had no choice but to murder, since it was metaphysically necessitated by his name.) Even when a name is introduced by description, the description doesn't 'travel with the name'—later users of the name can get into the naming practice without having any idea what the introducing description was. If, as Fregeans claim, the description gave the meaning of the name, we would have to say (incorrectly) that these later users didn't understand the name. The Kripkean view doesn't require this.

Kripke thus distinguishes between descriptive properties *giving the meaning of a name* and descriptive properties *fixing the referent of a name*. The Fregean view gives properties the first role, but on Kripke's view properties only (and only sometimes) play the second role. Another important question about reference is introduced here. The Kripkean and the Fregean agree that the property *committing the murders in London* plays an important role in the name 'Jack the Ripper', and both agree that the specific person Montague Druitt (if he in fact committed the murders) also plays an important role in the name. But the Kripkean and the Fregean would describe these roles differently. According to Kripke, the description is not part of the meaning of the name (i.e. the semantics of the name), but is part of the story about *how* the name gets the meaning it has (i.e. the *metasemantics* of the name). The referent Druitt then gives the meaning of the name. According to the Fregean, the property gives the meaning of the name, and the specific referent Druitt is not a *directly* linguistic fact, but is a worldly consequence of the linguistic facts.

Theoretical Explanations 1: *Semantics and Metasemantics*

In what follows we will appeal to the difference between a *semantic* theory and a *metasemantic* theory. A metasemantic theory tells us something about how the words of our language end up having the meanings they have. Some geometrical patterns (e.g. those you are reading now) have a meaning. Some have no meaning at all (e.g. :)**))___—**). A metasemantic theory aims to explain the difference. A semantic theory, on the other hand, starts from the fact that our expressions have certain meanings, and then tries to explain how these meanings combine to generate more complex meanings (how, for example, do we get from the meanings of 'Sam', 'kissed', and 'Alex', to the meaning of the sentence: 'Sam kissed Alex'?)

The reader might wonder whether we've got an actual dispute here. After all, as noted, both agree the property *committing the murders in London* is important and the person Druitt is important. Does it matter that for one the property is part of the 'meaning' while for the other it's 'meta-semantic'? Well, this turns on what theoretical role in our overall theory of communication we want notions like meaning and metasemantics to play. We may thus pose another question:

The Theoretical Role Question: Suppose, with Kripke, we identify one specific linguistic feature as the feature of *reference*, and distinguish it from other linguistic features such as *picking out an object descriptively*. It then becomes important to be clear on the theoretical role of each of these—does the distinction play an important theoretical role?

The next section starts to answer this question, which will further be addressed throughout this book. In Chapter 10 we end the book with some further reflections on the Theoretical Role Question.

1.7 Some Philosophical Ramifications of *Naming and Necessity*

Naming and Necessity didn't just introduce a new theory of names. It argued that this new theory of names has a number of important and wide-ranging philosophical consequences. For the most part in this book we'll be attending directly to questions about the post-Kripkean theory of reference and not on the further Kripkean philosophical arguments based on that theory, but we will quickly set out some of the central arguments here. We do this in order both to keep firmly in mind that we are not just considering narrow issues in the theory of language, but questions that will reverberate across many areas of philosophy, and so that we can from time to time mention bits of the subsequent history of that reverberation.

1.7.1 A Prioricity and Necessity

Before *Naming and Necessity*, there was a general assumption that the two categories of the a priori *knowable* and the *necessary* coincided: all necessary truths are a priori, and all a priori truths are necessary. *Naming and Necessity* made it clear that the categories are distinct, and neither subsumes the other. We can have contingent truths that are a priori and we can have necessary truths that are a posteriori.

Contingent A Priori: Our earlier discussion of descriptive names shows that there can be a priori claims that are contingent, rather than necessary. For original users of the descriptively introduced name 'Jack the Ripper', it is a priori that Jack committed the murders. But, as already noted, it wasn't *necessary* that Jack commit the murders. Jack, whoever he in fact was, could have lived a peaceful and murder-free life.

Necessary A Posteriori: Here is something you might not know: Marilyn Monroe is Norma Jeane Mortenson. Norma Jeane was her birth name and Marilyn her stage name. Not everyone knows that—you have to do some research to figure it out (you certainly don't know it just by being in a position to use the name: there could easily have been someone who knew her as Norma Jeane as a baby and had no idea that the famous actress she knows as Marilyn is identical to the baby she knew as Norma Jeane). But since the identity claim is true it is true *necessarily*. Here is why: both names are rigid designators. They refer to the same thing in every world. In this world they refer to the same person, and so in every world they refer to that person. So there is no possibility in which Norma Jeane isn't Marilyn. More generally, if A and B are proper names, then if A=B, it is necessary that A=B. But, as mentioned above, this necessary truth requires investigation to discover: so it is necessary *and yet* a posteriori.

Kripke extended his view of identity claims to the claims of natural science. According to him, natural kind terms like 'water', 'gold', and 'heat' are also referring expressions. They refer to natural kinds. Now scientists discover lots of identity claims. They have discovered that water is H_2O, that the planet Hesperus is the same planet as Phosphorus (Venus), and so on. These are identity claims. The terms 'water', 'H_2O', 'Hesperus', and 'Phosphorus' are referring expressions and so rigid designators. According to Kripke's view, these scientific truths are also part of the necessary a posteriori.

1.7.2 The Argument for Dualism

Kripke thinks he can use his theory of names to show that no physical state can be identical to a mental state, i.e. to show that the mental isn't identical to the physical. If this is true, it's a big deal, meaning that his theory of reference shows that physicalism is false. Here is the argument in summary form:

The physicalist thinks that a mental state—say, a pain or a thought—is identical to some physical state. Give both of those states a name: let the mental state be called A and the physical state be called B. The physicalist claims that A=B. Now, we know that A and B are rigid designators and that identity claims between rigid designators are necessary truths (if true at all). So it would have to be a necessary truth that A=B. But that's not true. It is possible, says Kripke, for the physical state to exist without the pain existing (if B is a brain state, it is possible for that brain state to exist without the person's pain existing). If the physicalist were to insist on the identity claim, she would have to accept that a pain, i.e. A, could have existed without being a pain. That, says Kripke, is unacceptable: being a pain is a necessary property of a pain (nothing can be A unless it is a pain).

This is but the briefest of introductions to what is one of the most controversial arguments in twentieth-century philosophy. One way to summarize many philosophers' reaction to Kripke's argument is to look at the cover of an influential book by Nathan Salmon on this topic. The cover of *Reference and Essence* (2005) shows a rabbit being pulled out of a hat. That, to many, was the reaction to the argument: it seems like magic that we can discover important facts about the connection between mind and body by thinking about reference and rigid designation. That said, the argument is still massively influential (it is, for example, at the core of David Chalmers' work on consciousness (Chalmers 1996)).

1.7.3 Necessity of Origin

Kripke also claims that he can use his view to prove that if a material object, say, a table, has its origin in a certain hunk of matter, some piece of wood, then nothing could be that table that did not originate in that piece of wood. Call this thesis the Essentiality of Origin Thesis. Here is Kripke's argument:

A principle suggested by these examples is: *If a material object has its origin from a certain hunk of matter, it could not have had its origin in any other matter* [...] in a large class of cases the principle is perhaps susceptible of something like proof, using the principle of the necessity of identity for particulars. Let 'B' be a name (rigid designator) of a table, let 'A' name the piece of wood from which it actually came. Let 'C' name another piece of wood. Then suppose B were made from A, as in the actual world, but also another table D were simultaneously made from C. (We assume that there is no relation between A and C which makes the possibility of making a table from one dependent on the possibility of making a table from the other.) Now in this situation B ≠ D; hence, even if D were made by itself, and no table were made from A, D would not be B.   (Kripke 1980: 114, footnote 56)

Again, the thesis of the rigidity of names (and the claim that identities of the form A=B are necessary truths (if they are true)) yields very surprising conclusions about the basic metaphysical structure of the universe.

As an extension of the above argument, Kripke argues that people's origins are essential, i.e. that we could not have had different parents from those we have. Kripke asks whether some arbitrary person, say Queen Elizabeth II, could have had different parents from the ones she had. He says no, and the argument mirrors the one above:

> Could the Queen—could this woman herself—have been born of different parents from the parents from whom she actually came? Could she, let's say, have been the daughter instead of Mr. and Mrs. Truman? [. . .] Not to go into too many complications here about what a parent is, let's suppose that the parents are the people whose body tissues are sources of the biological sperm and egg. [. . .] can we imagine a situation in which it would have happened that this very woman came out of Mr. and Mrs. Truman?   (Kripke 1980: 112)

What we can imagine, says Kripke, is that Mr. and Mrs. Truman had a child that was very similar to Elizabeth II. We can even imagine that, through some strange sequence of events, that woman became Queen of England. But, says Kripke:

> This still would not be a situation in which this *very woman* whom we call 'Elizabeth II' was the child of Mr. and Mrs. Truman [. . .] It would be a situation in which there was some other woman who had many of the properties that are in fact true of Elizabeth [. . .] It seems to me that anything coming from a different origin would not be this object.   (Kripke 1980: 112–3)

The more general version of this point is that any human essentially has the biological parents that they have—any person with different biological parents would have been a different person.

   Both the argument for dualism and the argument for the necessity of origin attempt to extract metaphysical conclusions from the theory of reference. That there could be conclusions of this sort should be unsurprising, whether or not one finds Kripke's specific examples convincing. The theory of reference is the theory of the way in which language hooks onto and allows discussions of the things that make up the world around us. So it should be expected that one way we might come to know more about those things is by thinking about our linguistic devices for discussing them, and about how those devices work.

   This issue introduces a further question:

The Metaphysical Question: What can we learn about the nature and constituents of reality by thinking about the nature of reference?

This will come up notably in Chapter 3 (on empty names) and Chapter 8 (on plurally referring expressions).

1.7.4 Anti-Individualism

One of the deepest influences that Kripke's work had on philosophy was the rejection of individualism about the mental. On Kripke's view, what you say, and what you think when you say it, are determined by factors *external* to the individual, such as their social and historical setting, others in their speech community, and the history of that speech community. This is a very radical departure from a view where meaning, thought, and other mental phenomena were thought of as inner states accessible only to the individuals having those states. Hilary Putnam, who also argued for anti-individualism, summed it up with the slogan: Meanings ain't in the head! (Putnam 1975). That is to say: even if you knew everything about an individual in isolation, i.e. her physical structure, what goes on in her brain, and so on, then you would not know what she is referring to when she uses a proper name. In order to know that, you need to look at her social and historical setting: what we mean and what we say isn't determined in an individualistic way.

If meanings ain't in the head, they'd better be somewhere else. Kripke's Causal-Communicative Model offers an alternative location for them: the referential facts about names are grounded in cultural and environmental facts about the use and transmission of names. But once the idea of anti-individualism has been introduced, a number of other anti-individualistic alternatives enter the discussion. Another important feature of the post-Kripkean literature on reference is thus:

The Metasemantic Question: Which factors determine what names refer to, and more generally determine what the meanings of our linguistic expressions are?

1.8 Plan for the Book: Eight Puzzles of Reference

In a way, our book takes the period around the publication of *Naming and Necessity* as its starting point. At that point, many in the philosophical community took Kripke to have done a very good job of refuting Frege. Since then, an extraordinary amount of fertile work has been done on topics related to those which Kripke talked about, both extending and refining his position, offering alternatives, and pushing back against his arguments. The rest of this book is an introduction to some of that literature.

The book is structured around eight puzzles. These puzzles can be appreciated in two ways. To a certain extent these puzzles should concern anyone—even someone with no knowledge of the theoretical debates we have sketched above. They are puzzles that arise simply from thinking about how names refer, and we have tried to present them as such. They are also puzzles that arise for those immersed in the debate between Kripkeans and Fregeans. This means that solving these puzzles might help us adjudicate between these competing theories. This is to say you can think of the chapters in two ways: on the one hand, they are introductions to intrinsically interesting puzzles and some possible solutions. On the other hand, the solutions to these puzzles provide ways into addressing the larger debates sketched in this introductory chapter.

The puzzles are:

- **A Puzzle about Belief, Reference, and Agency**: What is the role of referring expressions when they are used to describe what people believe?
- **A Puzzle about Referring to What Isn't There**: What does 'Superman' refer to? How do we refer to fictional objects?
- **The Puzzle of Essential Indexicality**: Do some referring expressions have a special connection to agency? Is such reference needed for us to act?
- **A Puzzle about Reference Determination**: Can what happens in the future or in other possible words help determine what we refer to now?
- **A Puzzle about Naming Arbitrarily**: How do arbitrary names refer? For example, what does 'Pierre' refer to in the sentence 'Let Pierre be an arbitrary Frenchman'?
- **The Puzzle of 'Every Alfred'**: How can we understand the fact that 'Alfred' appears to be both be a *predicate* and a *referring expression*?
- **The Puzzle of 'John and Paul and George and Ringo'**: How do terms that appear to refer to several things at once work?
- **A Puzzle about Intuitions and Methodology.**

We then close with a final chapter about whether we are better off without the notion of reference—i.e. whether the dispute between Fregeans and Kripkeans only arises because the two camps are using the word 'reference' to mean different things.

Central Points in Chapter 1

- There are two models that we can use for thinking about how names refer: the *Descriptive Model* favored by Fregeans, and the *Causal-Communicative Model* favored by Kripkeans.
- According to the Descriptive Model, names refer to things by being associated with descriptions which apply to the things referred to. On this model, reference determination is *Individualistic*.
- According to the Causal-Communicative Model, a name refers to something in virtue of i) an introductory event which associates the name with the thing (either via 'baptism' or an initial description), ii) the name being spread around in a linguistic community. What a name means, thus, is determined by the linguistic community in which it is used. On this model, reference determination is *Anti-Individualistic*.
- According to Kripke's view, the Descriptive Model is the correct story about some terms, such as quantified noun phrases, which are *transparent*, may be either *empty* or *superfluous*, and are *referentially unstable*. However, the Causal-Communicative Model is the correct account of names, which are *non-transparent*, cannot be either *empty* or *superfluous* (at least on first pass), and are *referentially stable* or *Rigid Designators*.
- Kripke gives three arguments against the Fregean view: i) that the Fregean view gives the wrong judgments concerning cases of descriptive underdetermination, in which a speaker has insufficient descriptions associated with a name to uniquely pick out one individual, ii) that the Fregean view gives the wrong judgments about misidentification cases, in which a speaker has false beliefs about a referent, and iii) that the Fregean view cannot explain the fact that names are rigid designators.
- Kripke's view allows that there can be *descriptive names* (such as 'Neptune', or 'Jack the Ripper'). In these cases descriptions play a role in the introductory event of a name. However, in these cases the descriptions only play a role in the *metasemantics* of the name, and are not part of the *semantics* of the name.
- Kripke's view of names has philosophical ramifications for debates about i) the relation between the a priori/a posteriori and the necessary/contingent, ii) physicalism and dualism, and iii) the necessity of origins.

Comprehension Questions

1. In your own words, give examples which illustrate each of Kripke's arguments against the Fregean picture of names:
   1.1. A case of descriptive underdetermination
   1.2. A case of misidentification
   1.3. A case concerning the modal properties of names.
2. Think of some other descriptive names. How widespread is this phenomenon?
3. Think of some other necessary a posteriori and—more difficult—contingent a priori truths (maybe think about descriptive names here).
4. We said that descriptions are referentially unstable: 'the president' stands for Trump now, but will stand for someone else—provided the world still exists—later. Can you think of any examples of stable descriptions?
5. We said above that descriptions are non-rigid—can you think of any descriptions which are rigid? How does this connect with referential stability? Is an expression rigid if and only if it's stable? If not, explain why not.

Exploratory Questions

6. We said that names are rigid. Can you think of non-rigid ones? Consider the following: we're looking at a list of names for the 2017 hurricane season in January 2017. Hurricanes are named alphabetically. 'Alex' is first on the list. In 'Alex will probably hit around July', could we say that the name is (temporally) non-rigid? If not, why not?
7. Consider the descriptive underdetermination cases, say, 'Gell-mann'. Can you think of any full description for 'Gell-mann'? What about 'the person Herman and Josh talked about by using "Gell-mann" in the first chapter of *Puzzles of Reference*'? Could that description refer to anyone else but Gell-mann?
8. The word 'cow' stands for the cows. Consider the models of the ropes and the viruses. Which model best captures how it does so?
9. If you like the dualism argument, try to clearly explain, in a few sentences, why you like it. If you dislike it, explain in a few clear sentences, why you dislike it.

10. Do you agree with the Kripkean thought that a person's origins are essential to them? Why?
11. What, if anything, do you think is the most notable difference between descriptions and names?
12. Give examples in which names refer to: i) no one, ii) different people at different times, iii) a group of people at the same time.
13. Members of different religions tend to have different beliefs about God. For example, Christians typically believe that Jesus is the son of God, and Muslims typically believe that Jesus was a prophet, but not the son of God. Do Muslims and Christians refer to the same thing when they use the word 'God'? What might Fregeans and Kripkeans have to say about this question?

Further Reading

The essential introduction to Kripke's views is Kripke 1980. Two good textbooks on the work of Kripke are Ahmed 2007 and Fitch 2004. Chalmers' famous work in the philosophy of mind begins with his accessible 1996 work. In addition to Kripke and Putnam, externalism is also argued for in the very influential Burge 1979. Two good recent anthologies are Burgess and Sherman 2014, on metasemantics, and Bianchi 2015 on reference. Williamson 2013 is a good example of the relevance of Kripke's (and Barcan 1946's) work for contemporary metaphysics.

2

A Puzzle about Belief, Reference, and Agency

2.1 The Puzzle

Kripke's view, as we have presented it, is that the content of a name—what it contributes to the meaning of a sentence or what is said by a sentence—is only its referent. So the meaning of the name 'Barack Obama' is the person, Barack Obama. There is no additional cognitive content (no additional associated descriptions) that contributes to the information content of sentences containing the name. In general, the meaning of a name is exhausted by its referent. This view might seem crazy for the following reason: in many cases we have different names that refer to the same object, but sentences that contain them seem to differ in meaning and differ in the information they convey. Here are a couple of cases which demonstrate this point:

'Marilyn Monroe' and 'Norma Mortenson' refer to the same person. So, according to the Kripkean view, which of the two names we use in a sentence should make no difference to the meaning of that sentence. This prediction seems wrong if we consider a sentence such as:

1. Jill just discovered that Marilyn Monroe is Norma Mortenson.

If you substitute Marilyn Monroe for Norma Mortenson you get:

2. Jill just discovered that Marilyn Monroe is Marilyn Monroe.

But that's not what Jill discovered. She already knew that Marilyn Monroe is Marilyn Monroe. It looks like we don't have a way to describe Jill's discovery without paying attention to *which* of the two names we use. So names must contribute something more to the sentence than their referents.

Next consider the two names 'Superman' and 'Clark Kent'. Those names refer to the same person. The following is true:

3.   Lois Lane believes that Superman can fly.

But it is not true that:

4.   Lois Lane believes that Clark Kent can fly.

Why is the first sentence true and the second sentence false when all we have done is substitute two co-referential names? Surely, if the only contribution a name makes to a sentence is the referent, then we should be able to substitute one co-referential name for another without a change in meaning. The sentences above make it look like we can't do that.

If names only contributed their referents to meaning, then we would be able to substitute the names without changing the meaning, but the above examples seem to show we can't do that. In what follows we will call sentential contexts which don't allow the substitution of names with the same referent **opaque**. These are sentential contexts where what matters is more than what is referred to—it looks like *how* we refer matters as well (the change in truth value shows that it matters). Trying to explain why the substitution of co-referential names is not possible is often described as the challenge of explaining opacity.

The challenge of explaining opacity is a point that many think gives an advantage to the kind of view which we, in Chapter 1, attributed to Frege. For Frege, each name has a meaning in addition to a referent. Remember our Jack the Ripper example: for Frege, the meaning of 'Jack the Ripper' is given by the property *being the one who committed the murders*. The meaning is not Druitt, even if he is the one who has that property. Turning to the Superman/Clark Kent example, we can note that the descriptions Lois Lane associates with 'Superman' differ from the descriptions she associates with 'Clark Kent', so according to the Fregean, we have different meanings. According to the Fregean, this difference in associated descriptions is what explains the failure of substitution (i.e. why we can't replace 'Superman' with 'Clark Kent' and vice versa).

Theoretical Explanations 2: *Opacity, Substitution, and Frege's Puzzle*

In order to get a good handle on the puzzle, we need to explain a bit more what opacity amounts to. First, let's introduce the notion of **substitution**. Take a sentence, for example 'snow is white and grass is green'. One thing we can do with such a sentence is substitute part of it with something else. We can substitute 'grass is green' with 'oranges are orange', for example, which would give us 'snow is white and oranges are orange'. An interesting thing to note about our example is that the original sentence is true, and provided you substitute a part of it with another true sentence, the sentence remains true. 'Snow is white and grass is green' is true, and no matter which sentence you substitute for 'grass is green', provided it is true, you get another true sentence (try it!)

Not all sentences are like that, however. Consider 'Alex believes that grass is green'. Let's try to substitute 'grass is green' in this sentence and see what happens. First, let's try 'oranges are orange', yielding 'Alex believes that oranges are orange'. Well, that might be true—it is pretty obvious, and Alex is smart enough, so she probably believes it. So can we substitute *any* other true sentence for 'grass is green' then? No. Imagine Alex is entirely ignorant of Russian literature. She's never heard either of Pushkin or of his verse novel *Eugene Onegin*. So she definitely doesn't believe that Pushkin wrote *Eugene Onegin*— that's just not one of her beliefs. Accordingly, 'Alex believes that Pushkin wrote *Eugene Onegin*' is false. This despite the fact that 'Alex believes that grass is green' is true, and 'grass is green' and 'Pushkin wrote *Eugene Onegin*' share the same truth value.

So that's a notable difference between 'snow is white and grass is green' and 'Alex believes that grass is green'. For the former, substituting a sentence with one of the same truth value always preserves the truth value of the original. For the latter, this is not so.

Now, finally, we can explain **opacity**. A part of a sentence is opaque if you can't substitute one expression for another having the same truth value or referring to the same thing while preserving the truth value of the sentence as a whole. Otherwise, it is transparent. Explaining opacity has been one of the foremost tasks in the philosophy of language, and it is frequently called 'Frege's Puzzle', because Frege introduced it in Frege (1892). For an English translation, see Frege (1948).

Our puzzle, then, is this: Kripke has given strong arguments *against* Frege's view that names have a meaning in addition to their reference. On the other hand, the data about the substitution of co-referential names in belief contexts just outlined seem to indicate that Kripke's can't be the full story. How can we reconcile these points?

In what follows we look at three attempts to respond to this puzzle:

- Kripke's solution to the puzzle: the Irrelevance solution;
- the Error Theoretic solution;
- the Pragmatic solution.

2.2 First Reply to the Puzzle (Kripke): Substitution Failures Have Nothing to Do with the Debate Between Fregeans and Kripkeans

Kripke argues that belief and other attitude reports are strange and complicated for reasons that have nothing to do with the choice between Kripkeanism and Fregeanism. Whatever puzzles there are in this domain, Kripke says, should be resolved independently of the choice between Fregeanism and Kripkeanism.

Kripke's argumentative strategy is the following: he presents us with another puzzle, one that is generated by principles that have nothing to do with the choice between Kripkeanism and Fregeanism. Just what he concludes from this is a bit hard to articulate, but our favored interpretation is the following:

Kripke's conclusion: Our practice of attributing belief is incoherent—it breaks down at various points. As a result, we should draw no general conclusions about reference from our practices of attributing belief. In particular, we should draw no conclusions about the debate between Kripkeanism and Fregeanism from our practices of attributing belief.

Why does he think the practice of attributing beliefs is incoherent? The basic structure of his argument is this: Kripke asks us to consider the case of Pierre:

a normal French speaker who lives in France and speaks not a word of English or of any other language except French. Of course, he has heard of that famous distant city, London (which he of course calls '*Londres*') though he himself has never left France. On the basis of what he has heard of London, he is inclined to think that it is pretty. So he says, in French, '*Londres est jolie.*'

The story continues. Kripke asks us to imagine that this Pierre guy moves to a very ugly part of London and hates it.

None of his neighbors know any French, so he must learn English by 'direct method', without using any translation of English into French: by talking and mixing with the people he eventually begins to pick up English. In particular, everyone speaks of the city, 'London', where they all live.

(Kripke 1979/2011: 143)

Speaking English, Pierre asserts: 'London is not pretty.' But note that Pierre doesn't know that 'London' refers to the same city as 'Londres'. So in French he asserts that London is pretty, but in English he asserts that London is not pretty. He can't translate between the two languages and so he doesn't recognize the inconsistency. Now it looks like we should say both that Pierre believes that London is pretty and that he believes it is not pretty. This, Kripke says, looks a lot like the substitution puzzles we started with (see Section 2.1 above).

2.2.1 What Follows from the Puzzle of Pierre?

One can try to resolve the puzzle of Pierre in various ways. However, what we want to focus on is the lessons Kripke wanted us to draw from it. Kripke developed this case as a response to the objection: If the meaning of a name is exhausted by its referent, then it looks like we should be able to go from *Lois Lane believes that Superman can fly* to *Lois Lane believes that Clark Kent can fly.* That, we said, seemed crazy. She clearly doesn't believe the latter, even though she believes the former. If it follows from Kripke's view that she does, we have to reject Kripke's view. The question we are now considering is the following: *how does throwing another puzzle at us help respond to that objection?* Kripke's thought is the following: the puzzle of Pierre didn't directly have to do with substituting one co-referential expression with another in belief contexts. It has to do with translation between languages. Nonetheless, we get a very similar result—Pierre both believes and doesn't believe that London is pretty. Kripke says the story of Pierre generates exactly the same absurdity as the original Frege puzzles. What this shows, according to Kripke, is that our practice of attributing beliefs in such cases (the Frege-puzzle cases and the Pierre-like cases) is defective. As a result, we should not draw any conclusions about the right theory of reference from them. In particular, the Fregeans get no advantage over the Kripkeans. Kripke says that when thinking about these puzzles we are:

in an area where our normal apparatus for the ascription of belief is placed under the greatest strain and may even break down. There is even less warrant at the present time, in the absence of a better understanding of the paradoxes of this paper, for the use of alleged failures of substitutivity in belief contexts to draw any significant theoretical conclusion about proper names. Hard cases make bad law.

(Kripke 1979/2011: 160)

Here are some options for how to interpret Kripke's conclusion, together with our replies to these interpretations:

FIRST INTERPRETATION OF KRIPKE'S CONCLUSION: The most natural interpretation is that Kripke thinks the puzzle of Pierre shows that we shouldn't draw any anti-Kripkean conclusions from the substitution argument.

REPLY: Why would a new puzzle lead us to put less weight on the original puzzle? A natural reply to Kripke, on behalf of the Fregeans, is this: You've articulated an interesting new puzzle, but that puzzle doesn't at all diminish the substitution arguments against your view. You've just articulated another problem, one that has nothing to do with the debate between the Kripkean and the Fregean. Why should that make us put less weight on the substitution argument we started out with?

SECOND INTERPRETATION OF KRIPKE'S CONCLUSION: The puzzle of Pierre and the classic Frege Puzzles are in effect the same puzzle. So whatever solution you propose to one of them should resolve the other. But the solution to the puzzle of Pierre has nothing to do with Kripkeanism vs. Fregeanism. So the puzzle won't help adjudicate that debate.

REPLY: Why think they are the same puzzle? The original substitution argument had nothing to do with translations between languages. The details of Kripke's Pierre argument (which we have skipped over here) rely on assumptions about translation and assertions and beliefs. That's a reason for thinking it's a different argument.

THIRD INTERPRETATION OF KRIPKE'S CONCLUSION: The puzzle about Pierre shows that the practice of reporting beliefs is incoherent— that is something Kripke seems to indicate when he says that 'our

> normal apparatus for the ascription of belief is placed under the greatest strain and may even break down.' He adds: 'Hard cases make bad law.'
>
> REPLY: The puzzle has done no such thing. It's just a new puzzle to work on. It's premature in the extreme to draw the conclusion that because there's this other puzzle, we should just ignore everything having to do with belief contexts when adjudicating between Kripke and the Fregean.

In sum: it is hard to see that Kripke's defense has the effect he hoped it would have. At the time of writing this book, it has been about thirty-six years since Kripke published his reply and it is fair to say that the lesson people have taken from this paper is not what Kripke intended. The effect has not been to deflect attention away from the substitution objection: people haven't taken it to make the original puzzle less urgent. It has, instead, been treated simply as another puzzle to be solved.

We turn now to two other efforts to respond to the substitution puzzle. According to the *error reply*, the intuitions or hunches people have about belief reports are wrong. We can substitute co-referential terms in belief contexts. End of story. On the other hand, the more concessive *pragmatic reply* introduces something like Fregean contents, not in the semantics, but at some other level. In other words, it grants something in the ballpark of Fregeanism at some level (thought or pragmatics), but denies that these Fregean contents correctly characterize the semantics.

2.3 Second Reply to the Puzzle: The Error Reply

The error reply says we **can** substitute co-referential expression in belief (and other attitude) contexts:

Error Reply: If Lois Lane believes that Superman can fly, then she also believes that Clark Kent can fly. When faced with the sentence, 'Clark Kent can fly', she will deny it, but she believes the proposition it expresses. She believes it because she believes that Superman can fly and Superman *just is* Clark Kent. So whatever she believes about Superman, she believes about Clark Kent.

Three points to notice about this kind of view:

i. **No deference to intuitions/hunches**: Those defending the error reply recognize that people will have a so-called *intuition* to the effect that this is wrong. Pre-theoretically, without theorizing, many will say that substitutions of co-referential terms just seem wrong. However, the Error theory puts very little weight on intuitions. Intuitions, they might say, are just hunches. Why should a theorist defer to whatever hunches we have? Physicists, psychologists, geologists, economists, and others are happy to override intuitions/hunches. Why shouldn't philosophers?

ii. **There's less error than you might think**: If you ask Lois Lane whether she believes that Clark Kent can fly, she would deny it. Nonetheless, the Error theory says, she does believe it. So the proponent of this view attributes a belief to her that she would deny having (i.e. she believes that that Clark Kent can fly, even though she doesn't believe that she believes it). That is why this is called an error reply. However—and this is a subtle but important point—*she also believes that she believes that Clark Kent can fly*. Here is why: remember, she believes *that she believes that Superman can fly*. According to the Error theory, we can substitute co-referential terms in belief contexts, so it follows in particular *that she believes that she believes that Clark Kent can fly*. In one way this is bad (we are attributing a contradiction to her), but on the other hand, she does believe one true thing (i.e. she believes that she believes that Clark Kent can fly).

iii. **Inconsistent beliefs despite being rational**: The Error theory attributes inconsistent beliefs to people who are entirely rational. Lois Lane appears entirely rational, but nonetheless the error reply describes her as both believing *that Clark Kent can't fly* and believing *that Clark Kent can fly*. So think of the Error theory as holding the view that irrationality is (at least in part) *to hold inconsistent beliefs that you can recognize the inconsistency of.*

The error reply is a very attractive way to defend Kripkeanism against substitution puzzles. It's a kind of 'stick to your guns' reply that yields no ground to the Fregean. It insists that the theory Kripke and others developed is right and that one thing we learn from it is that our pre-theoretic (hunch-based) assumptions about beliefs (and belief attributions) are wrong. Despite its great attraction, the view faces a number of objections. Below we present some of them.

2.4 Objection to Error Reply: Can't Explain Connection Between Beliefs and Action

Consider Lex Luthor. He's got hold of some kryptonite and wants to use it to kill Superman. As part of this murderous plan, he's having lunch with Clark Kent. Now consider what the Error theorist tells us about Lex Luthor:

i. He wants to kill Superman by throwing kryptonite at him.
ii. He believes that Clark Kent is sitting right in front of him.
iii. So he believes that Superman is sitting right in front of him (because, according to the Error theory, anyone who believes something of Clark Kent believes it of Superman as well).
iv. He also believes that he can throw his kryptonite at the person sitting right in front of him.

However, he does not act. He does nothing violent at all. He just has his little chat with Clark Kent and leaves. Now focus on the question: *Why didn't he throw the kryptonite?* He wanted to throw kryptonite at Superman, he believed that Superman was sitting right in front of him, and knew he could throw kryptonite at the person sitting right in front of him.

Some background for this objection. The practice of attributing beliefs to people is intimately tied up with the goal of explaining and predicting their behavior. If, however, we endorse the Error theory, it looks like the tie between belief attribution and action explanation is broken. So the Error theory has to give up one of the central goals of a theory of belief (and belief attribution). Surely, the objection goes, that is a great disadvantage of the theory. We should prefer a theory that doesn't have this consequence, such as a Fregean theory.

2.4.1 Reply to the First Reply: Fodor in Defense of Kripkeanism

Jerry Fodor in his book *The Elm and the Expert* (1994) presents a powerful response to this objection to the Error view. Fodor's argument goes as follows:

i. Fodor grants that our attribution of beliefs (or theory of belief) should have as a central role to account for the connection between beliefs and actions. In this respect Fodor goes along with the objection we outlined above.

ii. However, our goal is to develop so-called '*ceteris paribus* laws', i.e. laws that tolerate exceptions. Our goal is to develop laws (or theories) that explain what goes on in the *typical cases* where *nothing bizarre goes wrong*.

iii. The examples involving substitution puzzles are bizarre and unusual.

iv. So our theory of meaning (or more precisely the theory of belief reports) can ignore the kinds of cases that Fregeans tend to rely on, e.g. cases where one person or object is disguised in such a way that the agent doesn't recognize it.

The lesson of Fodor's view is that a Kripkean shouldn't worry about any of the Superman/Clark Kent-type cases. Fodor agrees with Kripke: 'Hard cases make bad laws' (Fodor 1994: 45).

Here is Fodor's illustration of this argument:

Ever since Frege, when philosophers think about the relations between content and action, *Oedipus* is the sort of plot that comes to mind. Oedipus didn't want to marry his mother, but he married his mother all the same. So, it appears, specifications of the contents of Oedipus' attitudes had better distinguish *wanting to marry Jocasta* from *wanting to marry Mother*.   (Fodor 1994: 43)

This looks like a problem for Kripkeanism (since according to Kripkeanism we can substitute 'Jocasta' for 'mother'[1] as they refer to the same thing). However, Fodor asks us to be cautious:

One might be well advised to bear in mind that in Oedipus' case *something went badly wrong* [. . .] *Prima facie, it is a bad idea to take a case where things go badly wrong as a paradigm for cases where they don't.*   (Fodor 1994: 43)

Suppose we go along with Kripkeanism and say that, despite intuitions to the contrary, Oedipus did try to marry his mother. This is the 'stick to your guns' defense of Kripkeanism. What, then, do we say about the aim of explaining the connection between action and belief attribution? We have attributed to him the desire to marry his mother, but we also want to say that he didn't want to marry his mother. Here is Fodor's reply:

There is, according to this revisionist proposal, a true and reliable broad intentional generalization: people try to avoid marrying their mothers. Full stop. Oedipus' case was an exception to this generalization; he did try to marry his

---

[1] For simplicity we assume here that 'mother' serves as a name and not a description.

mother. Well, you expect reliable generalizations to have occasional exceptions except, maybe, in basic physics. In psychology, as in any other empirical enterprise, the task when confronted with an exception to a generalization that you can usually rely on is to try to show that the case is unsystematic. This strategy seems entirely appropriate in the present case. What happened to Oedipus was exceptional enough to write a play about. Ceteris paribus, good theories want to treat exceptional cases as, well, exceptions.   (Fodor 1994: 44–5)

On this view, Oedipus's situation is so atypical that we shouldn't expect our theory to explain what goes on in it. More generally, the response to the standard kind of Frege puzzles is: *those are cases where something has gone wrong, and my general theory isn't trying to account for those*. Fodor, again: 'only a philosopher would consider taking Oedipus as a model for a normal, unproblematic relation between an action and the maxim of the act. Keep your eye firmly fixed on this: *Most people do* not *marry their mothers*; that, surely, should define the norm' (1994: 45). This is a pretty good defense of Kripkeanism against the substitution puzzles. It is, we think, the most promising non-concessive strategy ever developed.

However, there's a small wrinkle to all of this. Fodor's view doesn't stop with what we have outlined above. He goes on to say that we have to explain why a generalization fails when it fails. As Fodor notes, substitution failures 'do actually occur'—i.e. they are not extremely rare. So Fodor concludes: 'They can't, then, be merely dismissed; they have to be *explained away*.'

So much for Fodor's view. He thinks we are owed an answer to the question: 'Why was Oedipus an exception to the rule?' The first response we will consider is Dismissal: it's the answer that says: *We don't need to answer that question*. Fodor is wrong—not all such exceptions need to be explained. The question Fodor thinks should be answered deserves no answer.

2.4.2 More on Dismissal

Why did Oedipus try to marry his mother? According to the Error theory, he had the desire not to marry Mother, so he had the desire not to marry Jocasta. And he had the belief that he was marrying Jocasta. But he failed to *combine* the desire with the belief to produce appropriate (in)action. So why did he fail to combine the belief and the desire? Here is another way to ask that question: *Oedipus has the ability to engage in practical reasoning, but his ability failed in this case. Why?*

To answer this, let's briefly consider a more general question: what it is for an ability to fail in a particular case? Let's first consider an answer that we will call the *Tempting view*, which turns out to be false (according to the Error view):

The Tempting View: Jones failed to jump over the gap. Why? On the *Tempting view*, it's because Jones didn't have the ability to jump over the gap. Rather, Jones had the ability to *try* to jump over the gap, or the ability to tense certain muscles in certain ways. And he did successfully use that ability. It's just that, on this occasion, successfully using that ability wasn't enough to allow him to jump the gap. Inspired by such cases it's tempting to think of ability failures in the following way: whenever we seem to fail to do X, that's because we didn't really have the ability to do X—rather, we *really* had some infallible ability to do something else, Y, and on this occasion, doing Y wasn't enough to achieve X.

According to the Tempting view there aren't any *real* ability failures. This is how the Fregean thinks about Oedipus. Oedipus is infallible at combining Jocasta-beliefs with Jocasta-desires, and infallible at combining Mom-beliefs with Mom-desires. But because of his unfortunate situation, he can't use those infallible beliefs to avoid marrying his mother. The Error theorist will move us away from this way of thinking about abilities.

Against the Tempting View: The Tempting view is a controversial and counter-intuitive picture of abilities. On the face of it, we *do* have many fallible abilities. And it's quite hard to come up with any infallible abilities. Jones's ability to try to jump over the gap isn't infallible either. Jones might plan to try to jump, but then fail when the time comes (perhaps his nerve gives out). His ability to tense certain muscles in certain ways isn't infallible either. He might be tired and having trouble concentrating and fail to tense the right muscles. Of course, we can, in the face of these failures, just look further for the *really* infallible abilities. Maybe Jones can infallibly try to try to jump? But failures to try to try aren't hard to construct either. The Error theorist thus suggests that the Tempting view of ability failures is a mistake. Abilities sometimes fail, because abilities aren't manifestations of background infallible capacities.

But why did Oedipus's reasoning abilities fail in this case (i.e. why didn't he connect his Mom-belief/desires with his Jocasta-beliefs/desires?)? To answer that, let's consider briefly the more general question: *Why do generalizations sometimes fail?* Statements about abilities are, after all, closely connected to (maybe identical to) generalizations about what someone can do under certain conditions ('in general when you intend to tie your shoelaces, you do it'—though sometimes your ability will fail).

So how do we explain the fact that generalizations fail in specific cases? Sometimes it's because they come up against more specific generalizations. Generally, it rains in Seattle. But today it didn't rain. Why not? Because it's July, and it generally doesn't rain in July in Seattle. But, of course, the generalization that it doesn't rain in July in Seattle can also fail. That might be because it comes up against an even more specific generalization. It's cloudy, and it generally does rain on cloudy July days in Seattle. There are now three possibilities:

i. Eventually we come to an exceptionless generalization, so there's no further failure to explain.
ii. Eventually we come to a generalization with exceptions, but there's no explanation for those exceptions.
iii. We keep on going forever, because there is an infinite list of more and more specific generalizations.

The Error theorist wants to endorse the second of these three possibilities. If she's right in doing so, she's justified in simply *dismissing* the demand for an explanation of why Oedipus is an exception to the generalization that people don't try to marry their mothers. Option (i) is again a manifestation of the Tempting view we argued against above, i.e. the problematic Fregean thought that there's a level of infallibility here. To endorse it in this case would be to think that scientific theories that use *ceteris paribus* explanations are ultimately dispensable; that we could in the end replace the rough generalizations, admitting of exceptions, with precise rules that have no exceptions. Again, this is a bold and controversial claim. What's wrong with option (iii), i.e. the view that there is an infinite sequence of better and better generalizations? This view isn't favorable to the Error theorist, because the Error theorist wants to avoid giving an explanation of why Oedipus is an exception to the generalization. But it isn't favorable to the Fregean either, because while the Fregean *does* want to explain why Oedipus is an exception, he wants to give that explanation by citing a different, exceptionless generalization that does apply to Oedipus.

We find Dismissal the best reply on behalf of the Kripkean. However, it has not been the consensus view in the literature. Most of those trying to defend Kripke have made an effort to explain what goes wrong—why we seem to be unable to recognize sameness of content (e.g. between 'mother' and 'Jocasta' and between 'Clark Kent' and 'Superman'). We turn now to some theories that attempt to answer that question. The views we will survey have one feature in common: they preserve Kripkeanism at the level of *semantics* (or: as description of the content of names) but they try to add some content in addition to the referent at some extra-semantic level.

2.5 Third Solution to the Puzzle: The Pragmatic Reply

The Kripkean says that 'Lois Lane believes that Clark Kent can fly' and 'Lois Lane believes that Superman can fly' have the same content, and that if one is true, then the other is. Why do we, pre-theoretically, think otherwise? Why don't our actions track the real content (as witnessed by Oedipus and Lois Lane)?

What we call the 'pragmatic reply' is really a cluster of replies that have the following rough thought in common: in addition to what we literally, strictly speaking, say by uttering one of these sentences, we *convey* something more. This something more interferes with us seeing clearly that the two sentences mean the same (express the same proposition). That additional content also interferes with our actions: for example, it makes criminals react differently to 'Superman is on his way' and 'Clark Kent is on his way'. Below we sketch one way to spell out that view.

2.6 Believing Under a Guise

What is it to believe something? Here is a simple view:

Simple View of Belief: Belief is a relation between a person and a proposition.

On this simple view, if Lois Lane believes *that Superman can fly*, she also believes *that Clark Kent can fly*, because these are the same proposition and if she stands in the believing relation to one of them, then she stands in the believing relation to the other, just as, for example, if she is standing to the left of Clark Kent, she is standing to the left of Superman. If Lois also believes *that Clark Kent cannot fly*, then she also believes *that Superman cannot fly*. So she has an inconsistent set of beliefs.

One version of the pragmatic reply rejects this simple view. It holds, instead, that belief is a more complicated relation. We don't believe propositions *simpliciter*. Instead, we believe them *under a guise* or *a mode of presentation*. These ways of believing are in some ways like the descriptions that Fregeans think of as the meaning of a name, but, importantly, they are not part of the meaning of words. They don't enter into the content of names (and they don't help fix the referents of names). Instead, they enter into an account of *how* we believe propositions. Lois Lane, for example, believes the proposition *that Clark Kent can fly* (i.e. the proposition *that Superman can fly*) under a Superman guise or mode of presentation. She doesn't believe it under a Clark Kent guise. This view preserves Kripkeanism by introducing something very similar to Fregean meanings in the theory of belief while maintaining they have no role to play in our theory of language—so there's an important difference between a theory of meaning (e.g. an account of what 'A believes that p' means) and a theory of what belief is.

How does this theory of belief explain why, pre-theoretically, speakers think it is false to say that Lois Lane believes *that Clark Kent can fly* and true to say she believes *that Superman can fly*? The answer from the Guise (Mode of Presentation) theorist is that the sentences we use to report beliefs with *convey* something about how a proposition is believed. This is not because the names 'Superman' and 'Clark Kent' mean different things. It is because speakers use belief reports to convey something about *the way a proposition is believed*. On this view, if we say 'Lois Lane believes that Clark Kent can fly', we have *said* something true, but we have *conveyed* something misleading: we have conveyed that she believes this proposition in a certain way (for example, that she believes it under a Clark Kent guise).

Advocates of this view can explain why we don't think Lois is irrational. It is true that she both believes *that Superman can fly* and *that Superman cannot fly* (she even believes both propositions at the same time), but that's not irrational because she believes the former under the 'Superman' guise and the latter under the 'Clark Kent' guise. To be irrational she would have had to both believe and reject the same proposition under the same guise.

Note that this is not a view about the content of our sentences (and not about the meaning of the words). The view moves the debate about substitution away from the theory of reference and meaning. Instead, it focuses on the way in which we believe propositions and how our belief reports can convey information about that. To sum up, there are two core ideas:

i. We don't believe propositions directly; we believe them under a guise (or in a certain way).
ii. Belief reports convey (but don't express) information about how the subject believes a proposition.

The central challenges for such views is to explain *what* these so-called guises are. We are told that they are ways in which we believe propositions, but we are owed a theory of what such ways are. We need to know whether they change from moment to moment, from person to person, and what role they play in understanding. Do we, for example, need to know Barack Obama's guise for Trump to understand what he says when he utters 'Trump is now the president of the US'?

We also need to be told how guises (ways of believing propositions) help explain action. Recall the discussion above of the connection between belief and action. On the view we are now considering, someone who believes *that Superman is here* also believes *that Clark Kent is here*, but believing that proposition under the 'Superman' guise will trigger other actions than believing it under the 'Clark Kent' guise. The former way of believing it might motivate you to ask him about his crime-fighting accomplishments, while the latter will make you ask questions about journalism. What is it about guises that generates or explains difference in behavior? That is one of the central challenges for those who want to defend a Kripkean view by appeal to guises.

Central Points in Chapter 2

- According to the Kripkean view, the content of a name is just its referent. This view predicts that names with the same referent are intersubstitutable in sentences while preserving the truth value of those sentences.
- However, data from our belief ascriptions (from examples like the Marilyn Monroe/Norma Mortenson and Clark Kent/Superman cases) supports the claim that in some sentences ascribing belief, substitution of co-referential names will lead to a change in truth value.

(continued)

- The puzzle of substitution is to explain how the arguments for Kripkeanism can be made consistent with the data about substitution in belief ascriptions.
- Kripke's response to the substitution puzzle is to say that failures of substitution are irrelevant to the debate between Fregeanism and Kripkeanism.
- Kripke motivates this line by presenting the Puzzle of Pierre, which he claims supports the claim that our practice of belief ascriptions is just incoherent.
- There are various different interpretations of Kripke's conclusion from the Puzzle of Pierre.
- The second response to the puzzle of substitution is the *error reply.* According to this response, our judgments about the truth value of belief ascriptions under substitution of co-referential terms are incorrect. Contrary to common-sense judgment, substitution of co-referential terms *does* preserve truth value.
- One problem with the error reply is that it threatens our ability to use belief ascriptions to explain and predict actions.
- Fodor responds to this worry by pointing out that explanations of action are only *ceteris paribus* generalizations, and contending that Frege cases are ones in which these generalizations break down. There might be various explanations for why a generalization breaks down, but we have argued that the best response for the Kripkean is to simply dismiss the demand for an explanation of why the generalization breaks down.
- The third response to the puzzle of substitution—the Pragmatic response—is to appeal to the idea that belief is a relation between a person, a proposition, and a *guise.* Although the Kripkean cannot appeal to guises as part of the meaning of a name, they can claim that belief ascriptions pragmatically convey that the agent believes a proposition under a particular guise.

Comprehension Questions

1. Present a few other Frege puzzles, using different verbs ('wonders', 'knows', saw, etc.) and names other than the ones we use.
2. Say in a few simple words how Kripke's puzzle works (imagine you're trying to explain the puzzle to a younger sibling).
3. What do you think about the principles Kripke appeals to in his argument? Try to think of problems with them.
4. Think of a counterexample to the translation principle.
5. In your own words, distinguish the three interpretations of Kripke's response to the Puzzle of Pierre. Which is the most plausible?
6. Explain the error reply.
7. Do you like the error reply? If not, consider the following: 'Jones heard a noise and Smith called out'. Is this true in a scenario where Smith first calls out and then Jones hears him? If so, does it show that the truth value of a sentence may be other than it immediately seems? How might this help the error reply?

Exploratory Questions

8. Above, we consider the pragmatic reply in the case of belief. How might the Fregean pose a different kind of puzzle to the Kripkean, which doesn't involve belief? (Hint: think about your answer to Question 1 here and in particular what you said about 'saw'.) How might the Kripkean respond to this new puzzle?
9. Fodor argues above that we don't need to offer an explanation of why the cases of Pierre and Oedipus are exceptional. If one wanted to offer an explanation of why these cases are special, what might this explanation look like?

Further Reading

The puzzle has been around as long as philosophy of language has: see Frege 1948 for its introduction, and Textor 2010 and Soames 2010 chapter 1 for some textbook accounts. Some thinkers inspired by Frege include Dummett 1973 and Evans 1982. A recent version of Fregeanism which makes use of advances in logic is two-dimensional
(continued)

semantics: see Chalmers 2006, although it's tough going. A critical take on some of these views is the (difficult) Soames 2005. For Kripke's puzzle, see Kripke 1979, and McKay and Nelson 2014, Section nine, and references therein. For the error reply, see Fodor 1994, and for the pragmatic reply, see Salmon 1986 and Braun 1998. A slightly different view in the same vicinity is Crimmins and Perry 1989. Jennifer Saul has a range of papers on this topic: see e.g. Saul 1998, 1997.

3

A Puzzle About Referring to What Isn't There

3.1 A Puzzle

The name 'Berlin' refers to the capital of Germany, and the name 'Alexander the Great' refers to the famous student of Aristotle. But what does the name 'Sherlock Holmes' refer to? Maybe to *the detective who lives at 221B Baker Street*? But there is no detective who lives at that address. Does the fact that Sherlock Holmes does not exist interfere with saying that the name 'Sherlock Holmes' refers to Sherlock Holmes?

Figuring out what to say about the reference of 'Sherlock Holmes' requires thinking about what the notion of reference is doing for us in the first place. Why do we say that the name 'Berlin' refers to the capital of Germany? Because that city plays some important roles in explaining the properties of sentences involving the name 'Berlin'. Some examples:

- **Truth value:** The truth or falsity of sentences using 'Berlin' depends on how things are with Berlin. 'Berlin is in Europe' is true because of the location of Berlin, not because of the position of Paris. 'The Eiffel Tower is in Berlin' is false because of the geography of Berlin, not because of the geography of Paris. In both cases, this is because 'Berlin' refers to Berlin, and the truth value of a sentence depends on how things are with the objects referred to in the sentence.
- **Aboutness:** When someone says 'I love visiting Berlin', they are *talking about* Berlin, and not talking about Paris. Berlin, and not Paris, is the (or a) *topic* of their conversation. This is because 'Berlin' refers to Berlin, and a sentence is about the objects referred to in the sentence.
- **Cognition:** When Alex thinks of the capital of Germany that her grandmother grew up there, we can report her thought by saying 'Alex thinks that her grandmother grew up in Berlin'. That is because

'Berlin' refers to Berlin, and people's thoughts can be reported using words that refer to the objects their thoughts concern.

We can thus *discover* that 'Berlin' refers to Berlin by asking what object settles the truth or falsity of sentences using 'Berlin', asking what object people are talking about when they use 'Berlin', and asking what kinds of thoughts can be reported using the word 'Berlin'.

This strategy works well for names like 'Berlin' and 'Alexander the Great'. But how do things go when we consider 'Sherlock Holmes'? Suppose we start to wonder about the truth value of sentences using 'Sherlock Holmes', such as:

1. Sherlock Holmes lived at 221B Baker Street.

2. Sherlock Holmes doesn't exist.

3. Sherlock Holmes was first introduced in *A Study in Scarlet*.

4. Sherlock Holmes was a fictional character who was the basis for the television character Gregory House.

One difficulty is that it isn't completely obvious what the truth values of these sentences are. But even if we surmount that difficulty, it's also hard to say what object settles the truth value of the sentences. *Maybe* the answer is: Sherlock Holmes. But it's also natural to suggest that that answer can't be right, because there is no Sherlock Holmes. And even if that's not what we want to say in the end, how do we go about checking whether Holmes lived at 221B Baker Street? And if we can't check, what do we really mean in saying that the truth value of the sentence depends on him? Similarly, who are people talking about when they make utterances using the name 'Sherlock Holmes'? Not Holmes, we might think, because there is no Holmes for such claims to be about. And what kinds of thoughts can be reported using the name 'Sherlock Holmes'? Thoughts about Holmes? But what would it be for a thought to be about Holmes?

'Sherlock Holmes' is an example of an apparently non-referring name. Whether it is really non-referring is a question we will return to below, but certainly a puzzle is posed by a name like this. If 'Sherlock Holmes' does not refer, what determines the truth values and contents of sentences involving 'Sherlock Holmes'? And if it does refer, what could it refer to that would be *helpful* in determining truth values and contents? As we will see, languages are full of names like 'Sherlock Holmes'—talk about the nonexistent is a perfectly ordinary part of our linguistic practice. How can a theory of reference accommodate these sorts of 'empty names'?

We don't want to beg questions about *what* is problematic about 'Sherlock Holmes' by calling it an *empty* name, or a *non-referring* name, or even a *fictional* name. But 'Sherlock Holmes' is just one of a whole category of difficult cases, and we do want to have some label for those cases. So let's call them N-names. To get a sense for the range of the problem in language, consider some other N-names together with brief glosses on what makes them problematic:

- 'Frodo Baggins': (Almost) everyone agrees that there is no hobbit with a ring of invisibility out there. The name is introduced by a particular person (Tolkien) as part of a piece of fictional storytelling.
- 'Superman': (Almost) everyone agrees that there is no displaced super-powered person from Krypton out there. The name is introduced by a particular person (Siegel) as part of a piece of fictional storytelling, but the full Superman story, if there is any such thing, is a collaborative and open-ended thing with contributions from a great many people.
- 'Zeus': (Almost) everyone agrees that there is no thunderbolt-wielding deity living on Mount Olympus. The name emerges out of a developing practice, rather than being introduced by any particular person at any particular time, and is mistakenly believed by many of its original users to be a name of a real thing.
- 'Atlantis': (Almost) everyone agrees that there is no sunken island civilization out there. The name is introduced by a particular person (Plato) as part of a piece of fictional storytelling, but comes to be taken by some people as a name for a real place.
- 'Santa Claus': (Almost) everyone over a certain age agrees that there is no fat jolly man who leaves gifts for children at Christmas. The name begins as a name for a real person, the fourth-century bishop of Myra. Over time that person becomes associated with holiday gift-giving, and some false beliefs about his role in the gift-giving develop. Then the use of the name shifts so that it no longer refers to the bishop of Myra, but instead names another person generally taken not to be real, but believed by many children, at the time of their introduction to the name, to be real.

- 'Phaeton': (Almost) everyone agrees that there was no planet between Mars and Jupiter that fractured to form the asteroid belt. But in the nineteenth century a combination of the false Titius-Bode law and the discovery of the Ceres and Pallas asteroids led astronomers such as Heinrich Olbers to posit the existence of such a planet, and in the twentieth century the name 'Phaeton' was introduced for that planet by Sergei Orloff.
- 'Radioactive Man': (Almost) everyone agrees that there was no superhero with the ability to fire bursts of clean nuclear heat from his eyes. Furthermore, (almost) everyone agrees that there was no comic book writer Morty Mann who created the 'Radioactive Man' character. The name 'Radioactive Man' is introduced at a somewhat indeterminate (fictional) time by the fictional character Morty Mann, who is in turn introduced at a particular time by the writers of *The Simpsons*. Radioactive Man is thus merely fictionally fictional.
- 'Dimbo': Jack hallucinates a pink elephant. Knowing it to be a hallucination, he privately introduces a name 'Dimbo' for the hallucination.
- 'Alex': In a philosophy of language class, a professor uses the name 'Alex' in a sample sentence illustrating features of pronominal anaphora. The professor doesn't intend to refer to any particular Alex with the name, and the class doesn't take the professor to be referring to any particular Alex. Over the course of the semester, the name 'Alex' is repeatedly used in sample sentences, and the sample sentences are often chosen so that a vague narrative about Alex's life emerges.

Very roughly, we can divide N-names into two categories. First, there are *names of fiction*, which include all cases in which a name is introduced with the knowledge that there is no object (of the expected sort) to which it corresponds. Second, there are *names of error*, which include all cases in which the name introducer thought incorrectly that there was an object (of the expected sort) to which it corresponds. As the above list shows, many cases will be complicated to fit cleanly into one of these two categories, but the division gives a good approximate characterization. We will return to the necessity for the 'of the expected sort' qualification below.

3.2 Why the Puzzle Matters

Figuring out what things the world does and does not contain is the central project of metaphysics. But considering the way our language works can be a crucial part of that project. It's not hard to notice that the world contains trees and buildings, and scientists are on hand to tell us that it also contains quarks and gravitational fields. But until we think carefully about our use of sentences like 'The destruction of Carthage marked the final triumph of Rome over its enemies', it might not occur to us that the world also contains destructions and triumphs. If we are going to use language as a guide to metaphysics, we had better be clear about what's going on with N-names. Maybe N-names do refer, and there are more surprising objects to be found beyond destructions and triumphs. Or maybe they do not refer, in which case we need to know how to use the linguistic tools with proper caution.

Understanding N-names also matters for understanding how our minds relate to the world around us. On the one hand, we want our beliefs to be beliefs *about the world*. Our Berlin beliefs are really beliefs about Berlin, connecting us to the real capital of Germany. On the other hand, it seems to be in the nature of the mental not to be constrained by mere questions of existence. We can, in some sense, think about the nonexistent hobbit Frodo Baggins as easily as we can think about the long-dead philosopher Francis Bacon or the currently living Austrian base-jumper Felix Baumgartner. This lack of constraint contributes to worries of skepticism in epistemology, since it raises the specter of our thought systematically failing to connect to the world. Getting a better understanding of how N-names work should help us better understand how seriously these skeptical threats should be taken.

3.3 The Challenge of N-Names

N-names are particularly challenging for the Kripkean picture of reference. If the meaning of a name is exhausted by its referent, and the name 'Sherlock Holmes' doesn't refer to anything, then 'Sherlock Holmes' is simply meaningless. But if 'Sherlock Holmes' is meaningless, then it looks like perfectly sensible things we might say or think with the name 'Sherlock Holmes' will also be meaningless, such as:

5. Sherlock Holmes is a detective.

6. I wish I were as clever as Sherlock Holmes.

7. Sherlock Holmes doesn't exist.

This doesn't seem like an adequate picture of our talk and thought.

Fregeans, unlike Kripkeans, have a natural thing to say about N-names. They can hold that 'Sherlock Holmes' does not refer, but that its non-referential status does not leave it wholly without meaning, because it has a descriptive meaning such as 'detective living at 221B Baker Street'. This description gives the name a meaning even if the description does not (given the absence of detectives at that address) determine a reference.

Fregeans will thus say that 'Sherlock Holmes is a detective' is meaningful but false. On their view, 'Sherlock Holmes is a detective' is equivalent to 'The detective who lives at 221B Baker Street is a detective', and that latter sentence is not true, given again the absence of a detective at that address. Similarly, 'Sherlock Holmes does not exist' is equivalent to 'The detective who lives at 221B Baker Street does not exist', which in turn is equivalent to 'There is no detective who lives at 221B Baker Street', which is true. Not all the news is good: 'Sherlock Holmes is a fictional character' is equivalent to 'The detective who lives at 221B Baker Street is a fictional character', which is false (again because there is no detective at that address).

But Fregean approaches to N-names are vulnerable to arguments similar to those Kripke uses against Fregean views on ordinary names in *Naming and Necessity*. We can raise the Problem of Accidental Reference:

Suppose that, unknown to everyone, someone actually did perform all the deeds related in the Sherlock Holmes stories—he lived at 221B Baker Street, he fought Moriarty at Reichenbach Falls, and so on. Then according to the Fregean view, 'Sherlock Holmes' refers to that man. Call him Pseudo-Holmes, to give a neutral way of referring to him. The Holmes stories are then all true claims about Pseudo-Holmes. This is a bad result. The natural thought is that in this case Pseudo-Holmes isn't *really* Holmes, but just eerily resembles Holmes. (It is important that Conan Doyle too was ignorant of Pseudo-Holmes, and was not intending to write about his life or causally influenced by his life in writing the Holmes stories.)

The Problem of Accidental Reference can be made even worse. Charles Darwin did not perform the deeds of the Holmes stories. But he could have—there is some world in which everything said of Holmes in the stories is true of Darwin. According to the Fregean, then, 'Sherlock Holmes' refers to Darwin in that world, and 'Darwin is Holmes' is true in that world. The Fregean is thus committed to the claim that Darwin could have been Sherlock Holmes. If we also accept the widely held view that true and false identity claims are true and false necessarily, it will follow that Darwin actually is Holmes. This is an unacceptable result (especially if Pseudo-Holmes is Holmes in the actual world, because then, by the transitivity of identity, we are committed to the claim that Darwin is Pseudo-Holmes).

3.4 Some Options for Solving the Puzzle

To be able to evaluate theories of N-names, we need to know what we want those theories to do. Unfortunately, it is controversial in many cases what is the right thing to say about claims using N-names, so we cannot just have a straightforward list of data points to be accounted for. But we can have a list of important *decision* points, along with some brief remarks on the options at those points.

A theory of N-names should help determine the truth values of various sentences containing N-names, letting us say whether those sentences are true, false, or without truth value. In considering various options, we will focus on the following examples:

- **In-Fiction Claims**: Claims like 'Sherlock Holmes is a detective' report part of the content of stories about Sherlock Holmes. On some views, such claims will be true—the stories' saying that Sherlock Holmes is a detective is enough to make it the case that Sherlock Holmes in fact *is* a detective. On other views, such claims will be false. We cannot, on these views, make it the case that someone is a detective just by writing words on a page.
- **Metafictional Claims**: In addition to saying 'Sherlock Holmes is a detective', we can say 'Sherlock Holmes is a fictional character', or 'Sherlock Holmes appears in fifty-six stories by Arthur Conan Doyle'. Some views will hold that these metafictional claims are true, even if they think that the in-fiction claims are false.
- **Nonexistence Claims**: A special case of a metafictional claim is nonexistence claims involving N-names, such as 'Sherlock Holmes does not exist' and 'There is no Atlantis'. Those who accept *either* that Sherlock Holmes is a detective *or* that Sherlock Holmes is a fictional character will be under some pressure to reject these nonexistence claims, but others may want to endorse them.

- **Synonymy Claims**: Without taking a stand on *what* N-names mean, we can ask *whether* different N-names mean different things. We can thus consider claims such as '"Sherlock Holmes is a detective" means the same thing as "Veronica Mars is a detective"'. If neither 'Sherlock Holmes' nor 'Veronica Mars' refers to anything, and if meaning is exhausted by reference, it may be hard to avoid having such claims come out true.
- **Cognitive Claims**: In addition to asking whether 'Sherlock Holmes is a detective' is true, we can ask whether 'Alex believes that Sherlock Holmes is a detective' is true. Many, including some who think that it is not true that Sherlock Holmes is a detective, will think that Alex *does* believe that Sherlock Holmes is a detective (when Alex is unaware that the stories are fiction, for example).

We will distinguish two types of theories of N-names. (Note that it is possible to have different views about different kinds of N-names.)

- **Anti-realist** views say that N-names *do not refer*. The puzzle for anti-realist views is then to make sense of the communicative and cognitive role of language involving N-names, if there is nothing that those names refer to. Anti-realist views typically find it hard to make N-name-containing sentences get *any* truth value, let alone to have different sentences have different truth values in any satisfying way.
- **Realist** views, on the other hand, reject the apparent emptiness of N-names and say that N-names *do* refer. The puzzle for realist views is then to say what it is that those names refer to. Realist views thus incur a metaphysical burden to supply us with a plausible range of objects to be the referents of N-names, where those objects have properties that will give N-name-containing sentences reasonable truth values.

We will consider various developments of both anti-realist and realist views.

3.5 Anti-Realist Views

3.5.1 Anti-Realism 1: The No-Meaning View

Consider first the starkest version of Anti-realism, the *No-Meaning* view, according to which sentences containing N-names don't mean anything. The No-Meaning view makes no attempt to evade or soften the Kripkean anti-realist conclusion that N-names are meaningless, and in fact pushes that conclusion further by endorsing:

- **Contamination Principle**: A sentence with a meaningless part is itself meaningless.

The Contamination Principle can be motivated by considering examples such as:

8.   'Twas brillig, and the slithy toves did gyre and gimble in the wabe.

According to the principle, because 'brillig', 'slithy', 'toves', 'gyre', 'gimble', and 'wabe' are all meaningless made-up words, the whole sentence is also meaningless. It isn't true or false, nothing is said by uttering it, and no one can believe it.

Anti-realism together with the Contamination Principle entail that no sentence containing an N-name means anything. On the plausible view that only meaningful sentences can be true or false, it also follows that no sentence containing an N-name is true or false. The resulting view is quite stark. On this view, all sentences containing the name 'Sherlock Holmes' are meaningless and truth-valueless:

- 'Sherlock Holmes is a detective' is neither true nor false. 'Sherlock Holmes is a fictional character' is neither true nor false. 'Sherlock Holmes does not exist' is neither true nor false. The No-Meaning view thus must say that in-fiction, metafictional, and nonexistence claims lack truth values.
- There is no difference in meaning between the sentences 'Sherlock Holmes is a detective' and 'Frodo Baggins is a hobbit', because neither sentence means anything.
- Even if Alex takes all of the Arthur Conan Doyle stories to be true reports, the sentence 'Alex believes that Sherlock Holmes is a detective' is neither true nor false. On the plausible view that Alex's beliefs are given by the true belief reports about Alex, it follows that Alex does *not* believe that Sherlock Holmes is a detective.

The No-Meaning view, then, has some unwelcome consequences. To accept the No-Meaning view, we have to accept not only that we are massively in error in our beliefs about fictions (possibly about the contents of fictions, possibly about our theoretical views on fictions), but also that we are subject to vast cognitive illusions about fiction. We think that we have beliefs about Sherlock Holmes, but in fact we do not. Even our sophisticated theorizing can easily drift into error. Compare:

- 'Sherlock Holmes is a detective' is neither true nor false.
- It is neither true nor false that Sherlock Holmes is a detective.

The first of these is true, but the second isn't. The second isn't false either: it is truth-valueless, and indeed meaningless, because it *uses*, rather than just *mentions*, an N-name. Similarly, when we said above that Alex doesn't believe that Sherlock Holmes is a detective, we weren't correct, since our claim, using the N-name 'Sherlock Holmes', wasn't true (or false). (And, in fact, that previous claim also wasn't true or false.[1])

Theoretical Explanations 3: *The Use/Mention Distinction*
We use language to talk about the world. We use the name 'Kripke' to talk about a particular person in the world, as when we say:
 Kripke wrote *Naming and Necessity*.

But we also use language to talk about language itself. In addition to talking about Kripke the person, we can talk about his name. We could say, for example:
 Kripke's name has two syllables.

There are other ways of using language to talk about language, though. Philosophers are fond of using a particular convention for talking about names, and words in general. If you want to talk about a word, stick quotation marks around it, like so:
 'Kripke' has two syllables.

Note that this says something very different from:
 Kripke has two syllables.

---

[1] Distracting subtlety: given the way we've written the Contamination Principle, it's not clear that the first sentence ('Sherlock Holmes is a detective' is neither true nor false) is true. If the name 'Sherlock Holmes' is a part of this sentence, then the Contamination Principle applies, and it is meaningless (and thus not true). So the crucial question is whether quoted (mentioned) material is part of the sentence. We could write a more careful version of the Contamination Principle to clarify this, or we could change to slightly different examples. If we use: 'Sherlock Holmes is a detective. The previous sentence is neither true nor false.' then the second sentence is true, and outside the scope of the Contamination Principle.

ANTI-REALIST VIEWS 53

This latter sentence is false, perhaps nonsensical, while the former is true. Philosophers are also fond of using a bit of jargon to mark this distinction. If a word occurs without quotation marks and functions to talk about an object, it is being *used*. If it occurs with quotation marks and functions to talk about the word itself, it is being *mentioned*. (Note that non-philosophers often aren't as punctilious as philosophers are; even good writers sometimes talk about words without using quotation marks. But when doing philosophy it's an important distinction to keep track of.)

The No-Meaning view has important relations to the error reply to the belief puzzles discussed in Chapter 2. Both the No-Meaning view and the error reply require large imputations of cognitive illusion:

- According to the error reply, although it seems to us that Lois Lane doesn't believe that Clark Kent is Superman, she in fact does believe this—we are just subject to the cognitive illusion that she doesn't.
- According to the No-Meaning view, although it seems to us that Alex believes that Sherlock Holmes is a detective, she doesn't in fact believe this—we are just subject to the cognitive illusion that she does.

Just as the error reply can appeal to associated, possibly metalinguistic, beliefs, so can the No-Meaning view. Alex does not believe that Sherlock Holmes is a detective (*sic*), but she does believe that 'Sherlock Holmes' is the name of a detective.

3.5.2 Anti-Realism 2: Gappy Propositions

We can obtain a softened version of Kripkean Anti-realism by rejecting the Contamination Principle. On this view, although the *name* 'Sherlock Holmes' is meaningless, the *sentence* 'Sherlock Holmes lived at 221B Baker Street' is not. But what, then, does that sentence mean? One view is that it expresses a *gappy proposition*. To understand the idea of a gappy proposition, we begin with the idea of a *structured proposition*. Consider the sentence 'Winston Churchill was prime minister of Great Britain'. This sentence says something *about* Winston Churchill, about Great Britain, and about the property of *being prime minister*. We can think of its content as being built out of those parts. Now consider 'Sherlock Holmes lived at 221B Baker Street'. By analogy, we would like to say that the content of this sentence is built out of Sherlock Holmes, of 221B Baker Street, and of the property of living at. But there is no Sherlock Holmes, so one of the intended components of the structured proposition is missing. We are left with a structured proposition with a gap in it, where the missing part should have gone.

All of that is somewhat metaphorical. For our purposes, the crucial fact is that gappy propositions, like normal propositions, are the kind of things we can believe. So on the Gappy Proposition view, 'Alex believes that Sherlock Holmes is a detective' can be true. It is made true by Alex standing in the belief relation to the gappy proposition *that _____ is a detective*. But getting the cognitive facts right remains tricky. Since there is no Sherlock Holmes, 'Sherlock Holmes is a detective' expresses a gappy proposition whose sole component is the property of being a detective. But since there is no Zeus, 'Zeus is a detective' expresses a gappy proposition whose sole component is the property of being a detective. Thus 'Sherlock Holmes is a detective' and 'Zeus is a detective' express the same gappy proposition. But if Alex believes Sherlock Holmes is a detective because she stands in the belief relation to the gappy proposition *that _____ is a detective*, then she stands in the belief relation to the gappy proposition expressed by 'Zeus is a detective', so she also believes Zeus is a detective. But it is possible to believe that Sherlock Holmes is a detective and not that Zeus is a detective, so this is a problem for the Gappy Proposition view.

Notice that this problem is just another manifestation of the problem of opacity. The original problem of opacity was: 'Marilyn Monroe' and 'Norma Jeane Mortenson' refer to the same person, but it is possible to believe that Marilyn Monroe is an actor while not believing that Norma Jeane Mortenson is. Here we find that 'Sherlock Holmes' and 'Zeus' also refer to the same thing (because neither refers at all), yet it is possible to believe that Sherlock Holmes is a detective while not believing that Zeus is a detective. As a result, the same types of responses are available. The prospects for the Gappy Proposition view to give an adequate account of the role of N-names in cognition stand or fall with the general prospects for Kripkean views to resist the troubles of opacity.

The Gappy Proposition view also faces difficulties with getting plausible truth values for in-fiction, metafiction, and nonexistence claims. Here the crucial question is what to say about the truth value of gappy propositions like *that _____ is a detective*. The most plausible view is that gappy propositions are neither true nor false, because they don't have all the components that would be needed to determine a truth value. We cannot say that *that____ is a detective* is true, because it does not correctly ascribe the property of being a detective to someone who has that property. And we cannot say that it is false, because it does not incorrectly ascribe the property of being a detective to someone who lacks that property. But if gappy propositions lack truth values, then the Gappy Proposition view offers little advance on the No-Meaning view.

3.5.3 Anti-Realism 3: Operator Anti-Realism

The No-Meaning and Gappy Proposition views are difficult to accept because they systematically deny that N-name-containing sentences have truth values. This lack of truth value is the typical cost which offsets the benefit of the metaphysical simplicity of anti-realist views, but one remaining anti-realist option tries to avoid paying that cost. Perhaps, for example, 'Sherlock Holmes does not exist' is true. It's not true because 'Sherlock Holmes' refers to something that has the property of not existing, but rather because the gappy proposition expressed by 'Sherlock Holmes does not exist' *displays* the very lack of existence that it asserts. Tim Crane (2013) develops a version of Anti-realism that extends this strategy to a wider range of cases, claiming that, for example, 'Sherlock Holmes is a fictional detective' is true, despite the fact that 'Sherlock Holmes' does not refer to anything, because what it takes for that sentence to be true is not for the referent of 'Sherlock Holmes' to be a fictional detective, but for it to be fictionally represented that 'Sherlock Holmes' refers to a detective.

Compare the following two claims:

9.   There is a giraffe on the tarmac.

10.   According to Alex, there is a giraffe on the tarmac.

For the first of these claims to be true, there must be something on the tarmac—a long-necked mammal. But the truth of the second doesn't require anything on the tarmac. Rather, its truth depends on facts about Alex and what she says. The phrase 'according to Alex' creates an *opaque context*. A full theory of this sort of opaque contexts is beyond the scope of this discussion, but for a very simple view, suppose that 'According to Alex, S' is true just in case Alex has uttered the sentence 'S'. Since Alex has uttered some but not all true sentences, knowing that S is true won't tell us whether 'According to Alex, S' is true.

Operator Anti-realism is the view that although N-names do not refer, many uses of N-names are in opaque contexts. These opaque contexts are created by *implicit* 'in the fiction' operators. On this view, when we say 'Sherlock Holmes is a detective', what we mean is 'In the Conan Doyle stories, Sherlock Holmes is a detective'. 'In the Conan Doyle stories' then creates an opaque context, so even if 'Sherlock Holmes' does not refer and the simple sentence 'Sherlock Holmes is a detective' lacks a truth value, this won't settle the truth value of 'In the Conan Doyle stories, Sherlock Holmes is a detective'.

Again simplistically, assume 'In the Conan Doyle stories, S' is true just in case the sentence S occurs somewhere in the Conan Doyle stories. Then 'In the Conan Doyle stories, Sherlock Holmes is a detective' is true, because the sentence 'Sherlock Holmes is a detective' does appear in the stories. On the other hand, 'In the Conan Doyle stories, Sherlock Holmes is a giraffe' is false, because the sentence 'Sherlock Holmes is a giraffe' does not appear in the stories. Operator Anti-realism can thus give plausible truth values to in-fiction claims. Metafiction and nonexistence claims, however, are more difficult. We don't want to interpret 'Sherlock Holmes is a fictional character' as 'In the Conan Doyle stories, Sherlock Holmes is a fictional detective', because he isn't fictional *in the stories* (unlike Radioactive Man, who is fictional in the fiction). Nor do we want 'Sherlock Holmes does not exist' to mean 'In the Conan Doyle stories, Sherlock Holmes does not exist'. The operator anti-realist can, of course, hold that there is no implicit in-the-fiction operator in these claims—but then the one tool of the view is removed, and there remains nothing helpful to say about these cases.

The central struggle for all forms of Anti-realism is to produce plausible *variation* in the truth values of N-name-containing sentences. Since the anti-realist says the same thing about the *reference* of all N-names (namely, that they don't refer to anything), it is thus hard to get different N-name-containing sentences to have different truth values. But plausibly these sentences do vary. Some are true, some are false, perhaps some lack truth value. The No-Meaning view attempts the hard line of rejecting the plausible variation and holding that all N-name-containing sentences are alike in being meaningless. The Gappy Proposition, and Operator versions of Anti-realism use different tools for producing some variation. The Gappy Proposition view exploits a difference in *sentence meaning* to create difference in truth values of belief report sentences. Operator Anti-realism, on the other hand, makes use of implicit in-the-fiction operators to create difference in truth values of in-fiction claims.

3.6 Realist Views

Unlike anti-realists, realists think that N-names like 'Sherlock Holmes' and 'Phaeton' refer. As a result, there is a sense in which on the realist view, there is no special *semantic* problem of N-names—they, like all names, contribute their referent to meanings. The problems the realist faces are thus located primarily in *metaphysics*. The realist must tell us *what kinds of things the N-names refer to*.

3.6.1 Realism 1: Creationism

One view is that N-names refer to *fictional characters*. Fictional characters are certain kinds of *abstract objects* created by human activity. Kripke explains this idea as follows:

A fictional character, then, is in some sense an abstract entity. It exists in virtue of more concrete activities of telling stories, writing plays, writing novels and so on, under criteria which I won't try to state precisely, but which should have their own obvious intuitive character. It is an abstract entity which exists in virtue of more concrete activities the same way that a nation is an abstract entity which exists in virtue of concrete relations between people. A particular statement about a nation might be analyzable out in virtue of a more complicated one about the activities of people, or it might not: it might be hard, or maybe, because of problems of open texture, impossible to do so. But, at any rate, the statement about the nation is true in virtue of, and solely in virtue of, the activities of the people. I hold the same thing to be true of fictional characters. (Kripke 2013: 55)

Because Sherlock Holmes is an abstract entity created by human activity, Sherlock Holmes is not a detective. Detectives are concrete, not abstract. Sherlock Holmes is an it, rather than a he.

Call this view *Creationism*. Many details of the metaphysics of Creationism will need to be worked out. (Does Creationism require causal interaction between people and abstract objects? How much of a story needs to be told before a character is created? Do different Holmes stories (perhaps by different authors) create different Holmes characters?) We will not focus, though, on the details of the metaphysics. If creationist views are to cover the full range of N-names, creative acts had better not be linked too closely to particular forms of intentions, since (for example) introducers of false scientific theories involving N-names do not obviously have such creative intentions.

Creationist views take typical in-fiction claims to be false. When we say 'Sherlock Holmes is a detective', we say something about an abstract entity, but we say something false, because abstract entities cannot be detectives. Creationism could then optionally be supplemented with the 'in-the-fiction' operator of the anti-realist intentionalist. The creationist can think that although Sherlock Holmes (the human-created abstract entity) is not really a detective, it is true *in the story* that Holmes is a detective (in the same way that London in a story can have features that London really lacks).

Creationist views take standard metafictional claims to be true. Sherlock Holmes *is* a fictional character on this view, and there are many true things that can be said about that character. It is true that the character appears in fifty-six Conan Doyle stories, that the character is the most popular detective-representing character in existence, and so on. However, the specific metafictional claim of nonexistence will not be true. Sherlock Holmes *does* exist on this view, so 'Sherlock Holmes does not exist' is false. The creationist can, however, offer 'Sherlock Holmes is not concrete' as a nearby true replacement for the false nonexistence claim.

Similarly, on creationist views, cognitive claims are reasonably straightforward. Because Sherlock Holmes does exist, on this view, people can think about Sherlock Holmes (although there may be a puzzle about how they came to think about that particular abstract entity), and there can be true reports of those beliefs. On this view, someone who believes that Sherlock Holmes is a detective is massively confused—not confused because they think that someone exists who in fact does not exist, but rather confused because they think that something lives on Baker Street and investigates crimes, that is in fact an abstract object.

The price Creationism pays is primarily metaphysical—we have to accept a perhaps strange ontology of human-created abstract objects. Once we have accepted that ontology, the new supply of objects lets us, in effect, convert N-names into normal names, albeit with unexpected referents. From that point, the semantic theory goes smoothly, although (since the referents are not what we might naively have expected) getting particular sentences (such as 'Sherlock Holmes is a detective') to have the right truth value may pose extra challenges.

This extra challenge may in some special cases cause some of the problems that typically affect anti-realists to re-emerge for creationists. Consider the case of fictionally fictional names. Kripke, considering such cases, says:

> We can also have a pretence about a fictional character, as in the case of Gonzago. Only in the play *Hamlet*, or let's suppose so, is it said that there is such a play as *The Murder of Gonzago*. If so, we can say that there is no such fictional character as Gonzago. Here we are not reporting on what is in the play, because the play does say that there is such a fictional character as Gonzago. We are speaking now about the real world. There is in fact no such fictional character as Gonzago, though the play pretends that there is.   (Kripke 2013: 72)

Since it is not *true* that there is an author of *The Murder of Gonzago* who created the character Gonzago (just as it is not true that Sherlock Holmes is a detective), there is no character Gonzago. But then there is nothing for 'Gonzago' to refer to.

3.6.2 Realism 2: Possibilism

A second realist option is Possibilism. According to Possibilism, Sherlock Holmes is not an abstract object created by human action, but is rather a *possible* object. An initial question, then, is what possible objects are. There are two main categories of views here:

- **Possibility Anti-realism:** The phrase 'possible object' is misleading. There are no things that are possible objects. Rather, when we say 'Sherlock Holmes is a possible object', we are saying 'It is possible that Sherlock Holmes is an object'. That is, 'Sherlock Holmes could have existed'. On this understanding of 'possible object', Possibilism is not a species of Realism. We are not saying that 'Sherlock Holmes' refers, but rather that it could have referred.
- **Possibility Realism:** There are things that are possible objects (things whose features make true possibility claims). There are many views on what those things are like. For simplicity, we'll focus on David Lewis's *modal realism*, according to which possible objects are (typically) ordinary physical objects, but located in other possible worlds which are 'parallel universes' that are not spatially or temporally related to us.

Now suppose you are a realist about possibilities (you like the second view above). That is, suppose that you are a modal realist. How could you take advantage of that modal realism in dealing with N-names?

If you're a modal realist, you think there are many more things than people normally think there are. In addition to all of the normal speechless donkeys around here, there are talking donkeys elsewhere, in regions of space and time disconnected from our own. With all these additional things, the modal realist has many more options for providing referents for N-names. There is no detective living at 221B Baker Street *around here*, but in other regions of space and time, there is. That detective can be the referent of the name 'Sherlock Holmes'.

Actually, things are a bit more complicated than this. Other possible worlds don't have detectives living at 221B Baker Street, because other possible worlds don't have 221B Baker Street—that's a place in our world. So maybe 'Sherlock Holmes' refers to a detective who, in some other world, lives in some place suitably similar to 221B Baker Street. Or maybe the other worlds *do* have 221B Baker Street, because what it is to have 221B Baker Street is to have a place suitably similar to our 221B Baker Street.

This possibilist view is ideal for making in-fiction claims true. It's true that Sherlock Holmes is a detective, because the name 'Sherlock Holmes' really does refer to a detective (just one that's in another possible world). On the other hand, metafictional claims don't fare as well. 'Sherlock Holmes is a fictional character' doesn't come out true for the possibilist, precisely because Holmes is a detective, not a fictional character. (However, a possibilist could also be a creationist, and think that the name 'Sherlock Holmes' is ambiguous, referring on some uses to the nonactual detective and on other uses to the abstract object *the fictional character Holmes* that we created.)

Nonexistence claims are also, strictly speaking, false for the possibilist. Sherlock Holmes *does* exist, he just exists far removed from us. Of course, the possibilist says the same thing about talking donkeys: they too exist, but far removed from us. The possibilist then tries to soften that blow by pointing out that we often ignore distant and irrelevant objects in our claims. We can say, at a party, that everyone is having a good time, even though there are many people not at the party who aren't having a good time. And we can say, here in our little region of space and time, that no donkeys talk, even though there are many donkeys not around here that are talking. And in the same way, we can say, again in our region of space, that Sherlock Holmes doesn't exist, even though he is existing happily elsewhere.

The possibilist story is subject to the Problem of Accidental Reference, just as the Fregean approach is. Charles Darwin could have performed all of the deeds of the Conan Doyle stories, but we don't want to say that Darwin could have been Holmes. And if Darwin secretly actually did all of those deeds, we don't want to say that he *was* Holmes. A world might contain two people, both of whom performed all of the deeds of the Conan Doyle stories—we don't then want to say that it contains two Holmeses. (Or that those two people are identical, both being identical to Holmes.)

Obviously the plausibility of Possibilism requires the prior plausibility of a very expansive ontology. To see just how expansive, consider the range of stories we can tell. We are not limited to stories about things which, in any ordinary sense, we would call possible. We can tell stories about sentient numbers, colorless green ideas, and boxes that are both empty and full at the same time.[2] If we are to be possibilist realists, we will need possible entities for the characters in all of these stories.

3.6.3 Realism 3: Noneism

We now consider a subtle form of Realism that aims to achieve realism without metaphysical cost. The goal is to find a plausible way to say both:

11. 'Sherlock Holmes' refers to Sherlock Holmes.

And:

12. Sherlock Holmes does not exist, and there is nothing that 'Sherlock Holmes' refers to.

This doesn't look like an easy goal to achieve. How can a word refer to Sherlock Holmes, if there's no Sherlock Holmes to be referred to?

But we see a similar combination in other cases:

13. Dikaiopolis worships Zeus, but Zeus does not exist, and there is nothing that Dikaiopolis worships.

14. Ponce de León seeks the Fountain of Youth. But the Fountain of Youth doesn't exist, and there is nothing that Ponce de León seeks.

---

[2] See Graham Priest, 'Sylan's Box', available at: https://projecteuclid.org/euclid.ndjfl/1039540770

We could ask: how can Dikaiopolis worship Zeus, if there's no Zeus to be worshipped? And: how can Ponce de León seek the Fountain of Youth, if there's no Fountain of Youth to be sought? A view called *Noneism* says that we just shouldn't be puzzled by such questions. Dikaiopolis can worship Zeus without there being a Zeus to be worshipped, because that's just the way worshipping works. *Worshipping* isn't the kind of thing that demands existence of the thing worshipped.

Some verbs, then, are existence-demanding, while others are not. *Hitting* is existence-demanding. You can't hit Zeus, because there is no Zeus to be hit. *Seeking* is not existence-demanding. You can seek the Fountain of Youth, even without there being a Fountain of Youth. The question of *why* some verbs are existence-demanding and others are not is a hard one, and we won't try to answer it here. But the noneist will be satisfied if examples like *worship* and *seek* convince you that some verbs are not existence-demanding.

If there are verbs that aren't existence-demanding, then *refers* might be one of those verbs. And if it is, then the noneist can say that 'Sherlock Holmes' refers to Sherlock Holmes. The noneist agrees that there is no Sherlock Holmes, but just thinks (because refers isn't existence-demanding) that this is irrelevant to the claim that 'Sherlock Holmes' refers to Sherlock Holmes.

The noneist's goal is to have realism on the cheap. It's realism, because noneists say that N-names refer. But it's on the cheap, because we don't need some special kind of things (like created fictional objects or possible objects) to serve as the referents. According to the noneist, 'Sherlock Holmes' refers to Sherlock Holmes, but at the same time, there is nothing to which it refers, because there is no Sherlock Holmes. No thing means nothing to explain.

But no thing may also mean nothing to be helpful. The difficult question for the noneist is what use the reference facts are. According to the noneist view, 'Sherlock Holmes' refers to Sherlock Holmes. How does this help us settle the truth value of 'Sherlock Holmes is a detective'?

'Sherlock Holmes is a detective' is true if the referent of 'Sherlock Holmes' has the property picked out by 'is a detective'. According to the noneist, the referent of 'Sherlock Holmes' is Sherlock Holmes. So does Sherlock Holmes have the property of being a detective? Well, given that the noneist also tells us that there is no Sherlock Holmes, it's hard to know how to answer this question. We can't go find Sherlock Holmes and see what he's like, because there's no Holmes to be found. Noneism seems to make it possible for claims involving N-names to be true, but to give us nothing that would help us settle whether they are true.

One lesson to be learned here is that the metaphysical extravagances of Creationist and Possibilist Realism have been playing an important role in getting a plausible story about the truth values of N-name-containing sentences. As we saw in considering Anti-realism, we want different such sentences to have different truth values. Creationists and possibilists have a chance of getting this variation through variation in the natures of the objects provided by their extravagant metaphysics. But, precisely because Noneism doesn't provide any objects, it also can't account for the varying natures of those objects.

3.7 Cognitive and Metaphysical Lessons of N-Names

There is no easy solution to the problems created by N-names. Once we accept the Kripkean idea that names are centrally characterized by their referents, we inevitably confront the fact that natural language is extremely generous in its use of names. Something about the linguistic practice that lets us have a ready supply of names for objects far distant in space and time also lets us have names that apparently don't refer to anything. A Fregean view that takes descriptive meaning, rather than reference, to be central doesn't have to view N-names as unusual—they are simply names whose descriptive meanings, given the contingent state of the world, don't succeed in picking out referents. But this Fregean take on N-names is then subject to the same sorts of problems that Kripke points out for Fregean views more generally in *Naming and Necessity*.

Within the Kripkean framework, we can either view N-names as defective or anomalous aspects of the naming practice or find a way to accommodate them as normal parts of the practice. The anti-realist strategies set out above treat N-names as defective. The No-Meaning and Gappy Proposition views take N-names to be *failed attempts at names*. Both of these views, then, are examples of error theories: views that take us to be wrong about what's really going on. On these views, we think we are saying true things or communicating information in cases when we really aren't. The No-Meaning and Gappy Proposition views differ primarily in how much error they impute. For the Gappy Proposition view, error is limited to the realm of public communication, but stops at the internal mental realm, while for the No-Meaning view, error penetrates into the mind as well. Operator Anti-realism, on the other hand, doesn't treat N-names as defective names. Rather, it treats utterances using N-names as mere mock assertions. On this view, when we utter 'Sherlock Holmes is a detective', we aren't really asserting that anyone is a detective. Rather, we are doing a bit of storytelling, and *pretending* to assert that someone is a detective. But again, this is an error theory, since we don't normally take ourselves to be making mere mock assertions with N-names.

If we don't want to impute error where N-names are involved, we have to move to realist accounts. On realist accounts (as on Fregean approaches), there isn't anything fundamentally special about N-names. They are characterized only by referring to unexpected classes of objects: abstract entities created by authors, merely possible detectives, or things that don't even exist. We thus pay a metaphysical price for avoiding error theory: we have to expand our ontology to get enough objects to serve as referents for the profligate naming practices of ordinary talk. How high the price is then depends on how thoroughly we want to avoid error. Merely getting referents for N-names isn't enough to avoid all error—to be completely error-free, we need referents that have the properties we ordinarily impute to N-names. It's one thing to find some object or other to serve as a referent for 'Sherlock Holmes'; it's quite another to find a brilliant, pipe-smoking, cocaine-using detective as referent.

Central Points in Chapter 3

- Natural languages contain many names that don't seem to refer to anything. These can be classified as *names of fiction*, introduced as part of a deliberate practice of pretending to refer, and *names of error*, introduced as ordinary names, but under circumstances that don't provide a normal referent.
- Kripkean theories of names can approach N-names using either anti-realist strategies, which say that N-names don't refer and then offer alternative explanations of the properties of sentences containing N-names, or realist strategies, which offer expanded ontologies containing objects for N-names to refer to.

- No-Meaning and Gappy Proposition anti-realist views both agree that sentences containing N-names fall short of normal meaning. The No-Meaning view says that these sentences are completely meaningless, so that nothing true can be said or believed about Sherlock Holmes. The Gappy Proposition view says that these sentences express a special kind of *partial* proposition, which can be believed but which cannot have a truth value.
- Operator Anti-realism says that sentences containing N-names need to be understood as covertly expressing more complicated sentences saying that (for example) according to a story, Sherlock Holmes is a detective. Operator Anti-realism can then use the contents of stories to give plausible truth values to sentences.
- Creationist and possibility realist views both expand our ontology to provide referents for N-names. Creationist Realism takes Sherlock Holmes to be an abstract object created by Arthur Conan Doyle; on this view, Sherlock Holmes is fictional, but not a detective. Possibilist Realism takes Sherlock Holmes to be a merely possible person; on this view, he is a detective, but is not fictional.
- Noneist Realism attempts to combine the virtues of Anti-realism and Realism by saying that 'Sherlock Holmes' does refer, but that there is no thing to which it refers. Even if this is coherent, the view faces the challenge of then explaining what features (being a detective? being fictional?) the nonexistent Sherlock Holmes has.

Comprehension Questions

1. Explain the puzzle of N-names in your own words.
2. What is the Fregean response to the puzzle of N-names? What are the possible Kripkean responses?
3. Give three examples of each of the following:
    3.1. In-fiction claims.
    3.2. Metafictional claims.
    3.3. Nonexistence claims.
    3.4. Cognitive claims.

(*continued*)

4. Give two examples of sentences which seem to confirm the Contamination Principle, and two examples of sentences which seem to be counterexamples to the Contamination Principle.
5. Which, if any, of the realist and anti-realist views of fictional claims discussed above do you think is most common sense? Which least? (It might help to draw up a table with the different desiderata for a view of fictional claims on one side, and the different views on the other.)
6. The presence of the Eiffel Tower in Paris explains the falsity of 'The Eiffel Tower is in Berlin'. Does this make that sentence about Paris, or make 'Berlin' refer to Paris? What does this tell us about the relation between what a sentence is *about*, and what the words in it *refer* to?

Exploratory Questions

7. Are the following N-names: numerals (i.e. '1', '78'), abstract nouns (i.e. 'triangularity'), moral terms (i.e. 'goodness')? If so, can we learn anything from them about N-names in general? If not, can we use our understanding of them to help us understand the N-names of this chapter?
8. Consider a biography of Churchill which is full of errors.
    8.1. Are occurrences of 'Churchill' in this book N-names? If so, why? If not, why? Does your view change if you are told that the book is 99 percent in error?
    8.2. Why might this kind of example pose a problem to Fregeans?
    8.3. Why might this kind of example pose a problem to Possibilist Realism?
    8.4. How might the answer to 8.1 differ if the book was a work of historical fiction rather than a biography?
9. We suggested that if there was someone with all the properties ascribed to Holmes by Conan Doyle, it wouldn't be the case that 'Holmes' referred to him. Should the Fregean accept this? How might one argue that 'Holmes' would stand for Pseudo-Holmes in that situation?
10. Are you a realist or an anti-realist? Why? Which, in your view, is the strongest form of Realism/Anti-realism?

11. On the No-Meaning view, why exactly is the first sentence below true while the second is false?
    • 'Sherlock Holmes is a detective' is neither true nor false
    • It's neither true nor false that Sherlock Holmes is a detective.
12. Consider the following sentences:
    • Sherlock Holmes has two kidneys.
    • Sherlock Holmes has heard of Jack the Ripper.
    Assume that Jack the Ripper was sufficiently famous in the London of the Holmes stories that everyone had heard of him. Nevertheless, the stories of Conan Doyle don't mention this fact. Nor do they mention that Holmes has two kidneys. What would the operator view say about these sentences? Are these sentences true according to the operator view?
13. The creationist has a problem explaining the truth of in-fiction claims. Can you think of a way to resolve it—maybe reconstrue what is said by 'Sherlock Holmes lives at Baker Street'. Is there any property we could ascribe to Sherlock Holmes (as conceived of by the creationist) to make this true? (Hint: how might the creationist think of the predicate 'lives on Baker Street'?)
14. How might the idea that we believe propositions under a guise (which we talked about in Chapter 2) help us to explain some of the problems around N-names?
15. Some stories are told and retold in different ways. Consider the Sherlock Holmes stories as told by Conan Doyle, and the Sherlock Holmes stories as told by the recent BBC series (or in a fanfic version of the Holmes stories). These stories are going to share some in-fiction claims about Holmes (for example, that Holmes lives at 221B Baker Street), but other in-fiction claims are going to differ between stories (for example, the claim that Holmes has a mobile phone). How might the different views of N-names discussed above make sense of divergent in-fiction claims? (Think particularly about how these in-fiction claims might be handled by Operator Anti-realism, Creationism, Possibilism, and Noneism.)

Further Reading

A helpful survey article outlining the realist and anti-realist positions is Friend 2007. A recent version of the Gappy Propositions view is Braun 2005. Lewis 1978 is an account of the operator view. Sainsbury 2005 is a nice monograph devoted to empty names, which makes use of free logic. An anti-realist view is defended in Brock 2002. The long-awaited Kripke 2013 defends a realist view, and is very worth reading.

4
The Puzzle of Essential Indexicality

This chapter continues some themes from Chapter 2, but concerning a new class of expressions: *indexicals*. Indexicals are expressions such as 'I', 'now', 'here', 'that', 'you', 'yesterday', and 'she'. There's an important sense in which these expressions refer, as do names, but there are important differences. There is now an extensive literature on indexicals that originates in the work of Perry, Lewis, and Castañeda, and at the core of much of that literature is what we will call the *Puzzle of Essential Indexicality*. As we will see, that puzzle is very closely related to the puzzle about belief reports that we discussed in Chapter 2. Here is the connection: if indexicals are essential, it means that they cannot be substituted by other co-referential expressions. We will see the details of this below, but a basic idea behind essential indexicality is this: when Obama uses 'I', he refers to Obama, but many of his uses of 'I' cannot be substituted by uses of 'Obama'. If the arguments for essential indexicality establish this, then the efforts to argue against opacity in Chapter 2 will seem pointless: after all, if there's opacity with respect to indexicals, then the Fregean view wins anyway—there's little point fighting it in connection with names, if the phenomenon is established with respect to indexicals.

4.1 Preliminary: What Are Indexicals?

Consider the following sentences:

1. I'm happy now.
2. You came here yesterday.
3. She isn't here.

If we ask you what the indexicals in these sentences refer to (i.e. what the expressions 'I', 'now', 'you', 'here', 'yesterday', and 'she' refer to), you wouldn't know what to answer. You would be torn:

- On the one hand, those expressions don't refer to anything. The word 'I'—i.e. the word itself—has no referent.
- On the other hand, particular utterances of those words do seem to refer. If, for example, Nora uttered sentence 1, at 4 p.m. on October 23, 2015, then that utterance of 'I' would refer to her, i.e. to Nora. And that utterance of 'now' would refer to the time she was speaking, i.e. to 4 p.m. on October 23, 2015.

So the words, abstracted from particular utterances, have no referential properties. But when uttered, they do refer to something.

David Kaplan's 'Demonstratives' (Kaplan 1977/1989) provided a now widely accepted framework for thinking about indexicals. He distinguished between the *character* and the *content* of indexicals:

- **Character**: The character of an indexical, for example 'I', is a rule that tells you what that word refers to when it is uttered. The rule is fairly simple: a use of the word 'I' in a sentence refers to the person who uttered that sentence. Similarly, it is fairly easy to state the rule for 'now' (its character): it refers to the time of utterance of the sentence. Kaplan also described the character as a function: it takes context of utterance as inputs and yields referents as outputs.
- **Content**: The content of an indexical is the object it refers to. So when Nora utters the word 'I', *she* is the content of that utterance of 'I'. When we utter 'now' at 2 p.m. February 4, 2015, then that word refers to that time. If we utter 'that', pointing at a chair and intending to demonstrate it, then the demonstrative refers to that chair.

In some respects, indexicals are very much like names. There is of course one big difference. They don't refer to the same object in every context. In some contexts 'I' refers to Nora, in other contexts it refers to Barack Obama. It all depends on who is speaking. The same goes for other indexicals. They are context-sensitive. What an utterance of an indexical refers to depends on the context it is uttered in. That is not true for names. 'Barack Obama' refers to the same man, no matter what the context.[1]

---

[1] As with all philosophical views, there's no universal consensus on this: for dissenting voices, see Chapter 7.

There's another respect in which indexicals are different from names: their referents are all fixed by descriptions (what Kaplan called characters.) That is an important difference from names, whose referents are typically fixed by external factors—what Kripke called a communicative chain. According to Kripke, we don't need to have access to a set of descriptions that uniquely pick out the referent. In the case of indexicals, however, it looks like we do always have access to such rules.[2]

4.2 The Puzzle of Essential Indexicality and Indexical Opacity

We turn now to a presentation of a series of influential arguments— originating with Castañeda (1967), Perry (1977, 1979), and Lewis (1979)—that aim to show that indexical reference has some extremely peculiar features:

a. Indexical reference is essential for action: we can't understand the nature of agency unless we understand its connection to indexicals. No indexical reference, no action. Non-indexical reference (e.g. reference by proper names) is not essential for action in this way.
b. Indexical reference plays a distinctive role in gathering information: there's information you can only convey using indexical reference, which cannot be conveyed using names.

This is puzzling: *why does indexical reference have such features when reference with names does not?* Moreover, it seems to reintroduce us to the puzzle from Chapter 2: if indexical reference has such special powers, then indexicals can't be substituted for co-referential non-indexical expressions. For example, Obama's use of 'I' cannot be substituted with a use of 'Obama', *salva veritate*. If so, opacity again raises its ugly head and the efforts to fight it off in Chapter 2 will have been in vain.

---

[2] Note that, as in the case of descriptive names (e.g. Neptune and Jack the Ripper, discussed in Chapter 1), we can generate contingent a priori truths with indexicals: in some sense we know, a priori, that an utterance of 'I'm here now' is true, but it is contingent. This is not to say that these rules provide the meaning of the indexicals, i.e. that we can substitute the indexicals for the reference-fixing rule. To see why, consider the sentence: 'I am not speaking now'. Any utterance of this is false, but what it says could have been true (if the person actually speaking hadn't spoken). However, the sentence 'The person speaking now is not the person speaking now', couldn't have been true. This shows that you can't substitute 'I' with its character and preserve meaning.

There is powerful data in favor of both arguments a and b, and in what follows we outline that data and consider some replies on behalf of those who don't think that a and b are true. Section 4.3 lays out the case for a and Sections 4.4 and 4.5 respond to it. Section 4.6 lays out the case for b and Section 4.7 against it. Section 4.8 gives a positive account of how to understand the role of indexicality in action explanation.

4.3 Perry: Indexicals as Essential for Action

The view that indexicality is essential for action—that action would be impossible without indexical reference—is, at first blush, a surprising thesis. How could these little words, the indexicals, be necessary for human agency? Why should this kind of reference be so much more powerful than reference using ordinary proper names? The view might be surprising, but it is not much of an exaggeration to say that it is the orthodoxy today. We can find this view expressed in the following passages:

The present suggestion, then, is that indexical concepts are ineliminable because without them agency would be impossible: when I imagine myself divested of indexical thoughts, employing only centreless mental representations, I *eo ipso* imagine myself deprived of the power to act.   (McGinn 1983: 104)

It is widely agreed that agents need information in an egocentric form: they must think of places as 'here' and 'there', times as 'now' and 'then' if they are to be able to act on what they know (Perry 1979).   (Owens 2011: 267)

Practical guidance is, in Perry's phrase, essentially indexical, in the sense that its function depends not only on which of many propositions it expresses but also on how that proposition is determined by the context—specifically, on its being determined in the same way as the reference of indexical expressions such as 'I', 'you', 'here', and 'now'.   (Velleman 2015: 78)

The background for this view is a series of arguments first presented by John Perry, and later by David Lewis.[3] In particular, the view is motivated by a series of cases in Perry's paper, 'The problem of the essential indexical'. Here are two of those:

I once followed a trail of sugar on a supermarket floor, pushing my cart down the aisle on one side of a tall counter and back the aisle on the other, seeking the shopper with the torn sack to tell him he was making a mess. With each trip

---

[3] Both Perry and Lewis were inspired by the work of Castañeda, although they don't mention a specific work.

around the counter, the trail became thicker. But I seemed unable to catch up. Finally it dawned on me. I was the shopper I was trying to catch . . . I believed at the outset that the shopper with a torn sack was making a mess. And I was right. But I didn't believe that I was making a mess. That seems to be something I came to believe. And when I came to believe that, I stopped following the trail around the counter, and rearranged the torn sack in my cart. My change in beliefs seems to explain my change in behavior. My aim in this paper is to make a key point about the characterization of this change, and of beliefs in general. (Perry 1979: 3)

Ask yourself: what would make Perry stop and clean up after himself? Suppose he recognized that John Perry was making a mess. Wouldn't that suffice? No, it wouldn't. Not unless he recognized (or believed) that he was John Perry. Suppose he had forgotten his name or was an amnesiac—then being told that Perry was making a mess would have no effect on his behavior other than motivating a search for this guy Perry (who Perry doesn't know is himself). Coming to know that Perry is making a mess will make Perry stop only if he also believes something of the form: *I am John Perry.* That first-personal reference is, it seems, needed for agency to take place.

The second case makes the same kind of point with respect to 'now'. We are asked by Perry to consider:

A professor, who desires to attend the department meeting on time and believes correctly that it begins at noon, sits motionless in his office at that time. Suddenly, he begins to move. What explains his action? A change in belief. He believed all along that the department meeting starts at noon; he came to believe, as he would have put it, that it starts now. (Perry 1979: 4)

The point here is analogous to the point made about 'I' above: it is only when the time—i.e. noon—is referred to by the professor as 'now' that he will start moving. If he just keeps thinking to himself 'the meeting starts at noon', then no action will occur. He needs to come to a point where he is thinking 'Noon is now!' for action to take place.

4.4 Skepticism about Essential Indexicality

These powerful and vivid examples have led many philosophers to draw very strong conclusions. We saw some examples of this above. Recall what Perry had to say:

It is widely agreed that agents need information in an egocentric form: they must think of places as 'here' and 'there', times as 'now' and 'then' if they are to be able to act on what they know (Perry 1979). (Owens 2011: 267)

But do Perry's examples really show that indexical information is essential for action? There is now a growing literature that is skeptical of these radical conclusions—the opponents are still in a minority, but their views are getting more difficult to ignore (the skeptics include Millikan 1990, Cappelen and Dever 2013, Magidor 2015, Ninan 2016, among others). The skeptics argue as follows. There are two opposing views: on one view, a distinctly first-person (or other indexical) attitude is required in an adequate action rationalization. According to the other view, it is not required. Perry's cases have the form of thought experiments in which it is *stipulated* that at *t1* there is no action (and no relevant first-person or other indexical attitude) and then at *t2* there's action. By stipulation, the only difference between *t1* and *t2* is the addition of a first-person state. So we all say: fine, yes, that could happen—the first-person state could have that effect and so could play an important role in rationalization of that particular action. Note that this is at best very weak *inductive* support for the view that indexical reference is required for action. As Cappelen and Dever put it:

That indexical reference *can* lead to action in Perry's examples, doesn't show that it *has to*. Cases can be used as counterexamples to universal claims, but can't be used to (deductively) establish the latter. (2013: 41–2)

In other words, if there's an argument for the thesis that indexical reference is required for action, it has to go beyond just these famous examples.

Despite the fact that Perry's papers have convinced a very large group of philosophers, it is surprisingly hard to find articulated any real argument for this strong conclusion. As we have just seen, the examples, by themselves, don't establish the general conclusion. In what follows we look at some other considerations that Perry often appeals to. He says, for example:

Consider a transaction with a fax machine. To press certain buttons on it, I have to move my fingers a certain distance and direction from me. It isn't enough to know where the buttons were relative to one another, or where the fax machine was in the building or room. I had to know where these things were relative to me.
(Perry 1998: 87)

The basic idea is simple enough: in order to act on the world, we need to bring our bodies in contact with the objects around us. In order to do that, we need to locate ourselves (and in particular our bodies) relative to these external objects.

In response to this line of thought, the skeptic has two replies:

i. It is true that in order to act, our bodies have to be brought into engagement with the world around us. But what is not true is that for that to happen, we *must* represent ourselves in relation to the objects we engage with. Consider what Perry says about the fax machine: why do you *need* to know or have a belief about where the buttons are relative to you? In general, we don't need to have knowledge or beliefs of all the facts involved in our action. To move a finger, you have to tense various sequences of muscles. But you don't need to know or have beliefs about what those sequences of muscles are. Somewhere in the physical architecture, the relation of you to the muscles gets implemented, but it doesn't need to be a cognitive implementation. There is no reason why it can't be like that for you and the buttons. On the cognitive-representation level, it's just all about the buttons and their objective position in space. Then a bunch of neurons fire and our bodies end up doing the right thing. If there is no representation of the fingers (whether conscious or sub-personal), there is a fortiori no crucial *indexical* representation of the fingers.

ii. We just argued that we don't *need* to represent the external objects relative to our body in order to act. However, we do, of course, do that, sometimes. What we now want to emphasize is that when we do that, i.e. when the agent happens to think about the buttons' location relative to her, no argument has been given that she *has* to think about herself in a *distinctly first-person way* (e.g. that she has to refer to herself using 'I'). If the agent is Nora and she happens to represent Nora's relationship to the buttons, she could represent herself in a non-first-person way, e.g. as Nora.

In sum, the skeptic locates at least two mistakes in the line of thought expressed in Perry's passage about the fax machine:

- **Over-Representation Fallacy**: The fallacy of assuming that because the position of the body relative to the environment is involved in the movement, the body needs to be mentally represented. It could just be that the body's relation to the environment is implemented non-representationally.
- **Relational Fallacy**: The fallacy of assuming that if some part of the position of the body relative to the environment has to be represented,

it has to be *indexically* represented. It could just be that the position of the body relative to the environment is represented in non-indexical terms.

4.5 A Deflationary Interpretation of Perry's Examples: *It's All About Opacity*

It is important to note that sometimes Perry summarizes the lesson of his argument in terms of opacity. Perry says, for example, that when you use 'I' to describe one of your beliefs, it is especially important, because:

> When we replace it with other designations of me, we no longer have an explanation of my behavior and so, it seems, no longer an attribution of the same belief. It seems to be an *essential* indexical. But without such a replacement, all we have to identify the belief is the sentence 'I am making a mess'. But that sentence by itself doesn't seem to identify the crucial belief, for if someone else had said it, they would have expressed a different belief, a false one.   (Perry 1979: 3)

Here is one way to summarize Perry's claim:

Indexical Opacity: Indexicals cannot be substituted *without a change in truth value* in action-explanation contexts by any other co-referential expressions.

This, the skeptic points out, is an instantiation of the more general thesis:

Generic Opacity: Co-referential referring expressions cannot be substituted *without a change in truth value* in action-explanation contexts.

To see that Generic Opacity is true, note that cases analogous to those appealed to by Perry are easily constructed using proper names:

Superman/Clark Kent: Pushing my cart down the aisle I was looking for Clark Kent to tell him he was making a mess. I kept passing by Superman, but couldn't find Clark Kent. Finally, I realized Superman was Clark Kent. I believed at the outset that Clark Kent was making a mess. And I was right. But I didn't believe that Superman was making a mess. That seems to be something that I came to believe. And when I came to believe that, I stopped looking around and I told Superman to clean up after himself. My change in beliefs seems to explain my change in behavior.

Those skeptical of Perry's view take the Superman/Clark Kent case as showing that in general action explanations don't have their explanatory force preserved by substitution of co-referential singular terms. Seeing

Indexical Opacity as an instance of Generic Opacity suggests that there's nothing deeply central about indexicals here, the skeptic argues.

As we explained in Chapter 2, there's a series of powerful arguments that aim to deflate the arguments for opacity (to show that it's some kind of error to think that we can't substitute—see Sections 2.4, 2.5). Those arguments will now apply directly to the current debate. If the argument above is correct, then there is no distinctive argument in connection with indexicals—just the same kind of argument as was discussed and assessed in Chapter 2.

4.6 Lewis: Indexicality as Essential for Information Gathering

Many philosophers think that the following example from David Lewis shows that there is something distinctive about first-personal reference— in particular that it plays a distinctive role in gathering information about the world:

Consider the case of the two gods. They inhabit a certain possible world, and they know exactly which world it is. Therefore they know every proposition that is true at their world. Insofar as knowledge is a propositional attitude, they are omniscient. Still I can imagine them to suffer ignorance: neither one knows which of the two he is. They are not exactly alike. One lives on top of the tallest mountain and throws down manna; the other lives on top of the coldest mountain and throws down thunderbolts. Neither one knows whether he lives on the tallest mountain or on the coldest mountain; nor whether he throws manna or thunderbolts. Surely their predicament is possible. (The trouble might perhaps be that they have an equally perfect view of every part of their world, and hence cannot identify the perspectives from which they view it.)   (Lewis 1979: 520–1)

Lewis takes this case to show that there is knowledge about the world that can only be obtained when we use first-person reference. He calls this information 'self-locating' or *de se* information. *De se* information is the kind of information that the two gods are missing. It is the information they get when they are in a position to say or think: '*I am the god on the tallest mountain*'.

Here is another case (this time from Perry):

Consider an amnesiac, Rudolf Lingens, is lost in the Stanford library. He reads a number of things in the library, including a biography of himself, and a detailed account of the library in which he is lost. [. . .] He still won't know who *he is* and *where he is,* and no matter how much knowledge he piles up, until that moment when he is ready to say,

This place is aisle five, floor six, of Main Library, Stanford.

I am Rudolf Lingens.   (Perry 1977: 492; see also Lewis 1979: 519–20)

Again, the upshot is supposed to be that without those indexical thoughts, Lingens is missing important self-locating information.

These cases have led many to think that self-locating or *de se* information is distinctive in that it can only be accessed using indexical reference. So, again, we have an argument to the effect that indexical reference is significantly different from name-reference.

4.7 Response to Lewis from the Skeptic

Lewis's argument has been enormously influential (see Cappelen and Dever 2013: 6–9 for references). However, there are now also influential voices arguing that Lewis's argument fails, for much the same reasons that Perry's did. In what follows, we outline the skeptic's case against Lewis.

Recall that for Lewis's two gods argument to work, it is crucial that the omniscient gods still do not know who and where they are. Suppose Zeus is the god on the tallest mountain and Odin is the god on the coldest mountain. Then Zeus, despite his omniscience, does not know that he is the god on the tallest mountain. He does, however, presumably know that *Zeus* is the god on the tallest mountain.

So what Lewis is trying to explain is how Zeus can know (i) but not (ii):

(i) *Zeus* is the god on the tallest mountain.
(ii) *He* is the god on the tallest mountain.

But this, the skeptic argues—on analogy with the reply to Perry—is just a special case of traditional Frege puzzles. 'Zeus' and 'he' are co-referential and we can't always substitute one for the other while preserving truth value. The problem, the skeptic argues, belongs with the effort to explain how Lois Lane can believe that Superman is strong but not believe that Clark Kent is strong. In Chapter 2 we saw various efforts to reply to this challenge. The skeptic says: whichever one of those is your favorite, use it here. It is surely an adequacy condition on a theory of opacity that it be fully general. We don't want to have one theory explaining how one can believe Superman flies without believing Clark Kent flies, and a different one explaining how one can believe Hesperus is a planet without believing Phosphorus is a planet. Similarly, we don't want one theory explaining how one can believe Zeus is the god on the tallest mountain without believing Jupiter is the god on the tallest mountain, and a different one explaining how Zeus can believe Zeus is the god on the tallest mountain without believing he is the god on the tallest mountain.

Lewis does not give us any reason to think that his indexical versions of Frege puzzles are special in any way. So we are left with a problem: explaining opacity. But that has nothing specifically to do with indexicals (or self-locating beliefs or the *de se*), says the skeptic.

4.8 How Can Differences in Behavior Be Explained?

Now we focus on the need to capture difference in belief and desire among agents who are motivated to perform different actions. Consider a case where two agents have all the same objective, or non-indexical, information about the world. Not only can they be motivated to act differently, but what it is rational for them to do can differ. To see what we have in mind, consider this kind of example inspired by Perry: *Nora and Clara are out walking in the woods. Nora gets attacked by a bear. What happens? Nora climbs a tree while Clara calls for help.* Now one thing to note about this case is that we can imagine Nora and Clara having exactly the same beliefs when they are expressed without indexicals. Both of them think that Nora is being attacked by a bear. They have the same beliefs about where the bear is relative to Nora, and so on for every relevant objective fact about their situation. They also have the same desires and preferences: they would prefer for Nora not to be eaten by the bear. In sum: *we can imagine that they have the very same nonindexical beliefs and desires.* Then it becomes pressing to answer the question: why do Nora and Clara act differently? It is extremely tempting to answer: it is because Nora says (or thinks) to herself: 'I am being attacked by a bear', while Clara doesn't. Surely, that's the relevant difference. That's what explains the difference in behavior. According to the proponent of essential indexicality this explanation shows there's a special role for indexical reference.

Here is how Cappelen and Dever (2013) respond to this challenge: even if it were true that in some cases what makes it rational for A to perform an action, but not for B to do so, is that A has an indexical belief that B does not have, nothing general follows about the connection between indexicality and agency. All kinds of difference in beliefs can make a difference to what it is rational to do. The fact that action-explanation and rationalization contexts are opaque makes this particularly obvious. Consider the following case:

A and B are being threatened by Lex Luthor. They both see a person in the distance. A believes that the person is Superman; B believes that the person is Clark Kent. Now A has reason to refuse to give in to Lex Luthor's threats, since he has reason to think Superman will save him. But B has reason to submit to Lex Luthor's threats, since he has reason to think Clark Kent won't save him. A and B have all the same objective information and desires here, but have reason to act differently.

Notice that there's nothing distinctively *de se* and nothing indexical going on in this case. This is just another example of opacity. So the Perry phenomenon cannot in itself be an argument for the distinctiveness of indexicals. At most it can establish that there is a way that A is thinking of A that isn't the way that B is thinking of A. But that's no more than a familiar instance of opacity, nothing distinctive about indexicals.

Someone convinced by those criticisms might still wonder why it is the case that 'when you and I both apprehend the thought that I am about to be attacked by a bear, we behave differently' (Perry 1977: 494). More generally, an agent will have an indefinite number of third-person beliefs and desires about the world that don't result in or rationalize action by the agent. So we need to explain which ones produce action and which ones don't; we need a selecting mechanism of some sort. Call this 'the Selection Problem'. The *de se* proposal is that the first-person status is the selecting mechanism; only the first-person beliefs and desires give rise to the right sort of intentions, which then give rise to action/rationalization of action. What can be said about the Selection Problem if we don't appeal to *de se* states?

Here's a thought experiment that Cappelen and Dever offer as a replacement for the *de se* picture:[4]

The Action Inventory model. Every agent has a very wide range of third-person beliefs and desires that give rise to third-person intentions, which in turn rationalize or motivate actions (via their recognition). Not all of these intentions are going to produce action, at least in normal cases (perhaps in a god they would). This is because a given agent has an 'action inventory': a range of actions that he can perform. An agent constantly seeks to match his intentions with his action inventory, and when he finds a match, action occurs. When there's no match, the intention idles, and doesn't motivate or rationalize action. So the Selection Problem is solved by appealing to the physical or psychological constraints of the agent: only certain actions result because only certain actions were available in the first place.   (Cappelen and Dever 2013: 50)

The action inventory can include 'John throws a baseball through a window', 'That hand lifts a glass', or 'The car steers out of the skid'. The thought is that we're embedded agents who have a range of capacities directly to manipulate things in the environment. Some of those things are ourselves and our parts, but others are frequently and infrequently encountered objects, both proximal and distal. To think otherwise is to pursue the 'how to move my body' line of thought, which we have already argued against. According to our alternative picture, the belief-desire-obligation-intention sets produce a bunch of inputs— potential actions that are ready to go. Those inputs (i.e. potential actions) then hit the 'action center', which is a big switchboard with a bunch of available actions. If an input matches an available action on the switchboard, an action results. But no one has to 'look' to see if there's a match, and hence no one has to 'think about the available actions' in any way, let alone a first-person way. The actions have already been 'thought about' by the time they emerge as potential actions (and thought about just as the third-person action 'that *p*'); all that remains is to see if the actions are among the things that can be done.

Note that the Action Inventory Model is presented simply as an example of a way action *could* be structured. It is not the claim that we humans actually act like that. It is, rather, the claim that if we were

---

[4] For additional such models of action, see Cappelen and Dever (draft).

structured that way, it would count as acting. There are many ways that acting beings could be organized that let them be like enough to us in the relevant ways for them to count as really acting, but that don't require them to use first-personal beliefs and desires. No single one of these cases is argumentatively essential.

Central Points in Chapter 4

- *Indexicals* are terms like 'I', 'now', 'you', 'yesterday', 'she', and 'here'. Like names, indexicals refer to objects, but unlike names which object they refer to depends on the context in which they are used, and their referent is fixed by the description given in the character rule.
- The Puzzle of Essential Indexicality is to explain why indexical reference appears to i) be essential for action, and ii) have a distinctive role in gathering information.
- Perry and Lewis give a set of cases which aim to establish that indexicals are essential for action and information gathering, including the supermarket case, the professor case, the fax machine case, the two gods case, and the Lingens case.
- Proponents of essential indexicality claim that indexical information is *essential* for action and information gathering.
- Skeptics about essential indexicality claim that indexical information is *not essential* for action and information gathering. This view is compatible with indexical information sometimes being required for action.
- Skeptics argue that the proponents of essential indexicality commit the *over-representation fallacy*, and the *relational fallacy*, and aim to explain Perry's and Lewis's cases as examples of opacity, employing the same theoretical tools as they use to explain opacity in the case of belief ascriptions.
- In order to capture the differences in belief and desire among agents who are motivated to perform different actions, Cappelen and Dever offer the *Action Inventory model*, which aims to explain how action comes about without the need to appeal to indexical information.

Comprehension Questions

1. Give as many examples of indexicals as you can. Give the character rules for each of these terms.
2. Give an example in which an indexical term appears essential for action involving:
   2.1. 'Here'.
   2.2. 'Yesterday'.
   2.3. 'She'.
   2.4. In your own words, give an explanation of your cases: i) in terms of essential indexicality; ii) as examples of opacity.
3. Give an example of your own in which indexical information appears to be essential for information gathering.
4. In your own words, explain how the Action Inventory model works.

Exploratory Questions

5. How might the supporter of the error reply (see Chapter 2) explain cases of apparent essential indexicality? Does the supporter of the error reply have a good explanation of cases like Lewis's two gods example? What would their explanation of that case be?
6. How might the supporter of the theory of belief 'under a guise' (see Chapter 2) explain cases of indexicality? Do they have a good explanation of Perry's supermarket case? What might their explanation of that case be?

Further Reading
A good place to start for indexicality in general is Cappelen and Dever 2016, especially Chapter 5, Cappelen and Dever 2013, and the slightly more challenging Braun 2015. Two overview articles are Ninan 2010 and 2016. A recent anthology of papers on the topic is García-Carpintero and Torre 2016.

5

Reference Magnetism and a Puzzle About Reference Determination

5.1 A Puzzle

Castor and Pollux are twins, alike in every physical respect. But when Leda says 'Castor', she successfully refers just to Castor, and not to Pollux. Something must explain this referential fact. And the explanation can't just be that she uses *Castor's* name rather than *Pollux's* name. That explanation just pushes the problem back a step: now we need to know why 'Castor' is Castor's name and not Pollux's name.

The Fregean and the Kripkean agree that 'Castor' refers to Castor and 'Pollux' refers to Pollux. But they disagree about *why*. According to the Fregean, Leda associates a descriptive meaning with the word 'Castor'. So perhaps when she says 'Castor', she is thinking about the mortal twin who is the son of Tyndareus, and not of the immortal twin who is the son of Zeus. It's then because Castor is the mortal twin that she refers to Castor. According to the Kripkean, Leda was holding the mortal twin when she introduced the name 'Castor' (whether she knew that twin to be mortal or not), and it's because of this historical fact that she refers to Castor.

This disagreement between the Fregean and the Kripkean is a disagreement about the *metasemantics* of reference. As we noted in Chapter 1, the Fregean takes meanings to be in the head. The Fregean thus has an *internalist* meta-semantics. The explanations of why names refer as they do can appeal only to facts about the internal natures of speakers, because the descriptive meanings of names fix reference, and descriptive meanings depend on the way speakers are thinking about objects. But the Kripkean has an *externalist* metasemantics.

The explanations of why names refer as they do can include facts external to the speaker, such as facts about the origin of the causal chain of which the speaker is a part.

The case of Castor and Pollux provides a little challenge to any metasemantic theory. There are two candidate referents for 'Castor' that are very similar, so a good metasemantic theory must be sensitive enough to get the reference of each name targeted onto the correct object. It's only a little challenge, because despite the *physical* similarity of Castor and Pollux, there are important dissimilarities between them, such as the mortal/immortal distinction. But it's not hard to start creating more powerful challenges.

One path to better challenges is to start shrinking the resources available to the metasemantics. This is the path that Kripke takes in the Feynman/Gell-Mann case (Kripke 1980: 81–2). Feynman and Gell-Mann are less alike than Castor and Pollux, but we build the case so that the speaker knows little about either, so that the internal resources available to the Fregean metasemantics are so impoverished that they can't distinguish the two potential referents. (It was crucial above that Leda *knew* that one twin was mortal and one immortal.) On this way of thinking about things, the core problem with internalism is that it gives us very limited resources for fixing reference. Externalism is then just an opening of the floodgates to allow in more resources. We can't run a 'shrink the resources' argument against externalism, because externalism is just the view that there are no built-in constraints on what the resources are.

But another path to better challenges is to build better duplicates. From the Kripkean point of view, Castor and Pollux are lousy duplicates. That's because their perfect physical similarity doesn't matter to the Kripkean metasemantics. That metasemantics looks at causal chains and their origins, not at the descriptive features of potential referents. But it's not hard to build duplication cases that are problems for the Kripkean meta-semantics. Cases of *reference shift* have long been raised as challenges to Kripkean views. Gareth Evans discusses the case of 'Madagascar':

We learn from Isaac Taylor's *Names and their History* (1898) that 'In the case of "Madagascar" a hearsay report of Malay or Arab sailors misunderstood by Marco Polo . . . has had the effect of transferring a corrupt form of the name of a portion of the African mainland to the great African Island.' (Evans 1973: 11)

We have two candidate referents for 'Madagascar': an island and a piece of the mainland. In one sense these are lousy duplicates, because they are physically quite unalike. But in another sense they are excellent duplicates, because they bear very similar *causal* relations to our current uses of the name 'Madagascar'. There are causal chains of transmission and dubbing leading from us back both to the mainland and to the island. So the Kripkean faces the same sort of problem here that the Fregean faces with Feynman and Gell-Mann: the metasemantics depends on a body of determining information that doesn't successfully separate the candidate referents.

'Madagascar'-style reference change examples need not be fatal counterexamples to the Kripkean story. Perhaps they just show that the causal-communicative chain picture needs to be made more complicated and sophisticated. Evans's conclusion is that a better version of the story has reference track the *dominant source of the speaker's information* involving the name. Since our 'Madagascar' information is dominantly from the island, rather than from the mainland, it's the island-originating causal chain that wins out in the metasemantics.

But we can continue to look for better and better duplicates. In doing so, we find that a powerful *underdetermination* argument emerges, with roots in a wide range of philosophical work. The core of the underdetermination argument is this: *there are far more candidate ways of referring than there are plausible determiners of reference.* As a result, any one determiner will be compatible with many possible referents, and thus cannot be enough to fix what the name refers to.

Why are there too many candidate referents? Some interconnected reasons:

i. Ordinary physical objects are vague in their boundaries (Lewis 1993). One way of putting this point is that there are many mountains roughly where Mount Everest is. Consider some pebble on the slopes of Mount Everest. Our notion of a *mountain* is not so precise that it settles whether that pebble is part of the mountain. So we can say that there are two mountains there: one containing the pebble, and one not containing the pebble. Since there are an enormous number of pebbles, there are an enormous number of mountains, all overlapping with one another. We can then wonder what metasemantic story determines whether 'Mount Everest' refers to Everest1 or Everest2, where Everest1 and Everest2 differ only in whether the pebble is part of the mountain.

ii. In addition to ordinary physical objects, there are many idiosyn-cratically 'scattered' objects that we typically ignore. There is the Eiffel Tower, but there is also the object whose three disjoint parts are the Eiffel Tower, the left eyeball of Socrates, and a single atom of hydrogen in the star Betelgeuse. It's easy to see that there will be vastly more of these scattered objects than there are ordinary objects. We can then wonder what metasemantic story determines that 'the Eiffel Tower' refers just to the tower, and not to the *mereological sum* of the tower, the eyeball, and the atom.

iii. We can introduce even stranger objects by using scattered *features*. The most famous example of scattered features is Good-man's term 'grue' (Goodman 1955). Pick some time in the future, such as January 1, 2100. Then we can define 'grue' by saying that an object is grue if it either (1) is first observed (by anyone) before January 1, 2100 and is green, or (2) is first observed (by anyone) after January 1, 2100 and is blue. So an emerald found in 2015 is grue, and a sapphire found in 2115 is also grue. But it's not that grue objects *change their color*. The grue emerald found in 2015 is green the whole time, before and after 2100. The grue sapphire found in 2115 is blue the whole time, before and after 2100. Once we see how to define a term like 'grue', it's easy to produce more examples of the same sort. An emeruby is an object that is either (1) first observed before January 1, 2100 and is an emerald, or (2) first observed after January 1, 2100 and is a ruby. A ruberald is an object that is either (1) first observed before January 1, 2100 and is a ruby, or (2) first observed after January 1, 2100 and is an emerald. A motormelon is an object that is either (1) first observed before January 1, 2100 and is a motorcycle, or (2) first observed after January 1, 2100 and is a watermelon. And so on. We can then wonder what metasemantic story determines whether 'Hawaii' is the name of an island or the name of an isnana (an object that is an island if first observed before January 1, 2100, and a banana if first observed after January 1, 2100).

iv. Some of the objects we might want to refer to are infinitely complex, and are surrounded by an infinite number of objects very similar to them. Consider an example discussed by Kripke (1982). We use '+' as a name for the addition function. But the addition function is infinitely complex, because there are infinitely many pairs of numbers that can be added. We are finite, and so there will inevitably be some pairs of numbers that we have never added or considered adding. Take some pair we never get around to adding. (Kripke's example is 58+67. Of course, giving an example is immediately self-defeating.) Then along with addition, the function that delivers the *sum* of that pair, there are infinitely many other functions that deliver different answers, such as the *quaddition* function that acts just like addition for all pairs other than 58+67. We can then wonder what metasemantic story determines whether '+' refers to addition or to quaddition.

Each of these underdetermination arguments is complicated, and there are many ways of resisting the claim that all plausible reference determiners are too impoverished to pick out one of the many candidate referents. But many philosophers have concluded on the basis of these considerations that there is a genuine problem in giving an adequate account of what determines reference.

We will consider four solutions to this problem of reference determination. We briefly examine the skeptical 'solution', which simply accepts that there is no reference determiner, and a non-committal externalism, which says that reference is *somehow or other* determined by the entire history of the use of the word. We then look more carefully first at temporal and modal externalism, which show how the externalist determination base can be even more expansive than we originally thought, and at the idea that some objects are *reference magnets*, that naturally 'attract' words to referring to them, making reference determination easier than we expected.

5.2 The Skeptical 'Solution'

One response to underdetermination worries is a *skeptical* response. If our total usage history is insufficient to determine a referent for a word, says the skeptic, then no referent is determined. Quine (e.g. 1960) and Davidson (e.g. 1973) are both referential skeptics, holding that there will typically be many candidate referents compatible with our use and denying that there is then any fact about which of these candidates is 'correct'. In the case of vagueness, for example, the skeptical view might be that the reference-fixing facts are enough to determine that 'Mount Everest' refers to one of the many candidate tall mountains in the Mahalangur Range, but not enough to determine which of those many candidates it refers to. So it's incorrect to say that 'Mount Everest' refers to the Eiffel Tower, or to the Matterhorn. But it's no more correct to say that it refers to Everest1 than it is to say that it refers to Everest2. We might combine this with the view that we make true claims with a name just in case *all* of the candidate referents would make the claim true. So it will be true that Mount Everest is a mountain, because all of the candidate referents are mountains, but not true that Mount Everest contains a specific pebble, because some but not all candidate referents contain that pebble.

Kripke, in his 1982 exposition of Wittgenstein, is a radical referential skeptic, holding that in the end there is nothing more to say about reference than that we use words in certain ways, and that what matters to us is that our usage follows certain patterns, rather than that we are *right* in using the words as we do:

Any individual who claims to have mastered the concept of addition will be judged by the community to have done so if his particular responses agree with those of the community in enough cases, especially the simple ones (and if his 'wrong' answers are not often *bizarrely* wrong, as in '5' for '68+57', but seem to agree with ours in *procedure*, even when he makes a 'computational mistake'). An individual who passes such tests is admitted into the community as an adder; an individual who passes such tests in enough other cases is admitted as a normal speaker of the language and member of the community. Those who deviate are corrected and told (usually as children) that they have not grasped the concept of addition. One who is an incorrigible deviant in enough respects simply cannot participate in the life of the community and in communication.

(Kripke 1982: 92)

Kripke's skeptical 'solution' suggests that we shift our attention from what can be *said* about those who use language oddly (e.g. that they are *wrong*, because the words really refer to such-and-such) to what can be *done* about such people (e.g. that they be exiled, so that their strange usage patterns don't interfere with our own).

There is also room for a *fundamentalist skepticism*, which is skeptical not about the reference facts, but about the metasemantic explanation of the reference facts. The fundamentalist skeptic agrees that 'Aristotle' refers to Aristotle, but thinks that that is a fundamental and brute feature of reality that cannot be explained in terms of anything else. We will encounter this idea more in Chapter 6.

5.3 Non-Committal Externalism

The Kripkean picture of reference includes an externalist metasemantics. But not just *any* externalist metasemantics—it commits specifically to the picture of causal-communicative chains (even if it remains deliberately vague about some of the details of how those chains work). It's this specific commitment that allows us to construct problematic cases of reference shift like the 'Madagascar' case above. We could have been less committal, however.

Consider a non-committal externalism that says: given any name N, there is some total history of how that name has ever been used. This history will include all the utterances of the name, what sentences the utterances occurred in, what the speaker was thinking when uttering, what was going on in the world at the time of utterance, and so on. That's an enormous body of information, and it will let us separate many potential duplicates. In the 'Madagascar' case, for example, the island and the mainland are alike in being at the origin of causal chains of uses. But the island and the mainland definitely aren't alike in *all* the ways that are made available by the total usage history.

Of course, to say that reference is determined by total usage history isn't yet to have a real metasemantic theory, because we haven't said *how* reference is determined by usage history. It's rather to indicate what *sort* of metasemantic theory we want. Thus this is a non-committal externalism. But non-committal as it is, it's still possible to raise problems for the claim that total usage history will be enough. Consider a version of the problem of vagueness. Suppose an explorer encounters a river and names it 'Rushing River'. Unbeknownst to the explorer, however, many miles to the east, where neither the explorer nor anyone else has ever gone, the river splits into two branches—call them North River and South River.

One plausible view, then, is that the explorer has in fact encountered *two* rivers. These two rivers partially overlap, and the explorer encountered them in their region of overlap. (If this doesn't strike you as a plausible view about the nature of rivers, replace it with some other example in which we do have overlapping objects.) But then what river does 'Rushing River' name? Does it name North River or South River? The causal-communicative chain picture doesn't look helpful here, because it doesn't help us figure out whether North River or South River is the target of the original dubbing. But adding in the total usage history doesn't seem to help matters much, either. The problem is that the usage history is *symmetric* with respect to North River and South River. Every way that North River figures in the usage history is also a way that South River figures in that history. Even given the expansive body of information we've allowed for fixing reference, North River and South River are perfect duplicates.

5.4 Temporal and Modal Externalism

We are trying to solve the problem of underdetermination to find more things to do the determining of reference. One way to get more things is to drop a constraint that the Kripkean picture has been assuming. Both the Kripkean causal-communicative chain picture and the non-committal total usage history picture are *backward-looking* metasemantic views. They are both externalist, because they allow facts other than facts about what is in the speaker's head to help determine reference. But the reference-determining facts are always facts about how the world is at or before the time of utterance.

That's a natural constraint to impose. How, we might think, could things that *haven't even happened yet* determine what our words refer to? But it's not an inevitable constraint. *Temporal externalists* claim that what happens *after* the time of speaking can help determine reference. Temporal externalism (defended, for example, by Jackman 1999) is a more radically externalist view, allowing even more facts into the meta-semantic reference-determining base.[1]

We'll consider two versions of temporal externalism. On the milder version, the *present* intentions of the speaker combine with the *future* state of the world to determine reference. Consider:

- **Kaplan's Newman-1**: According to David Kaplan, we can introduce the name 'Newman-1' in the following way: 'Let "Newman-1" refer to the first child to be born in the 22nd Century' (1977/1989: 560 note 76). If a name can be introduced in that way, and if that name now has a referent (i.e. the firstborn child of the twenty-second century), we can now talk about that child, say by uttering: 'I hope

---

[1] This view is also defended in Jackman 2005, and Lance and O'Leary-Hawthorne 1997. Some criticism is found in Stoneham 2003.

Newman-1 will be happy'. What we refer to is determined by what happens in the future—the total history of the universe until the utterance won't suffice to determine reference of 'Newman-1'.

This is a mild version of temporal externalism, because even a Fregean can be externalist in this sense. We said that the Fregean was an internalist because reference was determined by descriptive meaning, and descriptive meaning was determined by the mental state of the speaker. But descriptive meaning determines reference only given the state of the world. A speaker uses 'Aristotle' to pick out the last great philosopher of antiquity. That fact is fixed by the internal state of the speaker. But this by itself doesn't tell us that 'Aristotle' refers to Aristotle. To reach that conclusion, we need the further information that Aristotle is the last great philosopher of antiquity.

Real externalism, then, requires that the internal state of the speaker doesn't even give us *instructions* for finding the referent. But in the Newman-1 case, the mind of the speaker does give us such instructions. They are instructions we can't follow for many years to come, but they are instructions nevertheless.

A more radical version of temporal externalism suggests cases in which the total state of the world up to the time of usage (including facts both internal and external to the speaker) doesn't even give us instructions for finding the referent, but in which adding in facts about the *future* does determine the referent. Consider again our case of the explorer who introduces the name 'Rushing River'. Suppose now that *after* introducing the name, the explorer continues along the river to the east. Eventually she comes to the branch in the river, and realizes that there are two rivers (North River and South River, although of course she doesn't have names for both). The explorer is now confronted with a choice: should she use 'Rushing River' to refer to North River, or to South River?

The temporal externalist thought is that *if* the explorer starts using 'Rushing River' to refer to North River, that then retroactively makes it the case that the name *always did* refer to North River. But if instead the explorer starts using 'Rushing River' to refer to South River, that retroactively makes it the case that the name always did refer to South River. What the early uses of the name refer to, then, depends on what will happen in the future.

Of course, the future determination doesn't need to be something so blunt as an explicit choice about how to refer. The explorer might continue to the east, not notice the branching, and just end up traveling along the North River branch. Continuing to call it 'Rushing River' (not realizing that anything has changed), she makes it the case that her early uses referred to North River. And the future determination needn't be in the hands of the original dubber. Maybe it is only generations later that travelers reach the branch, and something happens in the usage that retroactively fixes the referent as one river or the other.

Temporal externalism is not the only possible response to these sorts of cases. We might, for example, be referential skeptics here, claiming that the early uses of 'Rushing River' don't refer to either river, and that what the future events do is not make the name retroactively refer, but change the name from not referring to referring. The temporal externalist will claim that this gets the cases wrong. But we have seen in previous chapters (in particular in Chapter 2) that appeals to intuitions about cases can be methodologically suspect. Someone unimpressed by intuition-mongering might put little weight on these cases. If we reach a standoff of judgments on the cases, is there any further argument to be given for or against temporal externalism?

A more theoretical argument in favor of temporal externalism claims that it is ad hoc to draw a distinction between Kripke's original cases and the ones presented above. Surely, if what happened 1,000 years ago could determine what I refer to today, why can't what will happen in ten minutes do so too? If, with Kripke, you are happy with the idea that what happens thousands of miles away from you can determine reference, why couldn't what happens tomorrow do so as well?

This could seem to be simply a form of slippery slope argument: if you're willing to give me one dollar, why not give me four, and if four, why not eight, etc.? That is not a reliable way to get someone to give you a million dollars. That, however, is not the nature of the challenge. The question asked to the Kripkean externalist is this: what is the principled distinction between appealing to the past and appealing to the future and to other possibilities? Can some kind of principled theoretical reason be given for having reference depend on the past, but not on the future? The current literature contains no consensus on how to respond to that challenge.

5.5 How Much Does Temporal Externalism Help? Adding Modal Externalism

Temporal externalism expands the determination base for reference. It thereby eliminates more cases of duplicates, and reduces the underdetermination problem. But how much does it reduce it? Not enough, it's easy to see. At an abstract level, the total facts about the past weren't enough, because the total facts about the past were finite, and we could build cases with more potential referents than those finite facts could distinguish. But adding the future only doubles the amount of information in the determination base, and doubling isn't going to solve the problem.

And it's easy to build cases in which temporal externalism doesn't help. Suppose that after our explorer introduces the name 'Rushing River', she turns back. Neither she nor anyone else ever encounters the branch in the river, so no one is ever confronted with the choice between the North River and the South River, and no facts, past, present, or future, do the job of settling whether 'Rushing River' refers to the North River or to the South River.

Of course, we could again resort to referential skepticism in such cases. But another option is to push the externalism one step further to *modal externalism*. In addition to facts about how the word *was* used and facts about how the word *will be* used, there might be facts about how the word *would have been* used. Suppose that although the explorer turns back, it's true that had she continued, she would have used 'Rushing River' as a name for the North River when she encountered the branch. (For example, maybe the lie of the land guaranteed that she would have been heading northward when she encountered the branch.) The modal externalist then holds that that fact about possible usage is enough to make it the case that 'Rushing River' actually does refer to the North River. As with temporal externalism, modal externalism can be defended both by judgments about particular cases and by general theoretical considerations about what should follow from allowing 'remote' considerations to fix reference.

5.6 The Philosophical Significance of Temporal Externalism: Linguistic Negotiation

If temporal externalism is correct, then what we say is radically inaccessible to us. The facts that determine the meaning (referents) of our words have not yet come into existence. So this view is a rather extreme form of externalism. According to the kind of externalism described in Chapter 1, facts about the individual in isolation fail to suffice for fixing meaning, but at least we know that the community and its history fix it. Not so if we endorse temporal externalism: if it is true, there is nothing, now, in the entire universe that determines what we mean or what we talk about (assuming, not quite uncontroversially, that future events don't exist). Nonetheless, our words have meanings and refer to things (they refer to the things that the future determines that they refer to).

There is one phenomenon that this view throws interesting light on, which we call *meaning negotiation*: We often engage in something that looks much like a debate over the meaning of words. Here are some socially salient examples (in the sense that the debates over these words are public and in large part political): What should count as 'marriage', as 'democracy', as 'justice', and 'health'? These are important issues and issues where there's a great deal of disagreement among speakers of English. They are issues that are under continuous dispute and these disputes have great social significance.

Here is one picture of what goes on when we have such disputes: We want to change the meaning of the words. So at some time, say, *t1*, the words 'marriage', 'democracy', 'justice', and 'health' have certain fixed meanings. The goal is to change the meanings of those words, so that at some later time, *t2*, those words have different meanings (maybe in some sense improved meanings.)

On the alternative picture proposed by temporal externalists, such debates don't aim to change the meanings of terms, they aim to *determine* the meanings. Our words at *t1* mean what they are determined to mean at some point *t2* in the future. On this view, the effects of meaning negotiation debates are not just forward-looking—they don't just determine what words will mean in the future. They are backward-looking in the sense that their outcome determines what people said in the past: in some sense they determine the thought content of people a long time ago. So understood, temporal externalism gives us a very radical, and also exciting, perspective on certain kinds of social debates.

5.7 Reference Magnetism

The final response to the problem of underdetermination that we will consider centers on the idea of *reference magnetism*. Consider the following progression. The individualist has an underdetermination problem because the facts about the mental states of the speaker aren't rich enough to fix the referent of their words. So we broaden the base, allowing in non-mental facts about the speaker and the speaker's interactions with the environment and all of their words' potential referents. This helps, but not enough. At this point, we've exhausted what can come from *us*, so if there is going to be more progress, we need help from *the potential referents*. The reference magnetism thought is that the things in the world are ready to provide the needed help. Some objects out there are just *better* potential referents than others. Not because of anything we do—it's not that they fit better with our practices. Their referential superiority is an intrinsic feature of some objects. We then use that referential superiority to close the underdetermination gap. Our practice places some constraints on how our words refer, limiting them to some range of candidates. Within that range, the 'magnetic' force of the better referents takes over, and our words gravitate onto those objects.

So far the talk of 'reference magnetism' is just a metaphorical placeholder for some substantive theory of what intrinsic features of objects might make them better referents. We'll now consider three accounts of what reference magnetism consists in. The first account is just a toy story on which the magnetic feature is *existence*. The goal of the first account is primarily to help make the very idea of referential magnetism more plausible. The second account, which derives primarily from work by David Lewis, takes the magnetic feature to be *naturalness*. Naturalness magnetism is the dominant approach to reference magnetism in the contemporary literature. We'll then consider a third alternative, deriving from Sally Haslanger's discussions of the *ameliorative project*, which takes the magnetic property to be *goodness*.

5.7.1 Magnetism 1: Existence and Parsimony

One of the potential sources of underdetermination we discussed above was the existence of scattered objects. But not everyone thinks there are scattered objects. Scattered objects are an immediate consequence of *mereological universalism*, which is the view that given any objects, there is an object which has all of those objects as parts. Mereological universalism thus entails that there is an object that has the Eiffel Tower and Socrates's left eyeball as parts. But not everyone is a mereological universalist. Some people are mereological *nihilists*, who think that no objects have parts. Others think that only under certain special conditions do some objects form a further object having them as parts. If we aren't mereological universalists, we won't so automatically have many objects around to be potential referents, and the problem of underdetermination may be easier to solve. The Eiffel Tower will magnetically attract reference toward it and away from the mereological sum of the tower and the eyeball by virtue of the tower existing and the sum not existing. (This, of course, is just a fancy way of saying that the problem of selecting among duplicates is solved by there not being duplicates.)

In the same way, we can be parsimonious about properties, denying that there are grue-like properties, and thereby explaining why 'blue' means blueness rather than grueness. And we can be parsimonious about mathematical objects, denying that there are functions agreeing with addition on all cases we've considered but diverging on future cases, thereby explaining why '+' means *addition* rather than quaddition. If our ontology is parsimonious, then the things that actually exist are in a certain sense special by virtue of existing. It's then no surprise if by existing, they are better able to be referents than things that don't exist.

5.7.2 Magnetism 2: Naturalness

On David Lewis's view, it is the *naturalness* of properties which determines reference (1983, 1984). David Lewis's ontology is abundant, rather than parsimonious. He is a mereological universalist, and a universalist about properties in the sense that for any collection of objects, there is a property that all and only those objects have. He then recognizes the difficulty that this abundant ontology creates for him:

Because properties are so abundant, they are undiscriminating. Any two things share infinitely many properties, and fail to share infinitely many others. That is so whether the two things are perfect duplicates or utterly dissimilar. Thus properties do nothing to capture facts of resemblance [. . .] Likewise, properties do nothing to capture the causal powers of things. Almost all properties are causally irrelevant, and there is nothing to make the relevant ones stand out from the crowd. Properties carve reality at the joints—and everywhere else as well. If it's distinctions we want, too much structure is no better than none. (Lewis 1983: 346)

The 'joint carving' language at the end of this passage points to Lewis's way forward. Lewis's thought is that among the many distinctions that properties make, some 'carve nature at its joints', while others don't.

The property *being an electron* seems to carve nature at its joints, while the property *either wearing a purple scarf or being in orbit around Pluto* does not. We'll then call the joint-carving properties *natural* properties.

Talk of joint carving helps a bit, and some examples give us a start on getting the idea of naturalness. But it would still be helpful to have more to say about what makes some properties natural and others not. We could, of course, be *primitivists* about naturalness, holding that natural-ness is just a basic feature of the world that can't be better explained in other terms. But this won't do much to make reference magnetism an attractive proposal.

Alternatively, we can try to understand naturalness by understanding the role of naturalness in our philosophical theorizing. Dorr and Hawthorne, taking 'natural' as a theoretical term, rather than a label we are supposed to already understand, suggest we proceed as follows:

Our main strategy is familiar from Lewis's own treatment of novel theoretical terms (Lewis 1970). According to the model presented in that paper, any theory expressed using a newly introduced predicate 'F' is analytically equivalent to its *expanded postulate*—the claim that there is a unique property that does all the things that F-ness does according to the original theory.   (Dorr and Hawthorne 2013: 4)

They then extract from Lewis a description of the theoretical role of 'natural' (see Dorr and Hawthorne 2013: §2):

  i. *Supervenience*: All facts supervene on the facts about which things have which PNPs [perfectly natural properties]
 ii. *Independence*: The PNPs are mutually independent
iii. *Duplication*: Necessarily, x and y are duplicates iff some function from the parts of x to the parts of y preserves all PNPs and negations of PNPs
 iv. *Empiricism*: The right method for identifying instantiated natural properties is empirical
  v. *Laws*: The laws are the propositions that achieve the best fit between strength and simplicity of definition in terms of PNPs
 vi. *Length*: The more natural a property is, the simpler its definition in terms of PNPs
vii. *Similarity*: The more natural a property is, the more it makes for similarity among things that share it
viii. *Dissimilarity*: The more natural a property is, the more it makes for dissimilarity among things divided by it

ix. *Magnetism*: The more natural a property is, the easier it is to refer to

x. *Necessity*: Facts about how natural a given property is are non-contingent

It's beyond the scope of our discussion here to go through these ten roles carefully. What matters for our purposes is that if this is the theoretical role for naturalness, then there is only such a thing as naturalness if there's some one feature that can do all this work, that can make all these sentences come out true. According to Lewis, if there isn't anything that makes the ten claims true, then the term *denotes nothing*. So if one or more of the claims above are false, then, according to Lewis's own theory, 'naturalness' fails to refer:

'Phlogiston' presumably is a theoretical term of an unrealized theory; we say without hesitation that there is no such thing as phlogiston. What else could we possibly say? Should we say that phlogiston is something or other, but (unless phlogiston theory turns out to be true after all) we have no hope of finding out what? *Let us say, then, that the theoretical terms of unrealized theories do not name anything.* (Lewis 1970: 432)

Naturalness-based reference magnetism thus rests on a substantial metaphysical gamble: it assumes that there is a feature of naturalness of the sort Lewis describes. If there is, the proponent of naturalness-based reference magnetism can then hold that natural objects, or objects characterized by natural properties, preferentially attract reference, so that (roughly) our words refer to the most natural objects that are consistent with our usage, or to whatever objects maximize some combination of fitting our usage and being natural. But if there is not, then naturalness-based reference magnetism must be abandoned.

5.7.3 Magnetism 3: Goodness

Most discussion of reference magnetism has focused on naturalness as the magnetic feature. But it is quite compatible with the project of reference magnetism that some other kind of property is the 'magnetic' one. We'll now consider a sketch of an alternative reference magnetism, which takes the magnetic feature to be something like *goodness*. This will then lead us in the next section to consider the question of what would make one form of reference magnetism correct, rather than another.

Sally Haslanger has stressed the importance of *ameliorative projects* in philosophy, and in the philosophical process of considering concepts.[2] Ameliorative projects ask that we not just analyze our concepts as we find them, but also consider how we might *improve* those concepts, to make them better suited to serve various purposes. So, for example, in thinking about what gender is, we shouldn't just ask ourselves how people have in fact used the word 'gender'; we should also ask ourselves what concept of gender would be most useful in working toward a just and fair society.

Ameliorative projects can be given a *revisionary* or a *revelatory* reading. On the revisionary reading, the ameliorative project is proposing *changing* the referents of our concepts and words. We discover that as we have been using 'gender', it refers to one feature F1, but that having 'gender' refer to this feature interferes with pursuing social progress. We thus propose changing the referent of 'gender' to a new feature F2, a feature that it would be socially helpful to focus on. This revisionary reading doesn't involve reference magnetism, and is compatible with mild anti-individualism or even outright individualism about reference, since it takes our existing practice to have determined a reference, and just suggests that we *shift* to a new practice, thereby determining a new reference.

On the revelatory reading, on the other hand, the ameliorative project isn't proposing a change in our concepts, but is *discovering* what our concepts always referred to. On this view, 'gender' never referred to F1, but always referred to F2. We may have *thought* 'gender' picked out F1, because F1 was the feature that best fit our practice. But, following the general reference magnetism idea, fitting the practice isn't the only standard for reference. (It *can't* be, given the underdetermination arguments, on pain of skepticism.) On this version of reference magnetism, the magnetic features of the world are the features that it is *good* or *helpful* for us to talk about. F2 is better for us to focus on than F1, so our word 'gender' always picked out F2.

On the revelatory reading, an ameliorative project proposes a kind of reference magnetism, according to which the underdetermination in the referents for a term can be resolved by appealing to considerations of the

---

[2] See the papers collected in (Haslanger 2012), especially Chapters 7, 12, and 14.

goodness of those terms for the projects of achieving social justice. Perhaps our practice underdetermines the referent of 'woman', but considerations of social justice act as a magnet leading to the word picking out one referent: the one which is most useful for pursuing projects of social justice.

5.8 What's Magnetic?

As we've seen, multiple versions of reference magnetism can be formulated, on which different intrinsic features of objects carry the magnetic reference-attracting powers. But this raises a concern. Now, even if we decide to endorse reference magnetism, we need to decide which version of reference magnetism is correct.

Perhaps it's up to us which version of reference magnetism is correct. We might suppose that in one community, with one kind of linguistic practice, they act in such a way that it's the natural properties that do the work in closing the underdetermination gap. (They exhibit, for example, a special concern for classifying the world in a metaphysically fundamental way.) But in another community, with another kind of linguistic practice, they act in such a way that it's the socially helpful properties that do the work in closing the underdetermination gap. (They exhibit, in contrast, a special concern with addressing structural injustices.)

But there is a worry that if this is how reference magnetism works, the underdetermination property simply re-emerges. There are many functions similar to addition, and our unaided practice doesn't seem able uniquely to home in on one of them. But there are also many properties similar to the property of being natural (*is either natural or is instantiated by a banana orbiting Pluto*, various grue-like modifications of *natural*, and so on). So our practice won't be able to uniquely home in on one of those. And different properties in the similarity class around *natural* will yield different magnetic verdicts for our terms, so we'll still be faced with referential skepticism. Likewise, there are many properties similar to goodness.

We needed reference magnetism because we needed some reference determination that came from the world, and not from us. So we don't only need the magnetism to come from the world, we need the fact that the magnetism exerts an attraction on our reference also to come from the world. But that means the choice of whether it's naturalness magnetism or goodness magnetism (or some other form) needs to be coming somehow from the intrinsic nature of things (perhaps including the intrinsic nature of reference). That's not impossible, but it is rather mysterious.

5.9 Reference Magnetism and Philosophical Practice

We conclude the discussion of reference magnetism by noting that if the theories of reference magnetism are correct, they have the potential for significant and important consequences for our philosophical practice.

One important philosophical concern is coming to understand certain philosophical concepts, such as knowledge, truth, and justice. One standard way of proceeding is to propose a theory of one of these concepts, and then to test that theory by considering counterexamples to the theory. In his paper 'What Good are Counterexamples?' (Weatherson 2003), Brian Weatherson observes that for proponents of reference magnetism, this standard practice can't be so easily endorsed. Weatherson says:

> In assigning a property to a predicate, there are two criteria we would like to follow. The first is that it validates as many as possible of our pre-theoretic beliefs. The second is that it is, in some sense, simple and theoretically important [...] Lewis canvasses the idea that there is a primitive 'naturalness' of properties which measures simplicity and theoretical significance, and I will adopt this idea.
>
> (Weatherson 2003: 11)

He then applies this reference magnetism framework to the term 'knows'. An initially attractive theory of knowledge is that knowing that p is simply a *justified true belief* that p. (Call this the JTB theory.) This theory has fallen into disfavor due to a powerful class of counterexamples introduced by Edmund Gettier (1963). Here is a sample Gettier case:

> Jones believes that someone in his office owns a Ford. He believes this because he has seen Smith, who works in his office, with keys to a Ford. However, Smith does not own a Ford. He only had the keys because he had borrowed a Ford from a friend. But in fact Johnson, who also works in the office, does own a Ford. Jones, however, is unaware of this fact, and has never encountered any evidence that Johnson owns a Ford.

Jones's belief is *justified*, because Smith's possession of Ford keys is good evidence that someone in the office owns a Ford. And his belief is *true*, because someone in the office (namely, Johnson) owns a Ford. But most people have the clear reaction that in this case Jones doesn't *know* that someone in the office has a Ford. So we have a counterexample to the claim that knowledge is justified true belief.

Weatherson then argues as follows:

> Saying 'knows' means 'justifiably truly believes' does not do particularly well on the first requirement [of validating our pre-theoretic beliefs]. Gettier isolated a large class of cases where it goes wrong. But it does very well on the second [of being natural], as it analyses knowledge in terms of a short list of simple and significant features. I claim that all its rivals don't do considerably better on the first, and arguably do much worse on the second [...] That the JTB theory is the best trade-off is still a live possibility, even considering Gettier cases.
> (Weatherson 2003: 11)

Weatherson thus suggests that reference magnetism is sufficient to allow the naturalness of the JTB theory to override its poor fit with our practice as revealed in our reaction to Gettier cases, so that knowledge can, in fact, be justified true belief.

> There is an implicit folk theory of the meaning of 'knows', one according to which it does not denote justified true belief. I claim this folk theory is mistaken. It is odd to say that we can all be mistaken about the meanings of our words; it is odd to say that we can't make errors in word usage. I think the latter is the greater oddity, largely because I have a theory which explains how we can all make mistakes about meanings in our own language.   (Weatherson 2003: 10)

It's not our project here to settle whether the JTB theory is correct, or to settle whether Weatherson is correct in thinking that it would be the best option given naturalness reference magnetism. But we do want to emphasize that reference magnetism does have these revisionary consequences for philosophical practice. Reference magnetism takes reference to be determined through some interaction between our practice and the magnetic features—what is referred to is whatever does some overall best job of fitting our practice and of being a magnetic candidate. So in determining what knowledge is, and what truth is, and what justice is, we need to make sure we are looking to both of those factors. Our own reactions to cases, of course, provide information only about our practice, so we need somehow to incorporate in addition considerations about what is magnetic (natural, good, and so on, depending on the correct flavor of reference magnetism) in assessing philosophical theories.

Central Points in Chapter 5

- Metasemantics is the theory of how a referring expression refers to an object. We've been assuming a Kripkean theory according to which what determines reference is external facts about the speaker's use, community, and environment. But this view faces some challenges.

- We focused on the problem of underdetermination. For some expressions, it appears that the reference-determining facts don't suffice to pick out some particular entity as the referent of that expression.

- We considered this example. We come across a river and name it 'Rushing River', and go on, perhaps for years, using that name in conversation. Unbeknownst to us, many miles east, where we have never been, the river diverges north and south. It seems that our use of 'Rushing River' doesn't determine a single reference: it doesn't determine whether it refers to the north forking river or the south forking one.

- We then went on to consider several responses. A hard-line view would be to accept referential skepticism about this and other cases, arguing that frequently our terms fail to refer because of under-determination. This skepticism, like most skepticism, is hard to take seriously.

- More attractive was to expand the range of reference-determining facts, and in particular to consider how a term *will* be used in the future in working out what it *does* refer to now. Imagine that later we went east and discovered the forking river, and decided that the river going north was 'Rushing River'. Then, according to temporal externalism, 'Rushing River' *always* referred to the river that eventually forked north, even years earlier before we had discovered the fork.

- We saw that this view was also limited, and turned to another solution: reference magnetism. According to reference magnetism, some objects and properties are intrinsically better than others to be referred to.

- We surveyed several different forms of magnetism. On one account, the magnetic objects and properties are the ones which are *natural*. What naturalness is is contested, but consider the difference between the property with the extension all and only the red things and the property with the extension all the red things and one yellow banana. This latter property seems, in some sense, less natural than the former. An alternate view says that the magnetic property is goodness or usefulness.

- We went on to consider how appeals to naturalness can fundamentally change the nature of arguments in philosophy. For example, if we attempt to analyze a philosophically contentious notion, and are faced with a counterexample, we can nevertheless maintain our analysis if it is much more natural than any alternatives.

Comprehension Questions

1. What exactly is metasemantics about? How does it differ from semantics?
2. Explain the nature of the skeptical solution. Is it plausible?
3. Give some more examples of:
   - vague physical objects;
   - cases of reference shift;
   - cases in which an agent's knowledge is too restricted to distinguish between potential referents of a name;
   - predicates that behave like 'grue'.
4. Spell out exactly the difference between the more and the less radical versions of temporal externalism.
5. Explain the difference between the three forms of magnetism.

Exploratory Questions

6. Here's a natural sounding response to Kripkenstein: what determines that one means addition rather than quaddition is that you *intend* to speak about addition. Think carefully about whether this reply works.
7. Consider politically and socially important terms like 'woman' or 'latino'. Or, for another example, consider slurs, such as

(*continued*)

'queer' as used ten to fifteen years ago to talk derogatorily about gay people. Can reference magnetism help us analyze such terms? Do naturalness- and goodness-based accounts of reference magnetism have different things to say about these cases? What might temporal externalism have to say about projects to reclaim the meaning of words like 'queer'?

8. What do you think of the argument in favor of temporal externalism that leverages a similarity between the past and the future? Can you think of responses to it that turn on the dissimilarity between the past and the future?

9. Consider the modal externalist view according to which the reference of 'Rushing River' is North River because if an explorer had gone east down the river and discovered the fork, that's how they *would have used* that term. What if we drop the assumption that there's some one way they would have used the term—they could have used it to refer to North River, but they also could have used it to refer to South River. That's surely plausible. What would modal externalism say in this case? In general, is there a risk that modal externalism will seldom fix on any one referent for a given term, because it has many different merely possible uses?

10. What is the relation between goodness magnetism and naturalness magnetism? Can naturalness reference magnetism be swept into goodness reference magnetism by saying that natural properties are good/helpful for the purpose of scientific investigation? Will this move work for all concepts? (What about 'woman'?)

Further Reading
For more on Kripkenstein, see Boghossian 1989. For more on Davidson and Quine, see Soames 2003, Parts five and six. An interesting argument that all the physical facts about use, past, present, and future, won't determine reference is Kearns and Magidor 2012. For meaning negotiation, see Ludlow 2014 and Cappelen and Dever 2016, Chapter 11. A philosopher who puts magnetism to work is Sider—see his 2011. For more on negotiation, see Cappelen 2018 and Plunkett 2015.

6

A Puzzle About Naming Arbitrarily

When Aristotle's parents point to baby Aristotle and say, 'Let *Aristotle* be his name', they introduce a new name whose referent they're very well informed about. They definitely know what the name refers to: they've got the referent right in front of them. When Leverrier decides that an undiscovered planet must be responsible for irregularities in the orbit of Uranus and says, 'Let *Neptune* name the planet causing perturbations in the orbit of Uranus', he introduces a new name whose referent he's somewhat less well informed about. There's a clear sense in which he knows what the name refers to (the perturbing planet), but he knows little about that planet, and there's also a sense in which he doesn't know which heavenly object it is.

Consider the math professor who says, 'Let *n* be an arbitrary integer'. It looks like she, too, introduces a new name (she can go on to refer to *n* throughout her proof). But it looks like she knows even less about the referent of her name than Leverrier does about 'Neptune'. She has absolutely no idea which integer *n* is, and no idea what *n* is like (whether it is even or odd, for example). Indeed, we might start to wonder whether she has really introduced a name for an integer.

The theoretical practice of introducing 'names for arbitrary objects' is one that's largely unique to math. We don't in ordinary life find ourselves saying things like, 'Let Bessie be an arbitrary cow'. We might think that there's something odd going on in the mathematical talk, and that we don't need to take so seriously the appearance that new names are being introduced. But there are more ordinary ways of talking that share important features with the mathematical 'ordinary object' talk. Consider:

1. A student came to my office hours today. *He* wanted to complain about his grade on the paper.

The pronoun 'he' in this example gets its meaning from the earlier indefinite description 'a student' to which it is anaphorically connected. But the meaning of 'he' goes beyond the meaning of the indefinite. There could have been many students who came to office hours, but 'he' refers to a particular one of them. If only one of them complained about grades, then 'he' refers to that one; if more than one complained, then it refers to a particular one that the speaker has in mind (perhaps one the speaker plans to go on and relate an anecdote about).

If the complaining student is John, then 'he' in the example refers to John. It thus seems that 'he' can function as a referring expression just as much as proper names are. In fact, we can introduce names in the same sort of way:

2.   A strange man called me today. Let's just call him *Deep Throat*. He offered me information on scandals in the administration.

'Deep Throat' then refers to someone. It refers to the unique strange man who called, if there was only one, or the particular strange man that the speaker intends to refer to, if there was more than one.

These last two examples involve *anaphora*.

Theoretical Explanations 4: *Anaphora*

Some words acquire their meaning from the way that they are connected to other words in use. Pronouns like 'he' and 'she' are paradigms of this. Consider:

- When Alex entered the house, *she* took off her raincoat.
- Whenever a baseball player hits a home run, *he* is happy.
- A policeman was chasing a thief, and then *he* shot *him*.

'She' in the first sentence refers to Alex because it is linked to the earlier occurrence of 'Alex'. 'He' in the second sentence means what it does because it is linked to the earlier occurrence of 'a baseball player'. The third sentence is ambiguous because it isn't clear whether 'he' links to 'a policeman' and 'him' to 'a thief', or the other way around. Linguists call this sort of meaning inheritance *anaphora*. It is not limited to traditional pronouns. Consider:

- Alex has a brown dog, but Beth has a black *one*.
- Alex is happy, and *so* is Beth.

'One' and 'so' are anaphoric on 'dog' and 'happy' respectively. We might think of indexicals of the sort discussed in Chapter 4 as involving a kind of anaphoric linkage to the context: 'I' means what it does, on a particular use, because of the way that it is linked to facts about who is speaking.

The anaphora cases aren't fully analogous to the mathematical 'arbitrary object' cases, because there is a specific object the speaker intends to pick out. But other anaphora cases lack that feature. Consider:

3.   A Roman child typically left home at age 12. *He* worked as an apprentice for four years, and then opened his own business.

There were many Roman children, and there's no particular one of them the speaker intends to pick out. Rather, the speaker intends to make a *generic* claim about Roman children by having 'he' refer arbitrarily to a Roman child. Anaphoric connections, then, are an ordinary part of our talk that allow us to introduce things that look like the arbitrary names of mathematical talk.

Arbitrary names raise hard problems for a theory of reference. What do arbitrary names refer to? How do arbitrary names come to refer to what they do refer to, rather than to something else? Are these really referring expressions at all, or is there some other linguistic phenomenon at work here, masking itself as reference? Certainly the standard Kripkean toolkit will have a hard time with these cases. It's hard to see how there will be a causal chain of uses tracing back to an original dubbing when there doesn't seem to be any particular object that is the referent, and thus that is the object of original dubbing.

We will consider three theories of arbitrary names. The first theory puts the arbitrariness into the object, holding that arbitrary names refer to special kinds of objects called *arbitrary objects*. The second theory puts the arbitrariness into the reference relation, holding that arbitrary names refer to ordinary objects, but do so in an arbitrary way. The third theory returns to the thought that arbitrary names aren't really names at all, and suggests that we can better understand them as types of quantified noun phrases. All three theories face serious challenges, but taken together they also help us stretch the boundaries of our understanding of what reference is.

6.1 Arbitrary Objects

Kit Fine has suggested that when Alice says, 'Let Pierre be an arbitrary Frenchman', we should take her language fully at face value. Alice introduces a new name, and tells us exactly what that name refers to: an arbitrary Frenchman.

But what is an 'arbitrary Frenchman? Fine says:

In addition to individual objects, there are arbitrary objects: in addition to individual numbers, there are arbitrary numbers; in addition to individual men, arbitrary men. With each arbitrary object is associated an appropriate range of individual objects, its values: with each arbitrary number, the range of individual numbers; with each arbitrary man, the range of individual men. An arbitrary object has those properties common to the individual objects in its range. So an arbitrary number is odd or even, an arbitrary man is mortal, since each individual number is odd or even, each individual man is mortal. On the other hand, an arbitrary object fails to be prime an arbitrary man fails to be a philosopher, since some individual number is not prime, some individual man is not a philosopher.   (Fine 1983: 55)

Arbitrary objects, then, are objects *over and above* the ordinary objects we are familiar with. Consider the states in the USA. You probably think you know them well: Alaska, Alabama, Arizona, and so on. But according to Fine's theory, there is another one that has gone undetected: the *arbitrary state of the USA*. It is a state, but it is not any of the familiar states. It is not Alaska, Alabama, Arizona, or any of the others.

On Fine's view, we start with the idea of a *range of objects*. A range of objects is just any collection of objects, and for each range there is a corresponding arbitrary object. One range is the collection of integers. Corresponding to this range is the arbitrary integer. Another range is the collection of *positive* integers. Corresponding to this range is the arbitrary positive integer. Another range is the collection of all French citizens. Corresponding to this range is the arbitrary French citizen. And so on.

Arbitrary objects then have exactly the properties that are possessed by *every* object in the range to which they correspond. The arbitrary Frenchman, then, has exactly the properties that are had by every Frenchman. The arbitrary Frenchman has a heart, because every Frenchman does, but doesn't wear glasses, because not every Frenchman wears glasses.

In saying that the arbitrary Frenchman doesn't wear glasses, we have to be careful. We are not making the positive claim that the arbitrary Frenchman has a face unadorned by glasses. That wouldn't be right, because not every Frenchman is like that—some of them do wear glasses, after all. Rather, we are making the negative claim that the arbitrary Frenchman lacks the property *wearing glasses*. But for the same reason, the arbitrary Frenchman lacks the property *not wearing glasses*. So the arbitrary Frenchman neither wears glasses nor doesn't wear glasses. The arbitrary Frenchman is a *gappy object*, because there are some properties such that it has neither those properties nor their negations. Arbitrary objects in general will be gappy. If there is any *diversity* in their range—that is, if there is any property F such that neither all the objects in the range have F, nor do they all not have F—they won't have the properties marking that diversity.

Using arbitrary objects makes the theory of arbitrary reference pleasingly simple. It's straightforward to say what is referred to. In some cases ('Let *n* be an arbitrary prime number'), it's made completely explicit what arbitrary object is being referred to. In other cases, it's easy to figure out. When someone says:

3.   A Roman child typically left home at age 12. *He* worked as an apprentice for four years, and then opened his own business.

the use of 'he' refers to the arbitrary Roman child. And there's no particular puzzle about *how* the arbitrary name comes to stand in the reference relation to the right arbitrary object. The speaker has in mind a particular arbitrary object (and gets the right object in mind by thinking about the *range* that they want to make an arbitrary claim about), and then introduces a name for the object they have in mind. So this view fits nicely with the Kripkean framework outlined in the first chapter.

But the simple theory of reference comes with a metaphysical price. Arbitrary objects are strange things and have strange consequences. In addition to the simple surprising fact that (for example) in addition to the socks in your drawer that you knew about, there is one more sock in the drawer, the *arbitrary* sock in the drawer, there are a number of other troublesome consequences of the view.

i.   As we have seen, arbitrary objects are gappy, sometimes lacking both a property and the negation of that property. But logical contradictions threaten for gappy objects. Consider the arbitrary Frenchman Pierre. Pierre isn't right-handed, because not every Frenchman is right-handed. And Pierre isn't left-handed, because not every Frenchman is left-handed. But every Frenchman is *either right-handed or left-handed,* so Pierre is either right-handed or left-handed. But that means all this is true of Pierre:

4.   Pierre is either right-handed or left-handed.
5.   Pierre isn't right-handed.
6.   Pierre isn't left-handed.

These three sentences, though, are logically inconsistent. From *Pierre is either right-handed or left-handed* combined with *Pierre isn't right-handed,* we can derive *Pierre is left-handed,* which contradicts *Pierre isn't left-handed.* So we either have to accept contradictions or give up the principles of logic used in deriving the contradictions. Neither is appealing (although Fine is more sanguine about this. See Fine 1983: 61).

ii.   We've already noted that arbitrary objects are unexpected additions to the contents of the world. These unexpected additions create strange results in counting. Consider the question: *How many states are there in the USA?* You might have thought that the answer was fifty. But, as we saw above, there is also the arbitrary state. Since that's not identical to any of Alaska, Alabama, and so on, it's a fifty-first state in the USA. (We'll need to add another star to the flag!) The counting problems are even worse than they might seem at first. The arbitrary state in the USA is the arbitrary object corresponding to the range Alaska, Alabama, and so on. But there is also the *arbitrary state other than Alaska in the USA,* which corresponds to the range Alabama, Arizona, and so on. It's not the same as the other arbitrary object (it is south of Canada, for example, while the first arbitrary state isn't south of Canada). But it is a state in the USA, so now we're up to fifty-two states. Similarly for the range of Arizona, Arkansas, and so on, and for the range of California, Colorado, and so on. By taking various subranges of the fifty states, we're going to get quite a few states (the number will be in the quintillions). But things get really bad once we add in *second-order arbitrary objects.* We've seen several different arbitrary objects that are states in the USA. Take an arbitrary one of those. That's yet another thing, and it's also a state. As we add more arbitrary objects, we add more possible ranges for arbitrary objects, and those new ranges demand even more arbitrary objects. We'll quickly end up with infinitely many objects, and with the resultant danger of paradoxes of infinite size.

iii. The presence of arbitrary objects also creates unexpected *practical* problems. You might have thought, for example, that given the choice between saving two people and saving three, you should save three. But it turns out that you can't have just two people die. If there are two people, there is a third arbitrary person corresponding to the range of the two of them. If the original two both die, then the arbitrary person is also dead. And with the third arbitrary person added, there is a fourth arbitrary person corresponding to the range of the first two ordinary people along with the third arbitrary people. The fourth person also dies if the first two die. And so on—allowing two people to die is always allowing infinitely many people to die. So is allowing three people to die, of course, so now it looks like there's nothing to choose between saving two and saving three.

6.2 Arbitrary Reference

Fine's theory of arbitrary objects encounters difficulties due to strange features and consequences of the unusual objects that it posits. Breckenridge and Magidor (2012) have proposed an alternative approach to arbitrary names that places the arbitrariness in the reference relation rather than in the object referred to.

Imagine Alice says: 'Let Pierre be an arbitrary Frenchman. Pierre might like cheese and croissants.' Fine's view has it that Pierre refers to a special kind of object: the *arbitrary Frenchman*. On Fine's view, it then turns out to be false to say that Pierre might like cheese and croissants, because some Frenchmen definitely don't like cheese and croissants. According to Breckenridge and Magidor, on the other hand, there are no new arbitrary Frenchmen, but only the ordinary ones we already knew about. 'Pierre' refers to one of those ordinary Frenchman.

But to which one? On Breckenridge and Magidor's view, it could be any one of them. 'Pierre' could pick out French president Emmanuel Macron, or it could pick out former French footballer Zinedine Zidane, or any other Frenchman. Crucially, although Alice picks out some particular Frenchman, neither she nor anyone else knows which one she has picked out.

This picture of reference raises two obvious questions:

i. Suppose Alice's name 'Pierre' in fact refers to Macron. *Why* does it pick out Macron rather than, say, Zidane? Zidane would have served equally well as an arbitrary Frenchman, and Alice did nothing to single out Macron over Zidane.

ii. Furthermore, *how* does Alice's name 'Pierre' refer to Macron? Since on Breckenridge and Magidor's view, an arbitrary name just comes to refer to someone or other of the appropriate target group, there's no requirement that the namer have had causal contact with, or be able to think about, the named object. Alice might be wholly unaware of the existence of Macron and have never interacted with him. We thus can't use the standard Kripkean causal-chain picture to explain how the reference relation holds between name and named.

Breckenridge and Magidor's response to both of these questions is to endorse *primitivism* about reference.

Most views about reference are *anti-primitivist*. On anti-primitivist views, the name 'Barack Obama' refers to the forty-fourth president because of some other facts. On the Fregean view, the name refers as it does because people associate some descriptive meaning with it, and because the forty-fourth president then satisfies that descriptive meaning. On the Kripkean view, the name refers as it does because the forty-fourth president is at one end of a causal chain of uses of the name. The idea that names refer as they do because of some other facts is an instance of a more general pattern of things being as they are because of some other facts. For example, Berlin is the capital of Germany. But it's the capital of the Germany because of some other facts: it's because the Bundestag in 1991 voted to make Berlin the capital that it is the capital. And the fact that the Bundestag voted to make Berlin the capital is itself constituted by other facts—in this case, facts about particular members of the Bundestag voting as they did. But presumably this pattern of things being as they are because of other things can't go on forever. At some point we have to reach rock-bottom *fundamental* facts that just are the way they are, rather than being that way because of some other facts.

The Breckenridge and Magidor picture is that the reference facts are fundamental facts. There is nothing else in virtue of which 'Barack Obama' picks out the forty-fourth president—it just *does* pick him out. Similarly, then, with the arbitrary names. When Alice says, 'Let Pierre be an arbitrary Frenchman', 'Pierre' comes to be a name for someone— perhaps Macron. But there is no answer to the *how* question. 'Pierre' doesn't refer to Macron *because of* something else; it's just a fundamental fact that 'Pierre' refers to Macron. And because there is no answer to the *how* question, there is no answer to the *why* question either. As things are, Alice's name refers to Macron. But things could have gone otherwise, such that 'Pierre' referred to Zidane rather than Macron. There's then no *reason* that the world is the one way rather than the other—it's just a primitive fact that it's the way it is.

As we noted above, Breckenridge and Magidor's view entails a kind of ignorance that isn't present on Fine's view. For Fine, when Alice says 'Let Pierre be an arbitrary Frenchman', she can know exactly what her newly introduced name refers to: namely, the arbitrary Frenchman. But on Breckenridge and Magidor's view, it looks like Alice isn't in any position to know what 'Pierre' refers to. Maybe it refers to Macron and maybe it refers to Zidane, but Alice can never know which, and neither can anyone else. Breckenridge and Magidor take this to be a consequence of the primitivism about reference:

> You do not and cannot know what 'Pierre' refers to. Why? The obvious answer is that this is because nothing in the state of the world determines what 'Pierre' refers to.   (Breckenridge and Magidor 2012: 381)

They compare this to the flip of a coin in a truly random world: you cannot know in advance how the coin will land, because how it will land is not determined by the way the world is prior to the coin flip.

Consider two worries about this link between our ignorance of the reference of arbitrary names and the fundamentality of the reference of arbitrary names:

   i. The fundamentality of reference is, on Breckenridge and Magidor's view, a general fact about reference, and not special to arbitrary names. But invincible ignorance of reference looks like it is unique to arbitrary names. We can and do know who the name 'Barack Obama' refers to. If that reference relation is also primitive, what explains why we know who 'Barack Obama' refers to but not who 'Pierre' refers to?
   ii. Why would fundamentality be a barrier to knowledge? The suggestion seems to be that the only way to know what a name refers to would be by knowing the facts that *determine* what the name refers to. But if this is a general principle about knowledge, skepticism threatens. We then wouldn't be able to know any of the fundamental facts, because those facts aren't determined by anything, so we can't know them by knowing things that determine them. But if we can't know the fundamental facts, then we can't

know the things determined by the fundamental facts, so we can't know anything. If, on the other hand, the view is that there's some *other* way that we know fundamental facts, then we're left with no explanation of why we don't know what 'Pierre' refers to— the fundamentality of that reference fact is no longer a barrier to knowledge of the fact.

Let's now consider two general worries about the arbitrary reference view:

i. It looks like the view entails *one fact too many*. Suppose in a history class the professor says, 'Let's consider an arbitrary Roman citizen. Call him Lucius. What would Lucius's life have been like?' A student raises their hand and says, 'Is Lucius Augustus Caesar?' The natural thing to say is that the student's question is confused and displays a basic misunderstanding of what's going on in the discussion: that is, there is no sensible question about *which* Roman citizen Lucius is. The arbitrary object view does a decent job of capturing this natural thought. The professor can respond, 'No, Lucius isn't Augustus Caesar. He's an *arbitrary* Roman.' (Admittedly, the history class will take a sudden metaphysical turn if the student pursues the matter.) But on the arbitrary reference view, there wasn't anything wrong with the student's question (maybe Lucius does, in fact, refer to Augustus Caesar), and the best the professor can do by way of a response is to say 'It might—I don't know'. But this looks like it concedes too much determinacy about the reference of Lucius.

ii. It looks like the view requires *mysterious boundaries to the fundamentality of reference*. The natural thought is that 'Pierre' can't refer to Macron, because Alice hasn't done anything to *make* it refer to Macron. The primitivist response is then that Alice doesn't need to do anything to make it refer to Macron, since its referring to Macron can just be a fundamental fact, not explained by anything Alice or anyone else does. But Alice's actions aren't *completely* irrelevant to the reference of 'Pierre'. Her declaration that 'Pierre' be an arbitrary Frenchman is enough to make sure that 'Pierre' not refer to Donald Trump, for example. If the reference facts were really fundamental, why would anything Alice does be needed for any referential features of 'Pierre'? Why, for example, might it not turn out that 'Floofshmoot', which has never been used by anyone, all the time has referred to Alfred Hitchcock, just as a fundamental fact underived from any human usage facts? If we don't want to allow 'Floofshmoot' or the possibility that Pierre is Trump, we need the fundamentality of reference to take over just where Alice's referential plans give out, and go no further than that.

6.3 Arbitrary Names Without Naming

Both approaches we've looked at in this chapter—arbitrary objects and arbitrary reference—require some special maneuvering to get *truth* to come out in the right way. Consider again Alice's introduction of 'Pierre' as a name for the arbitrary Frenchman. The arbitrary Frenchman has a heart, but it's not true that the arbitrary Frenchman lives in Paris. So we need:

- 'Pierre has a heart' to come out true.
- 'Pierre lives in Paris' not to come out true.

With ordinary names, we rely on the objects referred to do the truthmaking work. 'Aristotle was a philosopher' is true because Aristotle himself had the property of being a philosopher. But with arbitrary names, the story gets more complicated:

i. On the arbitrary object view, 'Pierre has a heart' is true just in case this odd new object, the arbitrary Frenchman, in fact has a heart. But figuring out whether this arbitrary object has a heart is a very different matter from figuring out whether normal people have a heart. Ultrasounds and autopsies won't be of any help here. We need a special account of features of arbitrary objects: we say, as we saw above, that an arbitrary object has some feature just in case every object in the range correlated with that arbitrary object has that feature. Properties of arbitrary objects, then, flow from properties of ordinary objects.

ii. On the arbitrary reference view, 'Pierre has a heart' is true just in case some particular Frenchman (maybe Macron) has a heart. 'Pierre has a heart' is thus made true in the same way as 'Aristotle has a heart'. But the problem is that 'Pierre lives in Paris' might be made true in the ordinary way as well, if 'Pierre' happens to pick out a Parisian. So we make a distinction between what's *true* of Pierre and what we can *reasonably assert* about Pierre. Since we don't and can't know who Pierre is, the only things we can reasonably assert about Pierre are the things we can figure out without knowing which Frenchman Pierre is. Those things will be all and only things that are true of *all* Frenchmen. So what is reasonably assertable about Pierre flows from general facts about what's true about all Frenchmen.

Once we see these more complicated stories, though, we might start wondering whether we really even need arbitrary names to refer. In this section, we'll set out a view on which arbitrary names don't refer to anything.

On this view, when Alice says, 'Let Pierre be an arbitrary Frenchman', she doesn't do enough to introduce a real referring expression into the language. Let's start, then, by contrasting successful and unsuccessful attempts to add new expressions to a language.

When we introduce the name 'Aristotle', we have a specific individual on hand to whom we are attaching that name. When we introduce a new scientific term like 'DNA', we have a detailed scientific theory that tells us exactly what a thing needs to be like to fall under that term.

But we often do less than this, and thus less than is needed, to give a new word a fully determinate meaning. Such cases are common with slang expressions. No one sat down and determined exactly what it would take for something to be *cool* or *on fleek*. People just started using these expressions as more or less indeterminate terms of affirmation, and some vague boundaries of appropriate use grew up over time. That's enough to provide *some meaning* to the slang terms, but not the full determinate meaning we expect from fully successful terms. There is, for example, no definite property that 'cool' picks out.

Let's consider an example of incomplete meaning specification more carefully. We might introduce a new color term 'vermilion' by pointing to a particular object and saying:

7. Let 'vermilion' be the kind of red that that object has.

But 'vermilion' is intended to pick out a color range, and not one exact shade, and we haven't said what the boundaries of that range are. We've done enough to place some meaning constraints on 'vermilion'—it's definitely a color property, and a species of red—but not enough to assign an exact meaning to it.

If 'vermilion' hasn't been given a definite meaning, and doesn't pick out a definite color property, then what do we say about the truth value of claims using 'vermilion'? In some sense, saying:

8.   His blood is vermilion.

is like saying:

9.   The slithy toves did gyre and gimble in the wabe.

Both are sentences using words that don't mean anything, and thus aren't true or false. But the verdict seems harsher than necessary in the 'vermilion' case. 'Vermilion' isn't 'gimble'—it's not a word that's just completely made up, but rather a word that we, in a sense, started but didn't finish giving a meaning.

There are many different ways we could finish the job of giving 'vermilion' a meaning, and those different ways differ in the details of what 'vermilion' ends up meaning. But there are certain things we already know all these ways will have in common. All of them end up assigning *some shade of red* to 'vermilion', because we've already committed to that much. So consider:

10.   All vermilion things are red.

Perhaps this isn't *true*, because 'vermilion' doesn't have a precise meaning. But it's *assertable*, because it's reasonable to go ahead and say it on the grounds that we already know that whatever meaning we do eventually assign to 'vermilion', it will make our claim true.

Perhaps this kind of semantic indeterminacy is the source of the vagueness of color terms. Some objects will be definitely vermilion—for example, the original samples that we used in introducing the word, or objects that are perceptually indistinguishable from those samples. Other objects will be definitely not vermilion—limes, for example. But some objects will be kind of, but not overwhelmingly, similar to the paradigm sample, and it may be that nothing we've done in introducing the word 'vermilion' determines whether these objects are vermilion or not.

Return now to arbitrary names. When Alice says 'Let Pierre be an arbitrary Frenchman', she introduces a new word into the language, but fails to do all of the work needed to give it a precise meaning. She's required that 'Pierre' pick out a Frenchman, but not gotten around to saying *which* Frenchman it picks out. 'Pierre', then, doesn't refer to anything, because no one ever gave it a reference. It doesn't refer to *the arbitrary Frenchman* (and so we don't need such an odd object), and it doesn't refer arbitrarily to some Frenchman or other.

This view explains nicely why the student who responds to the professor's 'Let Lucius be an arbitrary Roman citizen' by asking, 'Is Lucius Augustus Caesar?' is confused. He's confused because he's taking the language to be more determinate than it really is—'Lucius' doesn't refer to anything at all, so in particular it doesn't refer to Augustus Caesar. But the view then confronts a problem in making sense of what the professor is saying. If 'Lucius' hasn't been given a full meaning, and thus doesn't refer to anything, then what is the professor doing when she goes on to say 'Lucius would have been exempt from torture by the state'?

Following the line we considered with 'vermilion', we say that claims involving 'Lucius' aren't true or false, but are reasonable if they would be correct *no matter how the language was made fully determinate*. When Alice says 'Let Pierre be a Frenchman', she does only part of the work of introducing a fully determinate name. There are many ways that Alice's work could be completed—it could be completed by further specifying that 'Pierre' refers to Macron or to Zidane, but it couldn't be completed by saying that 'Pierre' refers to Trump. So it's already reasonable to say:

11.   Pierre is French.

Because no matter how we finished the job of introducing 'Pierre' as a fully determinate name, that claim is assertable. We already know *enough* about what 'Pierre' could mean to know that that sentence can't come out false. But it's not reasonable right now to say:

12.   Pierre is a politician.

That might come out right if we eventually make 'Pierre' determinate by making it refer to Macron, but it might come out wrong if we make 'Pierre' determinate by making it refer to Zidane. Since it could go either way at this point, we shouldn't say that Pierre is a politician.

We need to say more, though, about what it means to give a *name* an incomplete meaning. With a descriptive term like 'vermilion', a partial meaning is something that determines whether *some* objects are or are not vermilion, but leaves unsettled whether other objects are or are not vermilion. But the story can't be so simple for names, because a name isn't dividing all objects into two categories (vermilion and not vermilion), but is picking out one specific object.

Some names are descriptive names, like Julius and Jack the Ripper. With descriptive names, there is a clear sense of what an incomplete meaning would be. A complete meaning for a descriptive name is a property that picks out a unique individual and thus makes that individual the referent of the name ('inventor of the zipper'). An incomplete meaning for a descriptive name is then a property that doesn't manage to single out a unique individual. This looks like what we have in Alice's 'Pierre' case. She does what looks like an introduction of a descriptive name, but then uses a descriptive property that is too general ('is a Frenchman').

But not all names are descriptive names. What would it mean for a non-descriptive name to have an incomplete meaning? On the Kripkean model, we could consider cases in which the original dubbing was incomplete—the original dubber, for example, makes a vague gesture toward a range of objects, rather than doing enough to dub a particular object. And we could also consider cases in which the causal chain was incomplete—the relation between uses of the name has some, but not all, of the causal features that we expect from a standard link in a Kripkean causal-communicative chain. Perhaps 'Madagascar' has a meaning that is incomplete in this sense.

6.4 Extending the View

We have been focusing on a somewhat unusual category of *arbitrary names* in this chapter. Our paradigm cases of arbitrary names have been those introduced by explicit statements of the form 'Let so-and-so be an arbitrary such-and-such'. Such introductions aren't uncommon in, for example, the context of mathematical proofs, but don't often show up in ordinary conversation. But, frequent or infrequent, they raise interesting foundational questions about what the role of reference is in our theorizing about language: what sorts of objects we need to provide referents for our terms, what determines what our names refer to, how much it matters for various purposes what we refer to.

How unusual arbitrary names are depends in part on how broad we take the category to be. As mentioned above, we can think of certain kinds of anaphoric pronouns as examples of arbitrary names. Consider two more examples:

13.   A woman dies of breast cancer every five minutes. (Dramatic pause) A woman just died. *She* would have lived if we had a cure. (Lewis 2013)

14.   Each conference participant must wear a name tag. *He* will find his name tag with his registration materials.

We can think of the pronouns in these examples as (i) referring to the arbitrary woman who died of breast cancer and the arbitrary conference participant, or (ii) referring arbitrarily to some woman or other who died of breast cancer and some conference participant or other, or (iii) incompletely specified names, whose meaning has been constrained to require reference to a woman who died of breast cancer and a conference participant, but whose referent hasn't been fully determined.

If we do include these anaphoric cases in the category of arbitrary names, then it would make sense to include *all* anaphoric pronouns in the same general category. Many cases won't require arbitrariness, either because the antecedent is already precise enough to settle non-arbitrary reference:

15.   An Austrian nobleman was assassinated right before World War I. *He* was Franz Ferdinand.

Or because the speaker intends one specific instance of the antecedent:

1.   A student came to my office hours today. *He* wanted to complain about his grade on the paper.

We can think of these as limiting cases of arbitrariness. The 'arbitrary Austrian nobleman assassinated right before World War I' just *is* Franz Ferdinand. Arbitrary reference to such an Austrian nobleman just is reference to Franz Ferdinand. And a name whose meaning is specified by the property *being an Austrian nobleman assassinated right before World War I* is a name that's been specified all the way to completeness.

If we're thinking of anaphoric pronouns as falling under the general banner of arbitrary names, then we might want to consider their antecedents as also falling under that general banner. In the above sentence, for example, 'a student' serves as antecedent to 'he'. Semanticists assume that there is some relation between a pronoun and its antecedent whereby the former derives its content from the latter. If we say, then, that 'he' is a device of arbitrary reference, it may make sense to say that 'a student' is one too. We could say the same about other quantified noun phrases. 'Most linguists', for example, might be taken to refer arbitrarily to some majority or other of linguists, or to the arbitrary majority of linguists.

This is only a vague gesture at a proposal, and much work would be needed to fill in the details. For example, we want 'A tiger ate Smith's dog' to be true just in case at least one tiger did the eating. That's not what we'll get if 'a tiger' picks out the arbitrary tiger (since the arbitrary tiger eats only what *all* tigers eat), and it's probably not what we'll get if 'a tiger' refers arbitrarily to some tiger or other (since it's unlikely to end up referring to the particular guilty tiger). And even when details are filled in, there will remain differences from ordinary names—we need 'a tiger' and 'most linguists' to come out non-rigid, which means we can't mimic the behavior of rigid names too closely. But even with these points of difficulty and difference, we're left with a picture that raises hard questions about how deep the divide between descriptive quantified noun phrases and referential names really is, and what the distinctive theoretical role of reference should be.

Central Points in Chapter 6

- Although we mostly use names and other referential devices to pick out some particular object, sometimes, in the case of arbitrary names, we do not.
- The most common instance of this is in mathematics. A mathematician wanting to prove something about all numbers may say: 'Let "n" be an arbitrary number'. She can then go on to use 'n' just like any other name. For example, she can go on to say: 'n is either even or odd'. We surveyed two extant views about such referential devices: arbitrary objects, and arbitrary reference.
- On the arbitrary object view, there is a special type of object which is what is referred to by 'n': an arbitrary object. These objects are associated with a *range* of normal objects. 'N' is associated with the numbers, for example. In 'Let Pierre be an arbitrary Frenchman', 'Pierre' is associated with the Frenchmen.
- An arbitrary object possesses a property provided all the objects in its associated range possess it. 'Pierre is a man' is true because all Frenchmen are men. 'Pierre wears glasses' is not true because some Frenchmen do not wear glasses.

(continued)

- Arbitrary objects give rise to complications concerning logic ('Pierre wears glasses or does not wear glasses' is true, but 'Pierre wears glasses' and 'Pierre does not wear glasses' are both false), and concerning counting (if the only two dire wolves in the world and they are on the table in front of you, then it may seem like 'there are two dire wolves in front of you' is true. But there's also the arbitrary dire wolf, and it is in front of you, so there are in fact three objects in front of you).

- On the arbitrary reference view, 'n' refers to some particular number, and 'Pierre' to some particular Frenchman. They do so, though, somewhat arbitrarily: there's no fact in the world that makes 'n' refer to 20 as opposed to 46, for example. It is just a primitive, inexplicable fact about the world that this is so.

- The arbitrary reference view can explain why it's ok for us to say things like 'n is either even or odd', but not ok to say 'n is even' or 'n is odd'. The reason is that because we can't know anything about the referent (how would we go about finding anything out?) apart from the fact that it's a number, we can only assert that it has properties we know all numbers to have.

- The arbitrary reference view also has problems, however. In the math class, having heard the stipulation, the student could ask the teacher 'Is n 17?' This sounds like the student has fundamentally misunderstood what's going on, but for the arbitrary reference theorist it's a fine question. Another problem is that the primitiveness of arbitrary reference is somewhat vague. It's not completely arbitrary—'n' can't refer to carrots, nor 'Pierre' to spaniels, and the made-up word 'floofschmoot' can't refer to anything.

- Finally, we sketched the beginnings of an alternative view, according to which arbitrary names are semantically underdetermined—in making an arbitrary reference stipulation, we don't do enough to pin the term down to any one referent. On this view, arbitrary names might be like vague terms, which, according to one view, are similarly underdetermined. Just as 'red' definitely stands for a color, but it may be indeterminate whether it holds of a given borderline red/green patch, so 'n' may definitely refer to a number even if it's indeterminate, whether it stands for 20 or 45 or eight billion and one.

Comprehension Questions

1. Say, in a couple of words, what the problem with arbitrary reference is.
2. Explain the difference between the arbitrary reference and the arbitrary objects view.
3. Spell out the semantic underdetermination view we presented in Section 6.3.
4. For the following sentences, say what the referring expressions refer to, and the truth conditions:
   4.1. Pierre is a friend of mine. He likes fish.
   4.2. Let 'Pierre' name the first person to tweet this morning (in EST).
   4.3. Let 'Pierre' name an arbitrary American president. He is a Republican or a Democrat.
   4.4. Let 'Pierre' name the present king of France. He is a king.

Exploratory Questions

5. Consider the following:
   5.1. The average man is 5 foot 9 inches tall.
   5.2. A madrigal is polyphonic.
   5.3. One must report to the guard before entering the building.
   Is there a case for saying that these uses of definite descriptions, indefinite descriptions, and pronouns, respectively, are devices of arbitrary reference?
6. The first sentence of this book reads: 'Killing Bill is no small undertaking'.
   How is 'Bill' functioning here? (For fans of postmodern American cinema, assume we are writing in a world in which Tarantino made no films, and thus that this isn't a name from fiction.)
7. Consider the case of what we could call arbitrary predicates. Can we say things like 'Let F name an arbitrary predicate. Obama is F or he is not F'? Does such arbitrary predication lead to any logical complications?

Further Reading

Fine 1985 is a monograph which treats arbitrary objects at more length than the paper cited in the text. Kearns and Magidor 2012 defends the claim of primitivism about reference. King 1991 is another view of how to understand reasoning involving what seem like arbitrary objects. A helpful introduction to the idea of semantic underdetermination is Sorenson 2016, Section 5, and its classic formulation can be found in the challenging Fine 1975.

7

Predicativism
The Puzzle of 'Every Alfred'

Reference is usually taken to be a distinctive feature of one particular grammatical category: *proper names*. 'Winston Churchill' is a proper name; it *refers* to the famous British prime minister. 'Jupiter' is a proper name; it *refers* to the largest planet in the solar system. 'No linguist', on the other hand, is not a proper name, but rather a noun phrase. It does not refer (what would it refer to?). Instead, it quantifies over the class of linguists. 'Duck' is not a proper name, but rather a predicate. It does not refer. Instead, it is *true of* some things (ducks), and not of others. 'And' is not a proper name, but rather a connective. It does not refer. Instead, it determines the truth value of a complex sentence in terms of the truth values of the component parts.

But what if there are no proper names? What's the place then for reference in our theory of language? *Predicativist* theories hold that there are no names, that the very idea that there is a distinctive grammatical category of names is a mistake. On predicativist views, 'Winston Churchill' and 'Jupiter' aren't names, but rather are predicates like 'duck'. An ambitious version of predicativism then holds that with names out of the way, reference disappears as well. 'Winston Churchill' and 'Jupiter' are predicates just like 'duck', and they refer no more than it does. At first glance, predicativism can seem obviously false. The expressions 'Winston Churchill' and 'duck' don't behave alike. We do refer to a particular person with 'Winston Churchill', and that's why we can say 'Winston Churchill was prime minister during World War II'. But we don't refer to any particular duck with 'duck', and that's why we can't say 'Duck is hungry'. We can say '*The* duck is hungry', or '*Every* duck is hungry', or '*No* duck is hungry', but not just 'Duck is hungry'. But sophisticated versions of predicativism have been developed that respond to this concern, and marshal substantial linguistic evidence in favor of treating 'Winston Churchill' like 'duck'.

7.1 Motivating Predicativism

Predicativism starts with the thought that philosophers have restricted their attention to an overly narrow range of uses of names. (Well, the predicativists don't think there are names, so from their point of view, this isn't the right way to put it. For convenience, though, we'll just use 'names' for what the predicativist would rather call 'expressions traditionally misclassified as names'.) We don't just say things like 'Winston Churchill was prime minister' and 'Jupiter is a planet'. We also say 'Many Kennedys have been politicians', and 'Some Alfreds are crazy; some are sane'. In these sentences, the words 'Kennedy' and 'Alfred' are combined with quantifiers 'many' and 'some' in the way that predicates typically are. Predicativists point out that we find an almost perfect parallel between the grammatical distribution of names and the grammatical distribution of predicates:

Every duck quacks.	Every Alfred laughs.
No cat quacks.	No Alfred laughs.
Several ducks in my house quacked.	Several Alfreds in my class laughed.
That duck quacked.	That Alfred laughed.
The duck in the pond quacked.	The Alfred in my class laughed.
Ducks quack.	Alfreds laugh.

Call this collection of data the *Predicate-Like Data*. If it looks like a duck and quacks like a duck, maybe it is a duck. The predicativist argues on the basis of this data that since names and predicates occur in all these same grammatical positions, names just *are* predicates.

Importantly, it's not just that names have the *grammatical* distribution of predicates. They are also playing a predicate-like *semantic* role in these sentences. What are we saying when we say 'Every Alfred laughs'? We are identifying a group of people (a group that includes Alfred Tarski, Alfred Hitchcock, Alfred Nobel, and many others), and we are saying that every member of that group laughs. The meaning is thus parallel to the meaning of 'Every duck quacks', in which we identify a group of animals (a group that includes Daffy Duck, Daisy Duck, Duck Dodgers, Howard the Duck, and many others[1]), and say that every member of that group laughs. Standard inference patterns are exhibited by both 'Alfred' and 'duck' sentences:

1a. Every duck quacks.	1b. Every Alfred in the class laughed.
2a. Donald is a duck.	2b. Alfred Tarski is in the class.
3a. Therefore, Donald quacks.	3b. Therefore, Alfred Tarski laughed.

(Note that the 'Alfred' argument creates pressure to treat the classical 'name-like' uses of Alfred in a way continuous with the 'predicate-like' uses. We'll return to the name-like uses below.)

Roughly, 'Alfred' is a predicate true of a bunch of people (Alfred Tarski, Alfred Hitchcock, Alfred Nobel, and so on). This explains why we can say 'Every Alfred laughs'. As with 'Every duck quacks', we are saying that every member of a certain class—the class of things satisfying the predicate—are a certain way.

7.2 The Uniformity Problem

Predicativists hold that treating 'Alfred' and 'Winston Churchill' as predicates just like 'duck' gives us the best explanation of the ability of *all* of these words to combine with quantifiers like 'some', 'every', and 'several'. But things aren't quite as smooth as the predicativists might wish. There are, in fact, some important grammatical differences between 'Alfred' and 'duck'. Consider:

The duck quacked.	*The Alfred laughed.
*Duck quacked.	Alfred laughed.

Call this collection the *Name-Like Data*. 'Alfred' can be used *bare* in the singular, with no accompanying quantifier. (It's this bare usage that philosophers have historically focused on.) But 'duck' cannot be used this way.

Furthermore, 'duck' can be used freely in combination with the definite article 'the', but 'Albert' cannot. (As we saw above, we can combine 'the' with 'Alfred' when 'Alfred' is further modified by some

---

[1] Overlook the fact that these are fictional names. We don't, unfortunately, know the names of any actual ducks.

additional description, such as 'Alfred in California', or 'Alfred who lost his jacket'. But 'the Alfred' by itself is unacceptable.) The Name-Like Data is unexpected for the predicativist, and bolsters the case for a traditional non-predicativist view.

Neither predicativists nor non-predicativists have a perfect story. 'Alfred' acts a lot like 'duck', but not exactly like 'duck'. One option is to drop the search for a unified story. Maybe predicativists are right about the predicate-like uses of 'Alfred', while traditional theorists are right about the name-like uses of 'Alfred'. But this option comes with a heavy cost. We have to accept that there are really two grammatically distinct words 'Alfred' in the language: one a predicate, and one a proper name. We would then need an explanation for why we sys-tematically find these pairs of words (whenever there is a proper name, there is an identical-looking predicate), and why the meanings of these pairs are always tightly connected. It's tempting, then, to take one of the two cases as basic, and try to explain away the other case. Predicativists then need to explain why 'Alfred' isn't acting exactly like 'duck'—they need to account for the Name-Like Data. Non-predicativists, on the other hand, need to explain why 'Alfred' is acting even a little bit like 'duck'—they need to account for the Predicate-Like Data.

7.3 Defending Names: Coercion Strategies

The non-predicativist strategy is to claim that the cases in the Predicate-Like Data are examples of *coercion*, in which we are forcing language into roles outside its normal function. Everyone agrees that words can tem-porarily and on the fly be pressed into service outside their normal grammatical category. The common observation that we can 'verb nouns' is itself an example of coercion. (As Calvin (of Calvin and Hobbes fame) says, in another example, 'Verbing weirds language'.) A proper name like 'Xerox', naming a corporation, gets pressed into service as a verb ('to xerox'), as a noun picking out the machines ('our office just got a new Xerox'), and as a noun picking out the products of the machines ('that's just a Xerox; I'll get you the original').

The coercion thought is that these non-standard uses of 'Xerox' don't give us reason to deny that in its standard uses, 'Xerox' is just a name for a corporation. The non-standard uses aren't evidence that the meaning of 'Xerox' is different from, or broader than, we previously thought. Rather, they are just evidence that language is our tool, and tools can be abused in addition to being used, and made to do things they weren't built for. 'Let me librarian that for you' isn't evidence that 'librarian' picks out an action instead of, or in addition to, an occupation—it's just evidence that we'll figure out what to do if we're called on to free-associate an action with the occupation.

Proponents of a coercion strategy make two points in its favor: first, they note that names become predicates in a number of ways. Earlier we treated 'Albert' as a predicate true of people named 'Albert'. But that's not the only option. When people called Slobodan Milošević the next Hitler, they weren't using 'Hitler' as a predicate true of people *named* 'Hitler'. Rather, they were using it as a predicate true of people *relevantly resembling Hitler*. When we say that the museum contains three Picassos, we aren't using 'Picasso' as a predicate true of things *named* 'Picasso', but rather as a predicate true of things *created by Picasso*. When we say that two Obamas came to the costume party, we aren't saying two people *named* 'Obama' came, but rather two people *dressed as* Obama came. And so on.

Coercion is an ad hoc strategy, a repair mechanism to make sense of language when it is being pushed outside its normal function. It's thus to be expected that the results of coercion will be varied and unpredictable. The more irregular and unsystematic the result of using names in predicate position is, the better things look for the coercion view. On the other hand, the more systematic things are, the better things will look for the predicativist, who claims that the predicativist use of names isn't a repair mechanism, but is their core semantic value.

Names can indeed become predicates in many and sometimes unpredictable ways. This is an important observation, and it's one that the predicativist owes an explanation for. But it's also important to note that there is a core systematic procedure of using name N as a predicate true of everyone named 'N'. The use of 'Hitler' to mean *genocidal nationalist leader* requires the right context and depends on strong cultural associations with Adolf Hitler, but the core predicative usage looks like it's available with any name in any context. A tempting response for the predicativist, then, is to agree that there is coercion, but it's coercion from the core predicative use. On this view, what 'Picasso' really is, is a predicate true of people named 'Picasso'. But in the right context we can press it into service as a predicate true of artworks created by Picasso.

The second argument in favor of coercion looks at the availability of Predicate-Like Data for words other than names. Coercion is a globally available repair strategy—there are few limits on what can be coerced into what. So if the predicative uses of names are a result of coercion, we should expect the phenomenon to be global in the way typical of coercion. Proponents of a coercion story can then point to two ways in which the phenomenon is global. First, names can be used in grammatical roles other than the noun role. For example, names can be pushed into the verb role. This is common with product names, as in the earlier example of 'Xerox'. It can also be done with names of people. Network television has taught us that sometimes one has to MacGyver one's way out of difficulties. Mathematicians learn how to Schönfinkel functions. Second, it's not just names that can be coerced into predicative role. After a vote, we can report that there were three 'yes's and two 'no's, coercing 'yes' and 'no' into predicative role. If we're organizing people for a land-or-water race, we can ask all the runs to go to one side and all the swims to the other.

However, many of these other coercion cases are much less natural than the predicative uses of names. Getting the coercion to work often requires setting up an explicit context (as done above) on which people are to be sorted according to some feature associated with the word being coerced into predicative role. The predicative uses of names, on the other hand, are smooth and natural, and require no special context. It's worth noting that pushing *pronouns* into a predicative role is much less successful than with names:

4.   #Every you in the class got an A on the exam.
5.   #No he came to the party—just a few shes.

This is surprising, given the many similarities between names and pronouns. The coercion story doesn't have any ready explanation for the fact that names move to predicate role much more smoothly than pronouns. (Predicativists can simply deny that pronouns are predicates, but then they will need to explain why pronouns have so many semantic similarities to names, despite being in different grammatical categories.)

The above considerations aren't fully decisive in either direction. There is room for the proponent of the traditional view to argue that the Predicate-Like Data is an instance of coercing language into non-standard roles. The burden on that view is then to explain why there is such a systematic, predictable, and easily available core phenomenon of predicate-like uses specifically of names. That's exactly what the predicativist would predict, but it's at best surprising for a coercion story.

7.4 Defending Predicativism: Hidden Determiners

To deal with the Name-Like Data, predicativists typically appeal to the idea of a *hidden determiner*. Hidden determiner views hold that when a name occurs with no visible determiner, there is a covert determiner that completes the phrase. So on some versions of the view, to say 'Alfred' is really to say 'That Alfred', with the occurrence of 'that' silent. On other views, it is to say 'The Alfred'. 'Alfred laughed' is thus 'That Alfred laughed', or 'The Alfred laughed', and its acceptability thus matches the acceptability of 'That duck quacked' or 'The duck quacked'.

The appeal to hidden, silent, covert words can seem mysterious. But similar appeals are not uncommon in linguistics. Standard stories, for example, say that both 'sharks' and 'fish' contain a plural number marker, but that while that marker is pronounced '-s' when combined with 'shark', it is silent when combined with 'fish'. Similarly, standard views hold that both of:

6. John wants Mary to be happy.
7. John wants to be happy.

have a word between 'want' and 'to' picking out the person to be happy, but that when that word refers to John, it remains silent. So the predicativist's move is not without precedent. But appeals to covert words should always be treated with a higher level of suspicion, calling for better confirming evidence, because it is otherwise too easy to make almost any view workable through extensive appeal to hidden words.

Predicativists often appeal, in defending the hidden determiner view, to the fact that, in many languages, normal uses of names do require overt determiners. In German, for example, we may say 'Hans eats' as 'Der Hans isst', using the definite determiner, rather than as 'Hans isst', without an article. The full cross-linguistic details are messy and complicated (see Matushansky 2008, for some discussion of the data). In many languages the use of the determiner is required for some types of names and not for others, and sometimes the determiner is not the same as the standard definite determiner. (Schoubye (2017), for example, notes that Danish contains both a definite determiner positioned before nouns, and a definite determiner suffix that can be attached to nouns, but that only the former can be used with names.)

English, in fact, has a limited use of names that require an overt determiner. One category is names of ships—we say *the Titanic*, rather than just *Titanic*. But when we have another determiner for quantification, the use of 'the' disappears, so that we can say:

8.   Every *Titanic* sinks on its maiden voyage.

So, on the predicativist view, it is in its nautical fragment that English reveals its often-hidden semantic stripes. These English cases can be helpful for examining whether these mandatory determiners have the normal semantic function of quantifiers. We can, for example, normally combine multiple determiners with a single noun, as in:

9.   The, or at least a, plumber will arrive soon.

Is the same construction with '*Titanic*' acceptable?

10.   The, or at least a, *Titanic* will arrive soon.

A full predicativist theory needs an account of *what* this hidden determiner is. There are two major views on this question. The earlier predicative views, such as Burge (1973), tended to hold that the hidden determiner is a demonstrative, equivalent to 'that'. More recent predicativist theories have preferred the view that the hidden determiner is a definite article, equivalent to 'the'. (Another option is that the hidden determiner is neither 'that' nor 'the', but a unique determiner of its own.) It is not always clear how much it matters what the hidden determiner is. We'll consider a possible semantic reason for caring shortly, when we discuss rigidity. Some grammatical evidence against so-called 'that'-predicativism has been given. Contrast the following pair of sentences:

11.   That Winston Churchill is a novelist, but this one is a prime minister.

12.   #Winston Churchill is a novelist, but this one is a prime minister.

The second sentence is markedly worse than the first, but 'that'-predicativism has no explanation for the difference. For 'the'-predicativism, however, we get the pair:

13.   #The Winston Churchill is a novelist, but this one is a prime minister.

14.   #Winston Churchill is a novelist, but this one is a prime minister.

'The'-predicativism predicts that the two sentences are equivalent, and we find that they are equally bad.

On the other hand, 'the'-predicativism owes us an explanation of why it makes sense to use a hidden definite determiner. If there are many Alfreds, why would it make sense to say 'The Alfred laughs'? Doesn't the use of the definite determiner assume uniqueness? When we say 'The queen of England is visiting', we make clear that we think there is a *unique* queen of England. The response is that the uniqueness behavior of definites is more complicated than this. There are many cases in which we use definite descriptions, even though absolute uniqueness obviously fails. These are cases of so-called *incomplete descriptions*, such as:

15.   The book is on the table.

In saying this, we don't commit to there being just one book (anywhere) and just one table (anywhere). The details are complicated and controversial, but roughly we commit to there being just one *relevant* or *conversationally salient* book and table. In the same way, when we say 'Alfred laughs', to express that *the* Alfred laughs, we don't assume that there's just one Alfred *anywhere*. Rather, we assume that there is a unique *relevant* Alfred.

Positing a hidden determiner is only part of the full response to the Name-Like Data. Suppose we endorse 'the'-predicativism, holding that the hidden determiner is a definite determiner. The naive prediction is then that when 'the' is combined with a name, it is mandatorily hidden. That explains why we get 'Alfred laughed', which on this view has a hidden 'the'. It also explains why we *don't* get 'The Alfred laughed', because 'the' is required to be hidden when combined with names. But the naive prediction is too naive, because there are cases in which 'the' occurs overtly with names:

16.   The Alfred in my class is happy, but the Alfred in your class is sad.

17.   The young Wittgenstein endorsed logical atomism, but the older
Wittgenstein rejected it.

In addition, as we've already seen there is variation across languages in
whether the definite determiner occurs overtly or covertly with names,
and there is variation even within English over categories of names on the
overt/covert behavior. More sophisticated versions of predicativism have
offered various more subtle rules controlling when 'the' occurs overtly
with names and when it occurs covertly. (See Sloat 1969 and Fara 2015 for
more discussion.) The need to posit complicated rules of this sort is a
significant cost to predicativism, and the more such rules look ad hoc and
dissimilar to other grammatical rules, the higher that cost will be.

7.5 On the Philosophical Significance of Predicativism

One ambition of predicativism was to eliminate a certain grammatical
category: the traditional category of proper names. We've seen now how
that elimination is supposed to proceed. But the grammatical revolution
of eliminating names doesn't by itself entail a *semantic* revolution. We
can distinguish between an unambitious and an ambitious version of
predicativism. In its ambitious version, predicativism is a thorough
rejection of the entire idea of reference. The ambitious predicativist
claims that there is no reference relation at all. On this view, it was a
mistake ever to think that there was a special referential relation in which
a particular word is hooked directly on to a particular object as a tag,
attaching directly to the object regardless of that object's properties. Rather,
there is just the predication relation, in which a word is associated with a
range of objects on the basis of the features of those objects. Language, on
this view, has only devices of predication. 'Winston Churchill' does not
refer to an individual, but rather holds true of various individuals: of all the
Winston Churchills—the British prime minister, the American novelist,
the seventeenth-century English soldier, and so on.

But there can also be an unambitious predicativism, which does not
seek to remove reference entirely from the theory of language. We can set
out three ways in which the scope of predicativism can be limited and the
theory made more cautious. First, predicativism could be a theory of
some, but not all, referring expressions. We can hold that proper names

like 'Alfred' and 'Winston Churchill' are predicates without thinking that all (apparently) referential terms are predicates. We might, for example, think that pronouns like 'I', 'you', 'he', and 'she' refer, and are not predicates. (As we saw above, pronouns don't easily fit the predicativist grammatical mold.)

Second, predicativism can be wrapped inside a referential package. In response to the Name-Like Data, the predicativist appeals to hidden determiners with bare name uses. But depending on our theory of those hidden determiners, we can recapture the referential status of names. Suppose, for example, we take bare 'Alfred' to come with a covert 'that' determiner, and thus to be equivalent to 'that Alfred'. If we think the demonstrative 'that' is referential, or creates a referential complex demonstrative, then we will think that the sentence 'Alfred laughed' involves *reference to Alfred*. We will distinguish the phrase '~~that~~ Alfred' (where a word's being struck through indicates that it is unpronounced), which refers to Alfred, from the single word 'Alfred', which merely predicates and does not refer. Those who think that definite descriptions are referential can say similar things about 'the Alfred'. On this view, the underlying predicative gives rise to a quantified non-referential expression when combined with some determiners ('no', for example), and to a referential expression when combined with other determiners. There are then still referring expressions (and referring expressions that look very much like names), but they are referring expressions with a soft predicative center.

Third, the predicative meaning of names might itself involve reference. We haven't said much yet about what *kind* of predicates names are, according to predicativists. But consider first an oversimplified view, which no actual predicativist seriously holds. Suppose 'Winston Churchill' is a predicate well glossed as 'person identical to WC', where 'WC' somehow really refers to Winston Churchill (and thus is not a further predicate). Then 'Winston Churchill' does not itself refer to anything, and in saying 'Winston Churchill is British' we say 'The Winston Churchill is president', and thus 'The person identical to WC is British'. 'The person identical to WC' is a definite description, so it also does not refer to anything (but rather denotes). But reference is *involved* in the predicate, since the predicate has its satisfaction conditions, and the definite description its denotation conditions, by virtue of a reference to Winston Churchill.

This oversimplified view isn't a very good one in general (though see McKeever 2016 for an attempt at a defense). In order to make sense of the fact that 'Winston Churchill' can also refer to the American novelist, we will have to say that the name is ambiguous. On one reading, it stands for the property *being identical to WC,* and on another it stands for the property *being identical to WC1,* where 'WC1' manages to really refer to the novelist Churchill. This means we won't be able to truly say things like 'There are two famous Winston Churchills', and we lose much of the potential virtue of the predicativist view. But when we look at more sophisticated predicativist accounts of the meanings of names-as-predicates, we can continue to track the question of whether the predicate meaning relies on an underlying notion of reference, and hence fits with a conservative predicativism, or whether it is a reference-free meaning that could fit with a radical predicativism.

If 'Alfred' is a predicate, what kind of predicate is it? What does it take for something to be an Alfred? There is variation among predicativists in the details of their answer to this question, but a common thread is that the predicate involves some notion of *naming.* Roughly, to be an Alfred is to be named or called Alfred. Being named can then be given a *metalinguistic* reading. On this approach, the predicative content of a name involves a mention of that name, or a quotational reference to the name. Bertrand Russell, for example, suggests that to be a Romulus is to be called 'Romulus' (2010: 79). On this view, we start with a bit of language (the word 'Romulus'), and then notice that certain people stand in an important relation to that word (the relation of having it as their name). Those people then form the extension of the 'Romulus' predicate. Other views are non-metalinguistic. Delia Fara argues that to be a Romulus is *to be called Romulus,* where *being called Romulus* is not a metalinguistic feature (Fara 2015: 65ff). On this view, being called Romulus is much like being called impetuous:

18. Alex calls Beth impetuous.

19. Alex calls Beth a brilliant chess player.

20. Alex called Beth Bethany.

We don't need a prior notion of what 'impetuous' or 'a brilliant chess player' *refer* to in order to understand Beth being called impetuous or a brilliant chess player. As long as we know what it is to be impetuous, we will know what it is to be called impetuous. So on this view, as long as we know what it is to be an Alfred, we will know what it is to be called Alfred.

But do we know what it is to be an Alfred? In particular, if we are trying to defend predicativism, do we know what it is to be an Alfred in a way that doesn't depend on some prior grasp of the notion of reference? We don't want to make it a requirement on a theory of meaning that it give us an *analysis* of being an Alfred. Theories of meaning in general aren't required to provide such analyses. A good theory of meaning can tell us that an object satisfies the predicate 'impetuous' just in case it's impetuous—it doesn't have to tell us *what impetuosity is*. That task can be left to the psychologist or the virtue theorist.

But we can say some things that help shed light on what it is to be an Alfred. We know that being an Alfred isn't an intrinsic feature like being bald or being strong. There's no particular height or weight or blood type that someone must have in order to be an Alfred. And we know that being an Alfred is somehow connected to our linguistic practice. If a baby is dubbed 'Alfred', and people systematically use 'Alfred' sentences when they want to pass on information about the baby, the baby will be an Alfred. The challenge for the ambitious predicativist is then to show that notions like *dubbing* and *aboutness* don't already involve reference.

7.6 Objections to Predicativism

Predicativism starts with the powerful observation that there are a wide range of uses of proper names that do not fit the orthodox view of names as simple referring expressions. Treating names as predicates then provides a simple and appealing account of the uses of names in combination with quantifiers, like 'several Alfreds' and 'no Winstons'. But predicativism, despite its revisionary origins, also wants to retain certain features of the traditional view. Grammatically, as we've seen, predicativism needs to be able to account for the Name-Like Data, and show why names can be used in (something like) the way traditional accounts say they are used. But the predicativist is also under pressure to preserve some traditional *semantic* features of names. Not *all* semantic features, of course, or ambitious predicativism would be impossible. But some semantic features will be supported by the data in a way that the predicativist needs to respect.

We'll focus on two such features. The first is the rigidity of names. The Kripkean arguments for rigidity can be run whether or not the predicativist is right, so we need to make sure predicativism has room for rigid names. The second is the easy transmission of names. Kripke emphasizes that hearing a name used is enough to get into the causal-communicative chain and start using it—one doesn't have to have any substantive information about the bearer of the name. Again, ideally the predicativist will be able to accommodate easy transmission.

How does rigidity fare under predicativism? The first thing to note is that we don't *want* predicate-like uses of names to be rigid. Consider the claim 'Two Winston Churchills attended the conference'. Suppose in the actual world this is true because both the British prime minister and the American novelist attended. Now consider a world in which the American novelist is not at the conference, but in which a Hungarian mathematician named 'Winston Churchill' is at the conference. It looks like 'Two Winston Churchills attended the conference' is true in such a world.

Similarly, the claim 'Three Winston Churchills could have attended the conference' is made true by there being a world in which the Hungarian mathematician named Winston Churchill also attends the conference. (It doesn't matter whether the Hungarian mathematician exists in the actual world, or whether he is named 'Winston Churchill' in the actual world.)

An important constraint on predicative theories is thus that they capture the rigidity of names in name-like uses and the non-rigidity of names in predicate-like uses. The non-rigidity of predicate-like uses falls out naturally from predicativism. Which people are called Alfred can vary from world to world, so the extension of the predicate 'Alfred' can vary from world to world. Predicativists then use two major strategies for explaining the rigidity of names in apparently referential uses:

1. **Rigidity Through Determiner:** If bare names are interpreted using hidden determiners, then the names can be made rigid using a determiner that creates rigidity. 'That', for example, creates rigidity in a way that 'the' does not. Compare:

   21. It could have been that that man wearing a red hat was wearing a blue hat.

   22. It could have been that the man wearing a red hat was wearing a blue hat.

The first of these is true, because 'that man wearing a red hat' rigidly picks out someone wearing a red hat in the actual world, and the sentence then says of that man that in some other world he wears a blue hat. The second is false, because 'the man wearing a red hat' picks out in each world the unique (contextually salient) person wearing a red hat in that world, and the sentence then says that in some world the person wearing a red hat in that world is wearing a blue hat. So if 'Winston Churchill' means 'that Winston Churchill', 'that Winston Churchill' is rigid in the same way that 'that man wearing a red hat' is rigid, and we explain the rigidity of bare 'Winston Churchill'. Rigidity Through Determiner requires that the hidden determiner be a rigidifying determiner like 'that', rather than a non-rigid determiner like 'the'.

2. **Rigidity Through Pragmatics:**   As noted earlier, most contemporary predicativists are 'the'-predicativists rather than 'that'-predicativists. But since definite descriptions, unlike complex demonstratives, are typically non-rigid, 'the'-predicativism faces special challenges in capturing the rigidity of name-like uses of names. Fara's response is that name-like uses correspond to a special class of definite descriptions that *are* rigid, and that the rigidity of names will then follow from the rigidity of that special class.

The special class is the class of *incomplete definite descriptions*. In incomplete definition descriptions, the descriptive content of 'the F' is not enough to pick out a unique object. Compare the following respectively complete and incomplete descriptions:

23.   The oldest person in Japan is over 100 years old.
24.   Alex left the book on the table.

Name-like uses of names will, on Fara's view, typically amount to incomplete definite descriptions. Since the 'Winston Churchill' predicate is satisfied by more than one person, 'the Winston Churchill' is incomplete—the predicate itself doesn't do enough to fix which specific person is being talked about, and context will need to do some work determining who that person is.

Fara's key thought is then that incomplete definite descriptions are typically rigid. When Beth says 'Alex left the book on the table' in a context in which it is clear that the book in question is *Naming and*

Necessity, she says something that is true in some other world only if
Alex left *Naming and Necessity* on the table in that world. No other
book will suffice for the truth of Beth's claim. So 'the book' as used by
Beth is acting rigidly, picking out the same object (*Naming and Necessity*) in all worlds. Of course, this is only a single case, so we don't have a
proof that incomplete descriptions are rigid. But if they are, and names
are incomplete descriptions, we have an explanation of the rigidity
of names.

The difficulty for Fara's view is that there are cases of non-rigid
incomplete definite descriptions. The most obvious cases involve relational expressions, such as 'the president', in which the incompleteness is
created by a failure to specify the other object in the relation. 'The
president could have been a Democrat', for example, is, on one reading,
true because Trump could have been a Democrat, but on another
reading true because Clinton could have been president. But other cases
can be found. Consider an example given by Kent Bach (2004):

25.   The rental car should have four doors.

Imagine this being said by the customer before a car has been assigned.
Then the description is incomplete, because there is more than one rental
car. And it is behaving non-rigidly, because there is no one car that is
relevant in all worlds to the truth of what the customer says.

The strategy for 'the'-predicativism is to tie the rigidity of proper
names to the rigidity of incomplete definite descriptions, so non-rigid
incomplete definite descriptions threaten to create the possibility of non-
rigid names. There are two ways of responding to this threat:

Isolate: We could identify certain types of incomplete definite
descriptions that behave non-rigidly, and then claim that names
never form those sorts of incomplete descriptions. We have already
seen that *relational* definites can behave non-rigidly, and plausibly the
predicates created by names are not relational in this way. Fara also—
following Bach (2004) and Rothschild (2007)—identifies a class of
role-type descriptions, in which 'it is presupposed that they will have
just one object that satisfies them, if any at all' and 'to satisfy the
description is to be the one to play a certain role' (2015: 104). Fara
claims that 'the rental car' is a role-type description. If names also
don't create role-type descriptions, then the non-rigidity of cases like
'the rental car' won't be any threat to the rigidity of names.

Accommodate: We could argue, by comparison with cases of non-rigid incomplete descriptions, that there *are* in fact non-rigid uses of names, and thus that 'the'-predicativism yields the right prediction in saying that such cases can occur. Fara gives the example:

26. Una should have been your first daughter (2015: 104).

She claims: 'If we imagine this as said to parents who are considering whether to give their second daughter the name "Una", then we are using the name as a "role-type" description' (2015: 104). The crucial question, then, is whether 'Una' can be read non-rigidly in this case. Not everyone agrees that this is so: Schoubye (2017) holds (of a similar case) that such attempts at non-rigid uses of names are odd.

What about the easy transmission feature of names? Suppose Beth has never heard of Aristotle, and Alex says to her, 'Aristotle was a philosopher'. How should the predicativist account for Beth's new-found ability to use 'Aristotle' to talk about Aristotle? On the version of 'the'-predicativism we have been discussing, Beth needs two things. First, she needs a grasp of the predicate *Aristotle*. That is, she needs to know what it is to be an Aristotle, or what it is to be called Aristotle. This does indeed look easy for Beth to get. She has already a general understanding of *being called something*, so once she encounters the word 'Aristotle', she can use that new word to extract an understanding of *being called Aristotle*.

Beth also needs the ability to pick out the right Aristotle. When Alex says 'Aristotle is a philosopher', according to the predicativist she is saying that *the* Aristotle is a philosopher, using the incomplete description 'the Aristotle'. But then how does Beth get on to the right understanding of the incomplete description? It looks like she needs to have an appropriate completion of the description available, or already have the right object in mind. But there's no reason that she should have either of these.

Since the predicativist claims that the name *is* an incomplete description, it's helpful to consider how things go with explicitly incomplete descriptions. Suppose Alex says to Beth, 'the book is in my office', in a context in which Beth doesn't know what book Alex is talking about. Does this easily transmit to Beth the ability to talk about that book? The answer is messy. *Within* that conversation, it looks like it does. Beth can now say, 'Did you find the book?' Even if she still doesn't know which book it is, she can bootstrap off of Beth's knowledge. But *outwith* the conversation, it doesn't. If Beth finishes talking to Alex, and goes off to talk to Charles, she can no longer say 'the book' to pick out Alex's book.

This looks like a disanalogy with names. When Beth acquires the name 'Aristotle' from Alex, she *can* go on to use it in conversation with Charles, and thereby pass on to Charles the ability to talk about Aristotle. But perhaps this is a special feature of this particular example, depending on the fact that Aristotle is already culturally well-known. Suppose Alex had said to Beth 'John is a philosopher'. Could Beth then talk to Charles about John and pass on the ability to refer to *that specific John*, or would she be under some obligation to tell him *which John* she meant?

7.7 Consequences of Predicativism for Reference

If predicativism is unambitious, its primary effect is to begin a complicated discussion about the grammatical form in which reference is realized in language. The unambitious predicativist, for example, might agree with the traditional theorist that in an occurrence of the sentence 'Aristotle is a philosopher', 'Aristotle' refers to Aristotle. There is a different story about why that is the case ('Aristotle' is short for 'the Aristotle', in which a predicate true of a number of people is combined with the definite determiner to create an incomplete description whose semantic function in that context is to refer to Aristotle), but the same final story about reference. Details matter, of course, and there may be much to learn from the different grammatical realization of reference.

Still, the more exciting prospect is ambitious predicativism, which promises a more radical revision of the landscape by getting rid of what had been taken to be a central semantic category. But it's worth reflecting briefly on what such an elimination of reference would amount to. Suppose the predicativist gives us a thoroughly convincing ambitious account of the nature of the predicate that gives the meaning of a name, so that it is clear that the notion of reference is in no way presupposed in that account. We can still observe the following. Some kind of important semantic relation holds between the name 'Aristotle' and Aristotle, the last great philosopher of antiquity. Maybe that relation isn't reference. After all, that relation is one which also holds between that same name and Aristotle Onassis, second husband of Jacqueline Kennedy Onassis. Nevertheless, it's a suspiciously familiar-looking relation.

Initially the baby Aristotle doesn't stand in this special relation to the name 'Aristotle'. Then Aristotle's parents do something—they point at the baby and say 'Aristotle', or some such. After this, Aristotle does stand in the special relation to 'Aristotle'. It's not by virtue of any intrinsic features of Aristotle that he stands in the relation to the word 'Aristotle'—he could have been shorter or taller, smarter or dumber, and so long as his parents did the same dubbing, he'd still stand in the special relation to 'Aristotle'. Other non-dubbers can use the word 'Aristotle' in that same special relation to Aristotle, even if they know nothing about Aristotle, have never met him, and cannot pick him out of a crowd. Aristotle continues to stand in the special relation to 'Aristotle' because the use of the term is passed from individual to individual over time. When we consider counterfactual circumstances, and ask who it is that stands in the special relation to the word 'Aristotle' in those circumstances, it's always Aristotle himself, regardless of what he's like in those circumstances, and regardless of what dubbings were done in those circumstances.

To say all that is to say that the semantic relation that holds between 'Aristotle' and Aristotle has all the functional markings that Kripke showed us were characteristic of directly referential names. It's a semantic relation typically induced by initial dubbings, preserved and transmitted by causal interactions between speakers, metasemantically fixed externally in a way that doesn't depend on the knowledge or intentions of speakers, and which holds rigidly, preserving the semantic relation under consideration of counterfactual circumstances. Maybe the predicativist is right and, despite all that, it's not reference that connects 'Aristotle' and Aristotle, but predication. In which case perhaps the most important lesson that comes out of consideration of predicativism is that we need to think more deeply about why the category of reference is supposed to be a philosophically interesting one.

Central Points in Chapter 7

- So far in this book we've been assuming that there is a special category of expressions, the function of which is to refer, of which names are the clearest example. This chapter considered a challenge to this view based on the fact that names appear, on closer inspection, to behave in some ways like predicates. Could it be that names aren't really referring expressions after all?
- The predicativist, in a sense, thinks so. Predicativism is based on the observation that names frequently behave like predicates: syntactically, they occur after determiners (like 'every') and can be pluralized, and semantically they sometimes talk about a range of objects (an extension) rather than a single object.
- Thus, we can say things like 'Every Alfred laughs', 'No Alfred laughs', 'An Alfred laughed', 'The Alfred at Berkeley laughed', and 'Alfreds laugh'. The 'names' in these sentences are functioning, or so it appears, as predicates.
- We noted that these facts needn't be fatal to the Kripkean analysis according to which names are in fact singular terms. It's a familiar point that expressions belonging to a given category can be coerced into another category. 'Beer', for example, is primarily a mass noun, but can be coerced to a transitive ('Beer me') or even a ditransitive verb (Andrew Bernard in *The Office* says things like 'Beer me that stapler'). We could then say that the same mechanism coerces names into predicates.
- Predicativists argue, as their name suggests, that we should take the data on its face value and conclude that names are predicates. To account for simple sentences like 'Alfred likes fish', which, for the predicativist, should be bad like 'Man likes fish' is bad, the predicativist posits a covert, unpronounced determiner preceding the name. The actual logical form is something like 'The Alfred likes fish', or 'That Alfred likes fish' but 'the' or 'that' is silent.

- Although the data supporting predicativism is impressive, the view faces some difficulties. In the first chapter we noted that rigidity is an important feature of names. Since definite descriptions aren't always rigid, and the most plausible version of predicativism claims that names are definite descriptions, predicativism has problems accounting for the rigidity of names. In the first chapter we also saw that a notable feature of names is that their use can be passed from person to person easily. This feature is hard to explain if names are as the predicativist claims.

Comprehension Questions

1. Outline in your own words the key differences between predicativism and the Kripkean theory of names.
2. We noted that the Kripkean can appeal to coercion to account for the data. Give some more examples of coercion in English, or other languages you know.
3. Some occurrences of names in English, as we saw, are preceded by a definite article. Think of some more examples besides those provided in the text. Is there any pattern to the data?
4. What is the distinction between 'the'-predicativism and 'that'-predicativism? Which do you prefer? Justify your answer.
5. Fara claims that the property corresponding to a name N is: *being called N*. Explain what this property is like. What other views might the predicate offer concerning the nature of this property?

Exploratory Questions

6. The predicativist relies heavily on the systematicity and reliability of the 'ordinary' predicative use of names. What do you think? Suppose William James and King James II are both in the room. Can we say that there are two Jameses in the room? If not, what's the notion of being called James that the ordinary predicative use relies on? Consider other problematic cases. What if one person has 'Jim' as a given name and one as a nickname? What if there's an Englishman named John and a German named Johann? What

(continued)

if there is a Catherine and a Kathryn? What if there is a Clara-with-a-short-a and a Clara-with-a-as-in-father?

7. Relatedly, predicativism depends crucially on the Predicate-Like Data being perfectly natural and robust. How true is it that 'Alfred' can be used in exactly the same way as regular predicates? Are these constructions marked at all? Are the stress patterns and intonations and phonology the same for these predicative uses of names as they are for traditional uses? What about combinations like 'Today I saw three sheep, two pigs, four Alfreds, and five cows'?

8. Formulate and defend *Millianismism*—the view that predicates and variables are proper names. Alternatively, formulate and defend *verbism*—the view that names are verbs. What assumptions are necessary to get these views to work? Can we learn anything about the debate by considering these wacky positions?

9. Can the traditional theorist hold that the predicativist still has a grammatical category of names? The predicativist has a division between predicates that obey a hidden-the rule and predicatives that don't obey a hidden-the rule. Why isn't that exactly the grammatical distinction that the predicativist was trying to reject? How satisfactory is it if the predicativist responds that the category of 'predicate' has always had subdivisions subject to different grammatical constraints? For example, we distinguish between count predicates and mass predicates, because mass predicates have different distribution with determiners than do count predicates:

9.1. All water is wet/All ducks quack.
9.2. Water is wet/#Duck quacks.
9.3. #Waters are wet/Ducks quack.
9.4. #Several waters are wet/Several ducks quack.
9.5. Much water is wet/#Much ducks quack.

Can the predicativist satisfactorily claim that 'names' are no deeper a grammatical category than mass predicates? Are there other examples of grammatical subtypes of predicates that provide helpful models for the predicativist? In languages other than English, for example, nouns carry gender marking. Could the predicativist appeal to this fact to argue that the division they posit isn't deep?

10. One argument for predicativism comes from the possibility of binding. Consider:

    10.1. If he has a child named 'Bambi', Bambi probably gets beat up.

    10.2. There's a gentleman from Hertfordshire named Earnest. Earnest likes hunting.

The thought is that the occurrences of 'Bambi' and 'Earnest' in the second sentences are bound by the preceding indefinite descriptions in the first. Now definites have bound uses. For example, I can say things like:

    10.3. If he has a child, the child probably gets beat up.

    10.4. There's a gentleman from Hertfordshire named Earnest. The gentleman likes hunting.

So, we might think, since names and definites pattern in this way, this gives reason for thinking, with the predicativist, that names are definites. Evaluate this argument. Consider all the data, including plural anaphora ('Two Mikes are in my class. They are bad students').

11. Names sometimes, functioning referentially, occur with indefinite articles, as shown by the following (inspired by McKeever 2016):

    11.1. A belligerent Donald Trump addressed Congress last night, and said he has no ties with Russia.

Try to find patterns in the data—are indefinites used with names only in particular circumstances? Do you think this supports or harms 'the'-predicativism?

Further Reading

Early versions of predicativism can be found in Quine 1960 and Burge 1973. Fara 2015 is destined to be a classic; other recent defenses include Elbourne 2005. Sloat 1969 and Matushansky 2008 are important works by linguists. For pragmatic accounts of the data which motivates the predicativist, see Leckie 2013, Rami 2015. Recent criticisms of predicativism include Schoubye 2017 and Jeshion 2015. Fara attempts to extend the predicativist strategy to descriptions in her 2001.

8

Plural Reference

The Puzzle of 'John and Paul and George and Ringo'

8.1 A Puzzle

'John Lennon' refers to the writer of 'Lucy in the Sky With Diamonds'. 'Paul McCartney' refers to the writer of 'Yellow Submarine'. 'George Harrison' refers to the writer of 'Here Comes the Sun'. And 'Ringo Starr' refers to the writer of 'Octopus's Garden'. But what about 'John and Paul and George and Ringo' or 'The Beatles'? Do these expressions refer? If so, what do they refer to? Our goal in this chapter is to consider the tools language has for referring to many things at once. We will see how various subtle pieces of linguistic data can help us distinguish different mechanisms for achieving this kind of plural reference, and see whether we can learn anything about the nature of groups and other collectives by thinking about our linguistic tools for talking about them.

Let's start with a list of some of the linguistic expressions of plural reference. We aren't at this point trying to do any theorizing about these examples, so it may turn out later that we want to treat different examples in different ways, or that we decide that some of these examples aren't really in any interesting sense plural. But it will be helpful to have some initial idea of what the target is.

- **Conjunctions of Names**: 'John and Paul and George and Ringo' refers to four people, because it conjoins four names, each of which refers to a person.
- **Plural Pronouns**: 'We' refers not just to the speaker, but to the speaker and some other people. 'They', in a context in which the speaker points to some people, refers to those people.

- **Demonstratives**: 'That dog' refers to one (demonstrated) dog, but 'those dogs' refers to many (demonstrated) dogs.
- **Group Names**: 'The Beatles' refers to a band with several members. 'The Boston Celtics' refers to a team with many members. 'Congress' refers to a legislative body with many members.
- **Bare Plurals**: 'Philosophers', in sentences like 'Philosophers attended the conference', 'Philosophers are lovers of wisdom', or 'Philosophers trace back to ancient Greece', refers to many philosophers, or refers to a kind (of person) with many instances.
- **Quasi-Group Names**: There are many entities that are group-like in that they have some special association with some objects (where the objects stand in some sort of membership or constitution relation to the starting entity). Apple is a company with many employees. The University of Texas is a university with many students. That flock is a collection of many birds. *Philosophical Troubles* is an anthology of many papers. Sequoia National Forest is a forest of many trees. Where we should draw the line between group-like and non-group-like entities is not clear—Is a skeleton group-like because it has many bones? Is a house group-like because it has many bricks? Is Mars group-like because it has many atoms?—and it may be that there is a spectrum here, rather than a real line to be drawn.

8.2 Why the Puzzle Matters

We will consider two main views on plural reference:

- **Plurality-in-Reference**: On this view, the reference relation holds between *one* word and *many* objects.
- **Plurality-in-Object**: On this view, the reference relation holds between *one* word and *one* object, but that one object is something group-like.

To get an initial sense of the difference between these two views, compare the following diagrams.

In Figure 8.1 we have one name ('The Beatles') and four objects (John, Paul, George, and Ringo). There are then four reference arrows from the name to objects, indicating that the one name stands in the reference relation to each of the four things.

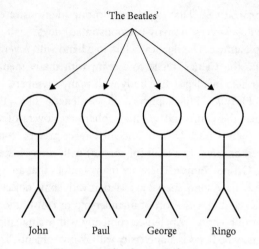

Figure 8.1 Plurality-in-Reference

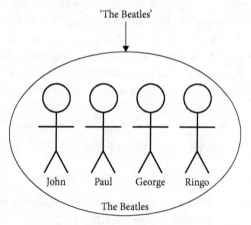

Figure 8.2 Plurality-in-Object

In Figure 8.2 there is again one name ('The Beatles'), but now there are five objects (John, Paul, George, and Ringo, as before, but in addition The Beatles). Here there is only one reference arrow, going from the name to the collective/group/plural object that is The Beatles. There are thus no reference arrows from the name to the individual band members.

Plurality-in-Reference puts the plurality into the semantics. On this view, there's nothing plural about the things being referred to. John isn't plural, nor is Paul, nor George, nor Ringo. But the reference relation is plural, because it relates a single expression ('The Beatles') to multiple objects. By contrast, Plurality-in-Object puts the plurality into the metaphysics. On this view, there's nothing plural about the reference relation—it relates a single expression (again, 'The Beatles') to a single object (the band, or the group of John and Paul and George and Ringo). But the thing referred to is plural, because it's a thing that has four members.

The choice between Plurality-in-Reference and Plurality-in-Object is thus a choice between two views on how rich the contents of the world are. Suppose Plurality-in-Object is the right view. Then if we set out to list all the things that there are, it's not enough to list John, and list Paul, and list George, and list Ringo. After listing each of the four of them, we will still have left something off: namely, the *plural object* The Beatles. We might then wonder about the nature of that object, and about what makes it different from the four individual objects we already listed. Suppose, on the other hand, that Plurality-in-Reference is right. Then there is no *extra thing* that is the Apple Corporation—talk about Apple is just talk about all of the things which make up the corporation. We might then wonder what those many things are, and how their properties and actions form the properties and actions of Apple.

8.3 Plurality-in-Reference

According to Plurality-in-Reference, the reference relation holds between the *one* expression 'The Beatles' and *four* things. But what does it mean to say that 'The Beatles' refers to four things? Normally when we say that an object stands in a relation to four things, we mean that it stands in that relation to each of the four things. For example, Montana borders four states. In saying that, we mean that:

- Montana borders Idaho.
- Montana borders Wyoming.
- Montana borders North Dakota.
- Montana borders South Dakota.

The *plural bordering* of Montana is just a number of *singular borderings*. If we say the same thing about plural reference, then the plural reference of 'The Beatles' just is the following four facts:

- 'The Beatles' refers to John.
- 'The Beatles' refers to Paul.
- 'The Beatles' refers to George.
- 'The Beatles' refers to Ringo.

But there's a serious problem with this proposal. 'The Beatles', on this view, refers to John. And John married Yoko Ono. So then we can reason as follows:

- 'The Beatles married Yoko Ono' is true, because 'The Beatles' refers to John, and John has the property picked out by 'married Yoko Ono'.

That's bad, because The Beatles didn't marry Yoko Ono—only John did. But the problem can be made even worse. We can also reason:

- 'The Beatles married Yoko Ono' is false, because 'The Beatles' refers to Paul, and Paul does not have the property picked out by 'married Yoko Ono'.

We are thus forced into unacceptable contradictions.

8.4 Collective and Distributive Predication

We need a better way to understand what it means for an expression to refer to many things, a way that doesn't just amount to its referring to each of those many things. A natural starting point for finding a better way is to look at the distinction between *collective* and *distributive* predication. Sometimes when we attribute a property to some things, we mean that each of those things has that property. So:

1.   Babe Ruth and Lou Gehrig hit home runs in the game.

means that Babe Ruth hit a home run in the game, and Lou Gehrig hit a home run in the game, not that working together they hit home runs. This is a *distributive* predication, because the attribution of the feature of hitting a home run distributes over the multiple subjects. But other times when we attribute a property to some things, we mean that those things together have that property. So:

2.   The police surrounded the house.

means that the police, all together, surrounded the house, not that each one of them individually surrounded the house. This is a *collective* predication, since the attribution of the feature is essentially to the collective, not to the individuals.

We got into trouble before by interpreting the Plurality-in-Reference commitment to the disquotational reference principle:

• 'The Beatles' refers to John and Paul and George and Ringo.

as a distributive commitment. Read distributively, the claim that 'The Beatles' refers to John and Paul and George and Ringo is a claim that entails further that 'The Beatles' refers to John. As we've seen, that's a bad result. But we can avoid the bad result by reading the claim instead *collectively*. Read collectively, it does not say that John and Paul and George and Ringo are *each individually* referred to by 'The Beatles', any more than:

3.   John and Paul and George and Ringo lifted the piano.

says that John and Paul and George and Ringo *each individually* lifted the piano. Given this reference principle, we can then say:

• 'The Beatles married Yoko Ono' is true iff the referent of 'The Beatles' has the property picked out by 'married Yoko Ono', and thus iff John and Paul and George and Ringo married Yoko Ono.

Since John and Paul and George and Ringo didn't marry Yoko Ono (because only John did), the sentence is false, as we want.

Appealing to collective readings in our understanding of Plurality-in-Reference reference principles creates a *circularity* worry:

Circularity: There is a worry that this account of plural reference begs the question. We pick out the right understanding of the reference principle for 'John and Paul and George and Ringo' by requiring that the predication of reference be read collectively, rather than distributively. But we get our understanding of the difference between collective and distributive predication by looking at sentences involving plural reference, which is what we were trying to understand in the first place.

What (Circularity) shows, though, is not that there is something *wrong* with this account of plural reference, but rather that the account depends on a prior understanding of plurality that cannot be *reduced* to or explained in terms of singular reference. We cannot reduce:

- 'The Beatles' refers to John and Paul and George and Ringo.

to:

- 'The Beatles' refers to John, and refers to Paul, and refers to George, and refers to Ringo.

Rather, we need to say that the reference relation holds between the expression and *them*. That won't be helpful to say to someone who doesn't already have the concept of plural reference, but it will be *correct*, and understandable by someone who does have the concept. And if the Plurality-in-Reference view is correct, we *do* have the concept of plural reference as part of our ordinary understanding of English.

8.5 Flexible Truth Conditions

Plurality-in-Reference reference principles are plausible only if read collectively. That collective reading then works beautifully in capturing the truth conditions of collective predications of plural expressions. Consider:

4. The Beatles performed 'When I'm Sixty-Four'.

Since 'The Beatles' refers collectively to John and Paul and George and Ringo, this claim will be true if the four of them collectively performed 'When I'm Sixty-Four'. And that's the right thing to say, because the performance *is* collective. No one of them performs the song alone, because performing the song requires producing vocals, guitar, bass, and drums.

But what about distributive claims? Consider:

5. The Beatles think *Sgt. Pepper's Lonely Hearts Club Band* will be a best-selling album.

The Beatles think this distributively. It's because each of them *individually* thinks it that the claim is true, not because they are somehow performing a collective action. A distributive reading of the reference principle would produce this distributive reading naturally, but we've already seen that a distributive reading of the reference principle has other disastrous consequences.

Suppose we've decided that 'John, Paul, George, and Ringo' refers collectively to John, Paul, George, and Ringo. Then we are committed to saying:

- 'John and Paul and George and Ringo think that *Sgt. Pepper's Lonely Hearts Club Band* will be a best-selling album' is true if, and only if, John and Paul and George and Ringo satisfy the condition 'thinks *Sgt. Pepper's Lonely Hearts Club Band* will be a best-selling album'. (Rather than: if, and only if, John satisfies this condition, and if, and only if, Paul satisfies it, and so on.)

But *do* John and Paul and George and Ringo collectively satisfy this condition? Nothing we've said yet tells us the answer to that question.

This is an instance of a more general question: When do objects satisfy conditions? One promising view here is that when we are theorizing about language, our commitments about satisfying conditions should be *flexible* and *minimal*. Suppose, for example, that we are trying to give truth conditions for the claim 'That is red'. The first step is to say that the referent of 'that' satisfies the condition 'is red'. But what does it take for an object to satisfy 'is red'? Should it be red on the outside or on the inside (consider apples and grapefruit)? Should it be colored red or produce red color (consider fire engines and pens)? Should it be entirely red or merely dominantly red (consider roses and stop signs)? If dominantly red, *how* dominantly?

The flexible view says that it is not the place of a theory of language to answer these sorts of questions. As theorists about language, we have finished our job when we say that the claim requires that the referent of 'that' satisfies the condition 'is red'. Anything beyond that should be left to the theory of color.

The flexible view, then, doesn't lay out reductive requirements for satisfying a condition, and is thus free to acknowledge that conditions can be satisfied in many different ways. Returning to plurals, we can then recognize:

- Sometimes, some things satisfy a condition C because each of them individually satisfies condition C. John and Paul and Ringo and George think that *Sgt. Pepper's Lonely Hearts Club Band* will be a best-selling album because each of them individually thinks it will be.
- Sometimes, some things satisfy a condition because taken together they satisfy it, because the individual things all collaborate in an effort that satisfies it. John and Paul and George and Ringo perform 'When I'm Sixty-Four' not because each of them performs it, but because they each do something that contributes to them performing it together.

- Sometimes some things satisfy a condition because some of them contribute to satisfying it, while others are idle bystanders. The falling rocks crush the goat because some of the individual rocks land on the goats, and the collective effect of the ones that do land on the goat is a goat-crushing, while other rocks miss the goat entirely.

This isn't intended to be an exhaustive list. Other ways of satisfaction can easily be found, especially when there are multiple plural expressions involved. (For example, 'The women dance with the men' is true because there is one-to-one pairing of the women and the men such that each pair of an individual woman and an individual man danced.)

8.6 The Transparency Problem for Plurality-in-Reference

We've now seen that the best version of Plurality-in-Reference combines a collective reading of the reference principles, so that 'John and Paul and George and Ringo' non-reductively refers to the four of them, not by referring to each of them individually, with a latitudinarian view of predication claims, on which John and Paul and George and Ringo can possess a property in many different ways. There is definitely a worry that the resulting view is too flexible: that it produces too many readings, and makes it too easy for claims involving plural expressions to be true. (The failure to capture the cumulative principle, explored in Question 6 at the end of this chapter, is a symptom of this worry.) But there is also a concern that despite its extensive flexibility, the view still can't capture all the claims we want.

We've been focusing on the plural expression 'The Beatles', which according to Plurality-in-Reference refers to John and Paul and George and Ringo. But that's not the only plural term that refers to the four of them. Consider also the conjunctive expression 'John and Paul and George and Ringo'. Plurality-in-Reference says that this expression *also* refers to John and Paul and George and Ringo. But then both expressions refer to the same thing. The result is a *transparency* conclusion: we should be able to substitute 'The Beatles' for 'John and Paul and George and Ringo'. (We have seen, in Chapter 3, that special contexts like attitude reports can call transparency into question. But here we will focus on cases that don't seem to have corresponding special features.)

In some cases, that transparency conclusion looks exactly right:

6. John and Paul and George and Ringo performed 'When I'm Sixty-Four'.

7. John and Paul and George and Ringo are The Beatles.

8. Therefore, The Beatles performed 'When I'm Sixty-Four'.

But, in other cases, the transparency conclusion is disastrously wrong:

9. The Beatles were formed in 1960.

10. John and Paul and George and Ringo are The Beatles.

11. #Therefore, John and Paul and George and Ringo were formed in 1960.

But John and Paul and George and Ringo were all happily in place long before 1960. The basic problem is that we want to say different things about John and Paul and George and Ringo, on the one hand, and The Beatles, on the other hand. Plurality-in-Reference doesn't give us any scope to say different things, because of the co-reference of 'John and Paul and George and Ringo' and 'The Beatles'.

8.7 Plurality-in-Object

Now let's move on to consider the Plurality-in-Object view. On this view, plural expressions don't refer plurally to many objects, but rather refer singularly to special objects that are somehow built up out of many objects. So 'John and Paul and George and Ringo' refers to the group of John and Paul and George and Ringo (where the group is one thing, not four people), and 'The Beatles' refers to the band, of which John and Paul and George and Ringo are members.

The transparency problems of Plurality-in-Reference can then be avoided if we can plausibly say that the *group* of the four of them is not the same thing as the *band* of the four of them. This points to a general commitment of Plurality-in-Object views: if we are going to say that plural expressions refer to special objects somehow built up out of many objects, we need to say *something* about what these objects are, and what they are like.

It isn't our goal here to get deeply into issues of metaphysics (although it is worth noting that this is another place where developing a theory of reference requires engagement with metaphysics), so we'll look only briefly at a few features of plural objects. For convenience, we'll call these plural objects *groups*, but we'll be using 'group' here as a neutral umbrella term covering any sort of plural object. We'll contrast groups with *pluralities*, where 'plurality' is an umbrella term for many objects, so that according to Plurality-in-Reference, John and Paul and George and Ringo are a plurality. (Note that the term 'plurality' unfortunately suggests that there is *one thing* that John and Paul and George and Ringo are, but this suggestion needs to be ignored. This is a very important point: a plurality is not a new sort of object; rather, we should think of sentences like 'John and Paul are a plurality' as equivalent to 'John and Paul are some objects'.)

- **Groups Overlap:** Two groups can have all the same members. John and Paul and George and Ringo can form a band, and also form a book group. But the band isn't the book group. (Perhaps the book group meets on Tuesdays, and is headed by John, while the band practices on Wednesdays, and is headed by Paul.) Two different pluralities, on the other hand, can't have different members. John and Paul and George and Ringo are trivially the same as Ringo and George and Paul and John.
- **Groups Change Over Time:** The Beatles can change members over time. Perhaps it used to be that Ringo wasn't in the group and Pete was. Pluralities, on the other hand, can't change over time. Ringo is always one of John and Paul and George and Ringo, and Pete never is.
- **Groups Can Change Modally:** Groups could have had different members than they actually do. Syd is never one of The Beatles, but he could have been one of them. Pluralities, on the other hand, have their members essentially. It isn't even *possible* for Syd to be one of John and Paul and George and Ringo.
- **Groups Can Be Nested:** Consider the group of John and Paul, and the group of George and Ringo. These are two groups. There's then a third group: the group of those two groups. This third group is a group of two things, so it isn't the same thing as the group of John, Paul, George, and Ringo. But since the plurality of John and Paul

isn't a *thing*, we can't combine it with George and Ringo to get something other than the plurality of John and Paul and George and Ringo (at least, it is commonly thought—see Rayo 2006 for a spirited defense of so-called superplural reference).

All of these points can be taken as anti-transparency observations: there are many contexts in which two names for groups with the same members can't be intersubstituted. The Plurality-in-Object view deals with such transparency failures by holding that they show distinctness of object, so considerations of these sorts can help us figure out how many different groups there need to be, and what sort of objects these groups are.

8.8 Plurality-in-Object and Truth Conditions

Just as there is a question about what it is for *some objects* to satisfy a condition, there is also a question about what it is for a group (or other plural entity) to satisfy a condition. 'The Beatles ate lunch' is true if the band ate lunch. But what is it for a *band* to eat lunch? The Beatles resemble The Monkees more than they resemble the Sex Pistols. But what is it for a *band* to resemble The Monkees more than the Sex Pistols?

We might worry that these two questions push in opposite directions. For a band to eat lunch seems to just be a matter of the individual members of the band eating lunch—it isn't as if the band itself has nutritional needs. (Although we can imagine strange cases in which the band itself does the eating.) So maybe the band satisfies a condition just in case the members of the band satisfy that condition (maybe distribu- tively, maybe collectively). But for a band to resemble another band seems to be a matter of the band itself. Even if each of The Beatles resembled the individual Sex Pistols more than the individual Monkees, the band could resemble The Monkees more than the Sex Pistols. (Perhaps because the band's music is more like The Monkees' music, and musical resemblance is what primarily makes for resemblance between bands.)

Another appeal to latitudinarianism seems in order here. A group can satisfy a condition by way of its members satisfying the condition, or by way of the group itself satisfying the condition. What is importantly different about the Plurality-in-Object strategy is that we have *another object* to work with in considering condition satisfaction—the plural entity, in addition to the various members of the plural entity. The addition of the plural entity allows us to capture the truth of various claims that in some sense *depend on* that entity—claims that we wouldn't be able to make true just using the members of the plural entity. Consider some cases:

True: The Los Angeles Lakers were founded in 1947.
False: Kobe Bryant, Julius Randle, and so on were founded in 1947.
True: The Constitution makes the Supreme Court the highest court in the country.
False: The Constitution makes Roberts, Kennedy, Thomas, and so on the highest court in the country.
True: Johnny Rotten could have been one of the Ramones.
False: Johnny Rotten could have been one of Joey Ramone, Johnny Ramone, Dee Dee Ramone, and Tommy Ramone.
True: The congressional committee on cybersecurity was expanded.
False: Langevin, McCaul, and so on were expanded.

These cases illustrate features that groups can have, that can't be had by the many objects that make up the plural entities. It's not clear that there is any precise characterization of these features, but they tend to be features focusing on change (over time or over alternative possibilities) on attitudes, and on rules.

Because one way a plural entity can satisfy a condition is by its members satisfying that condition, we expect Plurality-in-Object terms to create all of the readings created by their corresponding Plurality-in-Reference terms, in addition perhaps to some further readings. The result is an Inheritance principle. Suppose there is some property had by John, and by Paul, and by George, and by Ringo. (Perhaps the property of *being English*). Then the Plurality-in-Reference view, given latitudinarian truth conditions, will say that John and Paul and George and Ringo are English, by way of being distributively so. Similarly, the Plurality-in-Object view will hold that the band formed by John, Paul, George, and Ringo has the property of being English. In general, any property had by John, Paul, George, and Ringo is also had by The Beatles, since one way The Beatles satisfy a condition is by the members of The Beatles satisfying that condition. Of course, The Beatles will have further properties not had by John, Paul, George, and Ringo.

8.9 The Metaphysical Cost of Plurality-in-Object

It's often helpful to bring out the properties of groups by contrasting the behavior of, for example, 'The Beatles' and 'John and Paul and George and Ringo'. But on the Plurality-in-Object view, both of these expressions name groups; they just name groups of different sorts. 'The Beatles' names a band, which is a kind of group that can change its members over time. 'John and Paul and George and Ringo' names a group of a different sort (for which we have no convenient name), which cannot change its members over time.

It's thus easy to see that Plurality-in-Object is going to need there to be a lot of groups:

1. Whenever there are some objects, there needs to be a group of those objects. Given some objects, we can form a *list name* by conjoining the names of those objects. For example, given Winston Churchill, the Eiffel Tower, and Pluto, we can form the list name 'Winston Churchill and the Eiffel Tower and Pluto'. According to Plurality-in-Object, this name refers to a group, so there must be a group with exactly those three objects as members.

That's a lot of groups. (There is a quick argument that infinitely many groups result. Given the expression 'John and Paul', we need a list group of John and Paul. But then we can form the expression 'John and Paul and the list group of John and Paul', so there must be another list group corresponding to that expression. And then we can add a name for that object to our list, and so on.) The vast majority of the needed groups are odd ones that we wouldn't ordinarily recognize as groups. There is a worry that, in fact, it's so many groups that a paradox results. Some groups have themselves as members (the group of all groups, for example), and others do not. So there are some groups that do not have themselves as members. But if there is a group of all and only groups that do not have themselves as members, then a contradiction results, because there is no consistent answer to the question of whether this group is a member of itself (this is essentially the argument from Boolos 1984).

2. Even given a particular fixed list of objects, there may often be many groups with exactly those objects as members. By the previous point, there is always the 'list group' of John and Paul and George and Ringo, which has those four as members eternally and essentially. In this

case there is also the band they form, which does not have its members eternally or essentially. Maybe there is also a book club with those four as members. Are there also more esoteric groups, such as the group that has all four as members in 1969, but only John and Paul and George in 1968, or the group that actually has all four as members, and has John and Ringo essentially as members, but could have lacked Paul or George? Some heavyweight metaphysical considerations may be needed to settle these questions.

The metaphysical cost should be unsurprising. The general structure of things is this: Plurality-in-Reference is an ontologically parsimonious view that attempts to treat the linguistic phenomenon of plurality without adding new objects to our ontology. That strategy then comes up against the problem of transparency, as it is automatically committed to pluralities with the same members having the same features. Because much of our talk involving plurals is not in fact transparent, the Plurality-in-Object strategy emerges, explaining failures of substitution by claiming that different objects are involved. But that means that whenever we can make different claims about two plural expressions N1 and N2, Plurality-in-Object is committed to there being two different objects involved.

8.10 A Hybrid Strategy

We have been assuming so far that we face a *choice* between the Plurality-in-Reference and Plurality-in-Object views. But maybe we can get the best of both worlds by pursuing a hybrid strategy. According to the hybrid strategy, *some* plural expressions are Plurality-in-Reference expressions, which refer plurally to some things, and *other* plural expressions are Plurality-in-Object expressions, which refer singularly to special plural objects (groups).

A temptingly simple hypothesis is then that the Plurality-in-Reference terms are all and only the grammatically plural expressions ('we', 'they', 'John and Paul and George and Ringo', 'the birds in the tree'), while the Plurality-in-Object terms are all and only the grammatically singular expressions that are in some sense semantically plural ('The Beatles', 'Congress', 'The Yankees', 'the flock of birds'). Notice that this version of the hybrid view immediately avoids the first metaphysical cost worry above. We won't need 'list groups' corresponding to list expressions like

'John and Paul and George and Ringo'. List expressions are grammatically plural, so they fall within the domain of Plurality-in-Reference, rather than Plurality-in-Object. So there is no group that is (just) the group of John and Paul and George and Ringo. There are just the four of them, to whom we refer plurally with the list name.

This is only a gesture toward a fully worked out hybrid strategy. Given the latitudinarianism we have introduced as components of both the Plurality-in-Reference and the Plurality-in-Object views, there is enough flexibility built in that getting a precise characterization of the hybrid view is tricky. 'John and Paul and George and Ringo' doesn't refer to a group, but refers collectively to the four of them. They then have properties in some broadly latitudinarian way based on the individual properties of the four. John and Paul and George and Ringo sing because each of them sings; John and Paul and George and Ringo release an album because each of them contributes to the releasing. 'The Beatles', on the other hand, does refer to a group: the band, which is another object over and above the four members. The band then has properties in some broadly latitudinarian way. That includes having properties by way of its members having properties. The Beatles are happy because each individual Beatle is happy. And it includes having properties that aren't reducible to the properties of the members, such as the property of formerly including Pete Best.

But that's not enough for a full story. There are, for example, claims that can be made with grammatically plural claims that can't be made with grammatically singular claims for corresponding groups. As Moltmann 1997 observes, we can say:

12. The students are similar.

but not:

13. The class are similar.

Even when 'the class' names a group that has the students as members. Similarly, we have:

14. John cannot distinguish the students.

but not:

15. John cannot distinguish the class.

The division of cases into 'grammatically singular' and 'grammatically plural' is also an oversimplification. Note that 'The Beatles', which we have suggested treating using the Plurality-in-Object strategy, is grammatically plural both in that it has the plural '-s' morphology and in that it take plural verb agreement. ('The Beatles are', rather than 'The Beatles is'.) But this is an accident of the particular band name. The Velvet Underground lacks plural '-s' morphology and takes singular verb agreement, but surely its metaphysics is on a par with that of The Beatles.

Notice also that British English and American English have different rules regarding verb agreement with 'collective' terms. In British English we say:

16. The team are visiting Madrid.

While in American English we say:

17. The team is visiting Madrid.

One way to proceed in light of this is to hold that British English and American English have different ontologies. On the hybrid view, the plural verb in British English would mark 'the team' as a Plurality-in-Reference item, so there would be no further object above and beyond the individual team members, while the singular verb in American English would mark 'the team' as a Plurality-in-Object item, so there would be a team in addition to the team members.

Another way to proceed is to hold that noun phrase number and verb phrase number can come apart. On this view, 'the team' is grammatically singular, but British English, unlike American English, allows that grammatically singular noun to be combined with a plural verb. Notice that we get a similar phenomenon with pronoun agreement. Both British and American English allow a choice between:

18. The team is/are visiting Madrid. It arrived Sunday.
19. The team is/are visiting Madrid. They are enjoying the city.

On this approach, more syntactic work will be needed to figure out where Plurality-in-Reference and Plurality-in-Object apply.

8.11 Consequences

In Chapter 4, we saw that one challenge to an adequate theory of reference is that natural languages seem quite indifferent to the boundary between cases in which names have something to refer to ('Aristotle'), and cases in which names have nothing to refer to ('Sherlock Holmes'). This challenge pointed to a need to make the theory of reference match the indifference of the linguistic practice, either by smoothing over the ontological difference by providing referents for N-names, or by smoothing over the semantic difference by adopting a lightweight notion of reference. We see a similar phenomenon in the current chapter, but there are also important differences. Natural languages freely use expressions that appear to refer to only a single object, as in standard names like 'Aristotle', as well as expressions that appear to refer to many objects, such as 'John and Paul and George and Ringo' or 'The Beatles'. Again we would like to make the theory of reference fit with this natural language practice. But in this case it's not right to call the linguistic practice indifferent. Although the details are complicated, our practice does track some kind of *grammatical* distinction between singular expressions and plural expressions, and investigation shows that that distinction in turn tracks a distinction in what we are referring to.

The most promising views in this area combine two resources. One resource is a *semantic* resource: the recognition that reference can be a one-to-many relation that holds between one name and many objects. This resource allows us to explain the function of expressions like 'John and Paul and George and Ringo' without needing new things to refer to. The other resource is a metaphysical resource: the recognition that there can be *group-like* objects that have other objects as members. This resource allows us to explain the function of expressions like 'The Beatles', even when part of that function is to allow attribution of properties that don't depend on the properties of the individual Beatles.

If the hybrid view we sketched above is on the right track, then the distribution of these two resources is marked in language by the use of grammatically singular or grammatically plural expressions. This fact in turn would make it possible to use language as a tool for investigating the metaphysical nature of groups. Suppose T1 is a (Plurality-in-Object) term for some group we want to understand. We can introduce a list name for the members of the group named by T1. Call that list name T2. According to the hybrid view, T2 falls under Plurality-in-Reference, and doesn't call for a corresponding group. By then contrasting what can be truly said about T1 and what can be truly said about T2, we can work out what kinds of features the group needs to have, over and above the features of its individual members.

Central Points in Chapter 8

- So far in this book we've only been considering singular reference in which one expression refers to one object. But it appears that there is also plural reference. When I say 'John, Paul, George, and Ringo' I seem to refer to four objects. What's going on in such cases?
- An important distinction we drew was between collective and distributive predication. When I say 'John and Paul are from Liverpool' I am saying that each of John and Paul possess the property of being from Liverpool. John possesses it, and, as a separate matter, Paul possesses it. This is a distributive predication. On the other hand, we have collective predications. When I say 'John, Paul, and George surrounded Ringo (and begged him not to sing)', I am not saying that John surrounded Ringo and, as a separate matter, so did the others. It's not true that John surrounded Ringo—unless he was donut-shaped, that would be impossible. Rather, we're saying that the three *taken together* surrounded him. The three taken collectively satisfy the predicate 'surrounded Ringo', and this is an example of collective predication.
- We explored two theories of plural reference. On one, the pluralness of plural reference arises from the reference relation. Consider the property: being what is referred to by 'John, Paul, and George'. This could be construed either distributively or collectively. If the former, it says that John is the referent of 'John, Paul, and George' as is, separately, Paul, as is, again separately, Ringo; if the latter, that the three men taken together are the referent of 'John, Paul, and George'. This latter reading is what we want, and that's what the Plurality-in-Reference view claims.
- We went on to spell out this view in some more detail, and considered the transparency problem for it. This is that, according to the Plurality-in-Reference theorist, 'The Beatles' and 'John, Paul, George, and Ringo' co-refer, which leads to mispredictions such as the claim that 'The Beatles formed in 1960 iff John, Paul, George, and Ringo formed in 1960', which is false.
- We then went on to consider the plurality in object view. On this view, plurally referring expressions refer to just one object: what we called 'groups'. 'John and Paul and George and Ringo' refers to the group consisting of them. 'This bowl, Theresa May, and Wales'

refers to the group consisting of my cereal receptacle, the incompetent politician, and the birthplace of Dylan Thomas. In general, for any objects, there is a group consisting of it apt to be referred to by a plurally referring expression. We noted the problem with this view: it posits a lot of entities, and thus may seem ontologically unparsimonious.

- We ended by considering the possibility of a hybrid view that could overcome the problems Plurality-in-Reference and Plurality-in-Object face, and what we can learn about the concept of reference by attending to plural expressions.

Comprehension Questions

1. On the table there is a book and a pen. For the Plurality-in-Reference person, how many objects are there? What about for the friend of Plurality-in-Object?
2. Why do we need to appeal to flexible truth conditions?
3. List two true distributive and two collective predications, with different plural subjects, and then list two false ones for each.
4. What exactly is the transparency problem? Is it a big problem?
5. Just how much latitude do we have in plural predications? Our theory predicts 'falling stones killed the goat' can be true, even if some stones sailed safely past it. But how does it avoid predicting that 'the boys misbehaved' is true, even if only one boy in a class of ten misbehaved?

Exploratory Questions

6. Plural terms often satisfy a *cumulative principle*. If John and Paul are musicians, and George and Ringo are musicians, then John and Paul and George and Ringo are musicians. More generally, if plural term T1 satisfies condition C, and plural term T2 satisfies condition C, then the plural term 'T1 and T2' also satisfies condition C. Can you think of any counterexamples to that principle? What about 'The stones weigh ten kilograms', and 'The sticks weigh ten kilograms'?

(continued)

7. We saw that the Plurality-in-Reference view has problems with transparency. Is there any scope for making the sort of moves that are made in other cases of transparency? Could one dig in and say that yes, John, Paul, Ringo, and Paul *were* formed in 1960; it's just pragmatically odd, as it's pragmatically odd to say that Clark Kent can fly?

8. A problem for our hybrid strategy came when it attempted to make a division along grammatical lines between expressions which refer to a plurality and expressions which refer to a group. Can we avoid this problem by observing that there is some sort of anaphoric component to these claims? 'The students are similar to each other', but 'The class is similar to each other' is grammatically incoherent, because it lacks an antecedent for the anaphora. Are there other cases that don't have this anaphoric nature?

9. We noted that there are issues concerning agreement with expressions like 'team'. Do we get difference in verb number or pronoun number depending on the kind of predication we make?
   - The team is/are happy.
   - The team was/were founded in 1800.
   - The team played Barcelona. It/they won.
   - The committee was reorganized. It/they will be larger next year.

10. Another kind of plural expression we haven't discussed in this chapter is bare plurals, such as 'tigers', 'sharks', or 'ducks'. Consider four competing views about bare plurals:
    - Bare plurals are used to make universally quantified claims. 'Tigers are F' means that all tigers are F.
    - Bare plurals are used to make existentially quantified claims. 'Tigers are F' means that some tigers are F.
    - Bare plurals refer to kinds. 'Tigers are F' means that a particular kind of animal is F.
    - Bare plurals refer to stereotypes or normal instances. 'Tigers are F' means that the stereotypical, or perfectly normal, tiger is F.

    Now consider the following claims involving bare plurals. Make your best determination of the truth conditions for each claim, paying attention to possible ambiguities in each case. Then consider which of the above four views is best supported by the data provided by these claims. (Feel free also to introduce other claims involving bare plurals that you think provide helpful additional data.)

- Tigers are mammals.
- Tigers escaped from the Berlin Zoo on Thursday.
- Tigers are almost extinct.
- Tigers are dangerous.
- Ducks lay eggs.
- Sharks often attack people.
- Ducks aren't feared by people.

11. We set out a distinction between distributive and collective readings of plural claims. Some claims clearly allow both collective and distributive readings. *John and Paul lifted the piano* can be true because John and Paul cooperatively lifted the piano (collective), or because John by himself lifted the piano and then Paul by himself lifted the piano (distributive). Are there predicates that *require* a specific style of satisfaction—predicates that can only be read collectively, or predicates that can only be read distributively? Propose some candidates, and then consider whether the other readings can be obtaining by considering unusual circumstances in which normal assumptions about the world are abandoned. For example, *The police surrounded the house* might most naturally be taken to say that the police collectively surrounded the house, but if the police force is staffed by large donut-shaped officers, they can each individually surround the house.

Further Reading

Rayo 2007 is a good overview article, as is Linnebo 2014. For an approach from a linguistic perspective which covers some similar ground as here, see the classic Link 1983, as well as Moltmann 2012, Schein 2006, and Schwarzschild 1996. Rumfitt 2005 approaches the matter from more of a philosopher's perspective. Oliver and Smiley 2013 is very good on the history of thinking about plurals. Boolos 1984 is a pioneering discussion of the philosophical significance of plural reference, and Williamson 2010 gives a glimpse of some of the deep metaphysical issues that plural quantification can shed light on, as does Cotnoir 2013.

9

A Puzzle about Intuitions and Methodology

9.1 A Puzzle

The first chapter of this book outlined some competing views about reference and focused in particular on Kripke's arguments against Frege. But how did he go about finding evidence for these views? What is his method? If we are to say something about English and other natural languages, don't we need to do empirical research? Don't Kripke (and others working on these issues) owe us a better account of the evidential basis for their theories? So the initial puzzle we'll be concerned with in this chapter is: *What kind of evidence can be presented for and against theories of reference?*

A standard answer to these questions in philosophy is that *intuitions* serve as the fundamental evidence. Kripke says:

Some philosophers think that something's having intuitive content is very inconclusive evidence in favor of it. I think it is very heavy evidence in favor of anything, myself. I really don't know, in a way, what more conclusive evidence one can have about anything, ultimately speaking.   (Kripke 1980: 42)

But this answer to the first puzzle triggers another one: Why should intuitions be relied upon? What makes them so special? Are they reliable enough to play a role as foundations for philosophical theorizing? One might then have a very general concern, well articulated by Jaakko Hintikka (1999). He writes:

The most amazing fact about the current fashion of appealing to intuitions is the same as the proverbial dog's walking on two feet: not that it is done particularly well, but that it is done at all. For what is supposed to be the justification of such appeals to intuitions? One searches in the literature in vain for a serious attempt to provide such a justification. This blind faith is below the intellectual dignity of philosophers for whom unexamined intuitions should not be worth intuiting.

(Hintikka 1999: 130)

Hintikka is surely right that if philosophers actually do rely on intuitions as evidence, they owe us a story about *why* they rely on them. That is an extremely important challenge—a challenge that anyone who takes him or herself to rely on intuitions owes us a response to. Timothy Williamson describes the lack of an answer as a methodological scandal:

When contemporary analytic philosophers run out of arguments, they appeal to intuitions. It can seem, and is sometimes said, that any philosophical dispute, when pushed back far enough, turns into a conflict of intuitions about ultimate premises: 'In the end, all we have to go on is our intuitions'. Thus intuitions are presented as our evidence in philosophy. Yet there is no agreed or even popular account of how intuition works, no accepted explanation of the hoped-for correlation between our having an intuition that P and its being true that P. Since analytic philosophy prides itself on its rigour, this blank space in its foundations looks like a methodological scandal. Why should intuitions have any authority over the philosophical domain?   (Williamson 2007: 214–15)

9.2 Why the Puzzle Matters

Many philosophers, not just in philosophy of language, assume that theirs is a discipline that can be done from the armchair, so to speak. There's no need to get one's hands dirty. We just sit in our offices, reflect, trigger intuitions, and build theories based on our access to these intuitions. This entire cerebral image of philosophy is challenged by those who question intuitions. If philosophers rely on intuitions, and intuitions are suspicious, why should we listen to anything philosophers say? Maybe the entire history of (at least Western) philosophy is based on the illusion that intuitions can serve as the foundation of a discipline.

This puzzle in effect asks us to justify relying on the claims made in the first chapter. Chapter 1, recall, introduced some arguments in the recent debate about reference, but we didn't talk about the presuppositions of those arguments, or the legitimacy of the tools used to respond to them. We are now asking: what's the justification for employing any of those tools?

Some options for how to solve the puzzle

In what follows, we outline two options for how to resolve the puzzle:

- *Solution 1*: The evidential foundation is intuitions.
- *Solution 2*: The evidential foundation is not intuitions—instead, it's arguments and non-intuitive premises.

Solution 1 is the most popular (and, as we have seen, it's one it looks like Kripke endorses—although we'll question this later). It triggered one of the first and most influential experimental philosophy studies. We will discuss this study (and objections to it) in detail. *Solution 2* is advocated by Timothy Williamson, Max Deutsch, and Herman Cappelen (one of the authors of this book), and will be presented at the end of the chapter.

9.3 Introduction to *Solution 1*: Intuitions Are the Fundamental Evidence

We'll use *Naming and Necessity* as an illustration here (and throughout). Kripke, as we have seen, seems to be fairly explicit in his endorsement of the view that intuitions serve as evidence for his theory (see the passage quoted above).[1] It's hard to read that book and not get the impression that something called 'intuitions' play an important role in his theorizing. Kripke uses 'intuitive' and cognate terms extensively, applies them to ideas, notions, arguments, and claims; he talks about intuitions that are 'natural' (pp. 5, 15), or 'direct' (p. 14). When we consider the important argumentative junctures in *Naming and Necessity*, they all seem to involve what many would describe as appeal to intuitions about cases. Consider for example, this famous passage:

Suppose that Gödel was not in fact the author of [Gödel's] theorem. A man named 'Schmidt' [. . .] actually did the work in question. His friend Gödel somehow got hold of the manuscript and it was thereafter attributed to Gödel. On the [descriptivist] view in question, then, when our ordinary man uses the name 'Gödel', he really means to refer to Schmidt, because Schmidt is the unique person satisfying the description 'the man who discovered the incompleteness of arithmetic'. [. . .] But it seems we are not. We simply are not. (Kripke 1980: 83–4)

We are not, says Kripke. But what is the evidence that we don't use 'Gödel' to refer to Schmidt? On one influential interpretation the answer is: because we have an intuition that we don't. Kripke doesn't actually use the word 'intuition' in this passage, but to many of his readers it seems obvious that what he is doing is appealing to intuitions. What else could the evidence be?

---

[1] We say 'seems', since some people, such as Max Deutsch, have alternative interpretations of that passage—one we will return to later in this chapter.

Later in this chapter we will question this intuition-based interpretation of Kripke, but for now we'll go along with it.

9.4 *Solution 1* and Experimental Philosophy

Let's for a moment work on the assumption that Kripke is an intuition-monger—i.e. that appeals to something he calls 'intuition' play an important role in his argument. One might then have a very general concern: In what follows we present this as an argument with four premises and a conclusion.

In an influential paper, Machery, Mallon, Nichols, and Stich assume premise one:

> **Premise one:** Kripke's arguments are intuition-based.

Machery et al. say:

There is widespread agreement among philosophers on the methodology for developing an adequate theory of reference. The project is to construct theories of reference that are consistent with our intuitions about the correct application of terms in fictional (and non-fictional) situations. Indeed, Kripke's masterstroke was to propose some cases that elicited widely shared intuitions that were inconsistent with traditional descriptivist theories. Moreover, it has turned out that almost all philosophers share the intuitions elicited by Kripke's fictional cases, including most of his opponents. Even contemporary descriptivists allow that these intuitions have falsified traditional forms of descriptivism and try to accommodate them within their own sophisticated descriptivist frameworks.

(Machery et al. 2004: B3)

> **Premise two:** If there is variation in intuitions about a question, we should not employ those intuitions in our philosophical theorizing.

Machery et al. say: 'Suppose that semantic intuitions exhibit systematic differences between groups or individuals. This would raise questions about whose intuitions are going to count, putting in jeopardy philosophers' methodology' (2004: B4). If it turned out that significant groups of people didn't share the intuitions Kripke (allegedly) appeals to, we can at least conclude that it is wrong to assume that the intuitions are universally shared. If they are not universally shared, why should we trust our intuitions, and not those with the opposing intuitions?

> **Premise three:** We can empirically investigate people's intuitions.

This can be done using questionnaires: We present people with vignettes (little stories like those Kripke presents in *Naming and Necessity*), and then ask them questions about them. The answers people give to these vignettes will count as their intuitions.

> **Premise four:** Empirical testing of speakers' intuitions about Kripke's cases shows that there is variability between groups.

Machery et al. performed these experiments and found that the intuitions had by Kripke are not universally shared. More precisely, they found that undergraduate students in Hong Kong were less inclined to share Kripke's intuitions than undergraduates at Rutgers University in New Jersey.

> **Conclusion:** We should not employ intuitions about Kripke's cases in our philosophical theorizing.

On the basis of variability, Machery et al. concluded that we have reason to doubt Kripke's arguments against the descriptive theory of names. The intuitions used as the basis of that argument turn out to be idiosyncratic. They say:

We find it *wildly* implausible that the semantic intuitions of the narrow cross-section of humanity who are Western academic philosophers are a more reliable indicator of the correct theory of reference (if there is such a thing, see Stich, 1996, chapter 1) than the differing semantic intuitions of other cultural or linguistic groups. (Machery et al. 2004: B9)

This argument has been very influential, and there is by now a great deal of literature on it. In this literature one finds additional work by other experimental philosophers supporting Machery et al.'s result, as well as a wide range of responses from those defending Kripke. Moreover, the general strategy of trying to show that Western philosophers have relied on parochial intuitions can be extended to all areas of philosophy. Their results are, they claim, depressing: the foundations of Western philosophy—intuitions—are rotten.

In what follows, we first look at Machery et al.'s study in a bit more detail. We then consider three responses to it.

9.5 More on the Machery et al. Study, and an Introduction to the Responses

Machery et al. presented students in Hong Kong and at Rutgers with the following so-called vignette:

Suppose that John has learned in college that Gödel is the man who proved an important mathematical theorem, called the incompleteness of arithmetic. John is quite good at mathematics and he can give an accurate statement of the incompleteness theorem, which he attributes to Gödel as the discoverer. But this is the only thing that he has heard about Gödel. Now suppose that Gödel was not the author of this theorem. A man called 'Schmidt', whose body was found in Vienna under mysterious circumstances many years ago, actually did the work in question. His friend Gödel somehow got hold of the manuscript and claimed credit for the work, which was thereafter attributed to Gödel. Thus, he has been known as the man who proved the incompleteness of arithmetic. Most people who have heard the name 'Gödel' are like John; the claim that Gödel discovered the incompleteness theorem is the only thing they have ever heard about Gödel. (Machery et al. 2004: B6)

They then asked the following question:

When John uses the name 'Gödel', is he talking about:

(A) the person who really discovered the incompleteness of arithmetic?

or

(B) the person who got hold of the manuscript and claimed credit for the work?

Machery et al. found that significantly more of the Rutgers students endorsed the Kripkean intuition (option A), than students in Hong Kong. They have a hypothesis about why that is so:

The cross-cultural work indicates that EAs [East Asians] are more inclined than Ws to make categorical judgments on the basis of similarity; Ws [Westerns], on the other hand, are more disposed to focus on causation in describing the world and classifying things. This differential focus led us to hypothesize that there might be a related cross-cultural difference in semantic intuitions. On a description theory, the referent has to satisfy the description, but it need not be causally related to the use of the term. In contrast, on Kripke's causal-historical theory, the referent need not satisfy the associated description. Rather, it need only figure in the causal history (and in the causal explanation) of the speaker's current use of the word.

(Machery et al. 2004: B5)

Their prediction was that East Asians would be more likely to have intuitions that match the description theory, and that Ws would be inclined have intuitions that support Kripke's causal theory. If we take their view at face value, this is pretty much what they found.

Machery et al.'s study has been influential, and threatens the pessimistic conclusion that the foundations of philosophy, and thus the theory of reference, are unsound. However, this conclusion is far from unquestionable, and in the remainder of this chapter we will consider some responses. In particular, we'll consider three: i) that Machery et al.'s study doesn't test for the right phenomenon; ii) that the intuitions of the folk aren't the right kinds of intuitions to test philosophical theories against; and iii) that responses to questionnaires don't necessarily track intuitions.

9.6 First Reply to the Challenge from Experimental Philosophy: Speaker Reference or Semantic Reference?

One of the first issues that was brought up when Machery et al. published their paper was the question of whether the vignettes they used tested for the right phenomenon. According to the objection, Machery et al. tested for *speaker reference*, not *semantic reference*. What is the difference? Here is an illustration from Kripke:

Two people see Smith in the distance and mistake him for Jones. They have a brief colloquy: 'What is Jones doing?' 'Raking the leaves.' 'Jones', in the common language of both, is a name of Jones; it never names Smith. Yet, in some sense, on this occasion, clearly both participants in the dialogue have referred to Smith, and the second participant has said something true about the man he referred to if and only if Smith was raking the leaves (whether or not Jones was).   (Kripke 1977: 263)

The semantic referent of 'Jones' is Jones (he is the person that the word 'Jones' refers to). But, on this occasion, it is clear that the speaker wanted to use 'Jones' to refer to Smith. He is looking at Smith and wants to describe the person he is talking about—he's just wrong about the name of the person he is looking at. His goal was to refer to Smith, not to Jones. In such a case, the speaker referent was Smith and the semantic referent was Jones. Kripke's theory in *Naming and Necessity* is a theory of semantic reference. It is not a theory about speaker reference.

What did Machery et al. test for? Note that the question they asked was: 'When John uses the name "Gödel", what is he talking about?' This formulation is, at best, ambiguous, between asking for semantic reference and asking for speaker reference. The locution 'what is he talking about?' could be a question either about the object he had in mind, or the referent of the word. It is simply not clear. So one concern many had when first reading this paper was that it failed to clearly test for the right thing: intuitions about semantic reference. Of course, even if it failed to do that, it would have shown a difference in how the two groups interpret the question: East Asians are more inclined towards the speaker reference interpretation—we can then ask why that is, but the answer to that question seems less obviously relevant to a criticism of Kripke.

In response to this concern, Machery and others conducted new studies. They tried to formulate the studies in ways that more clearly targeted semantic reference. For example, in an effort to disambiguate, Machery et al. (2010) modified the question as follows:

When John uses the name 'Gödel', regardless of who he might intend to be talking about, he is actually talking about:

(A) the person who really discovered the incompleteness of arithmetic.
(B) the person who got hold of the manuscript and claimed credit for the work.

They thought that the phrase 'actually talking about' would help the participants target semantic reference, and make sure they didn't focus on speaker reference instead. The results seemed to support the original results from Machery et al.: there was still significant difference between responses from Westerns and East Asians. So, they concluded, the original results were robust: the Kripkean intuitions were biased in favor of one culture. The challenge remains: why assume that the intuitions of Western academic philosophers are a reliable indicator of the correct theory of reference when those intuitions are not widely shared?

However, the dispute didn't end there. It didn't take long for people to point out that the ambiguity still wasn't eliminated: 'actually talking about' is still about the speaker, not about the word. Remember, it is the word that has a semantic referent—not a use of that word and not the act of talking.

In sum: to get the readers of the vignette to focus on the referent of the word, as opposed to whatever the speaker has in mind or is talking about, is really hard!² This leads us to the second objection to the challenge from experimental philosophy.

9.7 Second Reply to Experimental Philosophy: The Expertise Reply

Here is one way to think about the first objection: the distinction between semantic reference and speaker reference is not one that ordinary speakers (those not trained in philosophy and semantics) have. You have to learn that distinction in order to get clear on it. So if you ask non-experts about their reactions to vignettes, as Machery et al. did, you will never get them to focus on the right phenomenon, because the phenomenon (i.e. semantic reference) simply isn't identifiable for people without the relevant training.

This objection is an instance of a more general objection to experimental philosophy. According to this view, it is a mistake to describe philosophers as relying on intuitions in general. They rely on *expert intuitions*, not on the intuitions of lay people. Here is how Weinberg et al. (2010) describe the so-called expertise defense:

[T]he practice of appealing to philosophical intuitions about hypothetical cases, properly construed, should be the practice of appealing to philosophers' intuitions about hypothetical cases. And so studies conducted on the intuitions of untutored folk can provide no evidence against the practice of appealing to philosophical intuitions as evidence.   (Weinberg et al. 2010: 333)

Here is Michael Devitt expressing this view in connection with semantic intuitions:

Still, are these referential intuitions likely to be right? I think we need to be cautious in accepting them: semantics is notoriously hard and the folk are a long way from being experts. Still it does seem to me that their intuitions about 'simple' situations are likely to be right. This having been said, we should prefer the intuitions of semanticists, usually philosophers, because they are much more expert (which is not to say, very expert!). Just as the intuitions of paleontologists,

---

² Machery et al. are not unaware of this. They say, for example: 'It is sometimes possible to understand 'actually talking' as bearing on speaker's reference and 'intending to talk about' as bearing on semantic reference, precisely the reverse of the readings we intended in formulating the probe!' (2015: 71). Note that they think they have a solution to the problem, but the point here is simply to emphasize that they are aware of the difficulty.

physicists, and psychologists in their respective domains are likely to be better than those of the folk, so too the intuitions of the semanticists.   (Devitt 2011: 426)

Machery nicely summarizes the concern with the following analogy:

because the reliability of the judgments about the historical origins of pot shards depends on the expertise of the intuiters, we treat the judgments made by archaeologists as the relevant evidence to decide whether some pot shards are of Sumerian origin, and we are not concerned if lay people's judgments are haphazard.   (Machery 2012: 43)

The 'expertise reply' to x-phi says that we should focus on the intuitions of experts, not of lay people. We should no more expect lay people to have accurate intuitions about semantics than we should expect them to have accurate intuitions about pot shards of Sumerian origin.

Machery has responded to this objection. At the center of his response is the idea that in order to assess the expertise reply, we need empirical data about the effects of expertise on intuitions. In the paper, 'Expertise and Intuitions about Reference', Machery investigates what, as a matter of fact, happens to people's intuitions when they acquire expertise. The tentative result of these studies is that expertise does not improve the reliability of intuitions. According to Machery, when you look at people with relevant expertise, they are all over the place—there is no consistent effect of expertise. For more on this, see Schwitzgebel and Cushman (2012), Nado (2014), and Andow (2015).

9.8 Third Objection to Experimental Philosophy: Intuitions Are Not Revealed by Answers to Questionnaires

We turn now to a third line of response to the experimental philosophy. This reply was developed in response to experimental philosophy more generally (not specifically as a response to Machery et al.). John Bengson (2013) agrees with the first premise of the experimentalist's argument— i.e. that Kripke relies on intuitions. What he denies is the second and third premises of the argument: that responses to questionnaires test for intuitions.

In order to understand this line of thought, we first have to say more about what an intuition is supposed to be. So far we have not said much about just what it takes for a judgment to be an intuition. So here is a general strategy for responding to the experimental philosophy data:

  i. Intuitions are judgments with features F.
 ii. Responses to questionnaires about vignettes don't exhibit F.
iii. So: the results we get from experimental philosophers don't concern intuitions.

In sum: don't assume that just because you have discovered a pattern in answers to questionnaires (say, that East Asians respond differently from Westerns), you have discovered a pattern in intuitions.

This kind of argument can be spelled out in different ways, all depending on what one takes intuitions to be—i.e. what one takes the relevant F to be in the argument above. We will use Bengson's version as an illustration here. For Bengson, a judgment—e.g. that a use of 'Gödel' doesn't refer to Schmidt—is an intuition if it expresses how it strikes you, or how it seems to you, where this striking or seeming has a somewhat distinctive feel. For our purposes right now it is not important to be very precise about just what this 'striking' or 'seeming' is. What is important is that it is a distinctive kind of judgment.

With that notion of an intuition in hand, it is open to respond to the experimental philosopher as follows: *You have no way of knowing that the responses you get express intuitions or whether they express judgments driven by other factors.* Here is a vivid example from Bengson:

Open-minded is asked the following question: 'Might incest between consenting adults—who may or may not enjoy passionate sex—ever, in some situation, be morally permissible?' He asks himself whether there might be *some* situation— even just one—in which incest between consenting adults is morally permissible. It strikes Open-minded that there could be at least one such situation. But as he tries to imagine this situation, one which may involve passionate sex between siblings—perhaps even him and one of his own siblings!—he finds himself having a strong negative emotional reaction. On the basis of this reaction, he answers that incest can never be morally permissible. (Bengson 2013: 509)

The important feature of this example is that it strikes Open-minded as true that incest could be morally permissible in certain situations. But that is not what he answers. His answer is driven by other considerations—the powerful impact of the imagination. This makes Open-minded deny his intuition.

More generally, if an intuition is a sort of judgment with distinctive features, we need evidence that the responses to vignettes belong to that sort. So far, according to Bengson, we have no such evidence.

9.9 Solution 2: The Evidence for Theories of Reference Is Arguments and Premises of a Non-Intuitive Kind

In this final section, we consider the response that we find most promising. This response denies the first premise in the experimentalist's argument. That is to say, it denies that Kripke's argument relies on intuitions. The entire project of experimental philosophers is built on the assumption that philosophers rely on intuitions in their argumentations. That is an empirical assumption about how philosophers argue. It can be investigated, and several recent investigations have thrown doubt on this assumption.

This line of argument has been pressed by, among others, Max Deutsch (2009, 2015), Timothy Williamson (2007), and Herman Cappelen (2012). You can think of this as line of argument as having three components:

i. The relevant passage by Kripke doesn't mention intuitions at all.
ii. In the passages that mention intuitions, the occurrences of those words can be interpreted in other ways.
iii. The judgments Kripke makes don't have any of the distinctive features that intuitive judgments are supposed to have.

We consider these in turn.

9.9.1 The Apparent Irrelevance of Intuitions in Kripke

We will focus on Deutsch's version of this objection. Deutsch points out that in the passage where Kripke presents the Gödel case, he doesn't explicitly appeal to intuitions. Deutsch says:

Kripke insists that, in the circumstances he imagines in his story about Gödel and Schmidt, we 'simply are not' referring to Schmidt when we use the name 'Gödel' (Kripke 1980, 83). It is not that it is *intuitive* that we are not talking about Schmidt; it is that we are not talking about Schmidt, period. Facts about which propositions are intuitive appear to play no role at all. Instead . . . it looks as though . . . Kripke [is] appealing to facts that are not purely psychological—the fact that we simply are not referring to Schmidt when using 'Gödel' (Deutsch 2015: 44–5)

The point here is that there's an important distinction between the following two argumentative moves:

i. Kripke's evidence against descriptive theories is this: in the imagined scenario, 'Gödel' refers to Gödel, and not to Schmidt.

ii. Kripke's evidence against descriptive theories is this: we have the intuition that in the imagined scenario, 'Gödel' refers to Gödel, and not to Schmidt.

If (ii) is true, then we have opened the door to the objections from the experimental philosophers. If, however, (i) is the right interpretation, then it looks like issues about intuitions are totally irrelevant. What we have to check is *whether it is true* that 'Gödel' refers to Gödel and not Schmidt, not whether people have the intuition or not. According to Williamson, Deutsch, and Cappelen, (i) is the correct interpretation. If that is right, then experimental philosophy is, in Cappelen's words, 'a big mistake'.

9.9.2 How to Interpret the Passages where Kripke Does Use 'Intuition' Vocabulary

We mentioned at the beginning of this chapter that *Naming and Necessity* uses 'intuitive' and cognate terms extensively. So even though the particular passage doesn't use that terminology, one might be excused for thinking that intuitions were central to much of Kripke's thinking as Hintikka, and later the experimental philosophers, came to think.

That, however, would be a mistake. From the fact that a philosopher uses the term 'intuitively' a lot, it does not follow that he or she relies on intuitions. Cian Dorr addresses this point in a particularly elegant way. Dorr is addressing those who accuse metaphysicians of relying on intuitions—in particular, those who base those accusations on the use of 'intuitive' and cognate terms. Dorr says:

Often, saying 'Intuitively, P' is no more than a device for committing oneself to P while signaling that one is not going to provide any further arguments for this claim. In this use, 'intuitively...' is more or less interchangeable with 'it seems to me that...'. There is a pure and chilly way of writing philosophy in which premises and conclusions are baldly asserted. But it's hard to write like this without seeming to bully one's readers; one can make things a bit gentler and more human by occasionally inserting qualifiers like 'it seems that'. It would be absurd to accuse someone who frequently gave in to this stylistic temptation of following a bankrupt methodology that presupposes the erroneous claim that things generally are as they seem. But the sprinkling of 'intuitively's' and 'counterintuitive's' around a typical paper in metaphysics is in most cases not significantly different from this. It may be bad style, but it is not bad methodology, or any methodology at all, unless arguing from premises to conclusions counts as a methodology.   (Dorr 2010)[3]

Dorr is certainly right about this—that an author likes to use the word 'intuitively' doesn't mean he or she is relying on an intuition. As Cappelen states, this way of talking has become a kind of verbal virus. It has affected the way people talk, but has had hardly any impact on first-order philosophy. It is, as Dorr says, maybe bad style, but not an indication of bad methodology.

9.9.3 The Judgments Kripke Makes Don't Have Any of the Features Intuitive Judgments Are Supposed to Have

Let's put aside the question of how Kripke (and others) use 'intuition' vocabulary. You might think that it's irrelevant anyway: someone might rely on intuitions, even though she does not explicitly say, 'Now I'm relying on an intuition', or in some other explicit way mark that reliance. Compare perception-based judgments: we rely on our perceptual input all the time, without making it explicit. Nora can say: 'There's Josh!' and base that judgment on visual input. She doesn't typically say: 'I can see that that is Josh!' or 'I see Josh so I infer that Josh is coming', or anything like that. So a judgment can be based on an intuition, even if it is not marked as such. This raises the questions: How would we tell that a judgment is intuition-based? What are the characteristics of such judgments?

What we are looking for here are diagnostics for a judgment being intuition-based (diagnostics to be used in the absence of the use of 'intuition' vocabulary). There are many options for such diagnostics, but three are most commonly cited (see Cappelen 2013, Chapter 7, for further discussion).

   i. **Snap**: They are judgments that are made without reflection—a kind of gut reaction. This is the most salient notion in the psychological literature on intuitions.

[3] Cappelen (2013) develops these points in detail. In particular, see Chapters 2–4.

ii. **Special Feel**: They are accompanied by a certain phenomenology—a distinctive feel. (Cappelen 2013: 101–2).

iii. **Unjustified Justifier**: They have a distinctive epistemic status—they justify, but need no justification. They are the kinds of judgments that serve as justifiers, even though they themselves cannot be justified. (Chalmers 2014: 536).

We now have a new research project—one that has to be engaged in prior to doing experimental philosophy. Experimental philosophy is done on arguments that rely on intuitions; it is an empirical question as to which arguments do. One way to check that is to investigate specific arguments by appeal to diagnostics 1, 2, and 3 above. If the argument in question—e.g. Kripke's arguments in *Naming and Necessity*—has one or more of features 1, 2, or 3, we have evidence that the argument is intuition-based. If, on the other hand, the argument has none of these features, then we have good reason to think the argument isn't intuition-based, and experiments on intuitions become irrelevant.

What is striking is that Kripke's arguments in *Naming and Necessity* don't fit either 1, 2 or 3:

- **Kripke and the Snap Feature**: There is no evidence that Kripke wanted the reader to make a quick, non-reflective judgment. There is also no evidence that he made a quick, non-reflective judgment about any of the cases. On the contrary: this is philosophy, and we are all encouraged—indeed required—to think very carefully about each judgment.
- **Kripke and the Special Feel**: There is no evidence in any of Kripke's writings that he thought the judgments about his cases—e.g. the Gödel case—was (or should be) accompanied by a special feeling. As a matter of fact, it is not.
- **Kripke and the Unjustified Justifier**: Kripke argues for the conclusion about each of these cases—he does not treat his judgments as unjustified justifiers.

This is, of course, a tentative conclusion. There is an empirical project here, one the experimental philosophers have neglected: to make clear exactly what they mean by 'intuition', and then show, argument by argument, premise by premise, that their targets are intuition-based.

Central Points in Chapter 9

- At the center of this book are Kripke's arguments against Frege. And at the heart of those arguments are certain claims, such as that even if Gödel hadn't discovered incompleteness, 'Gödel' would still refer to him and not Schmidt. What is our evidence for such claims?
- A common answer is that such claims rest on intuitions. Kripke himself, for example, seems to talk approvingly of intuition as a source of knowledge. But what are intuitions? And why should we think intuitions are reliable? If we don't have answers to these questions, it seems as if philosophy rests on insecure foundations.
- We presented some reasons to be worried if philosophy does depend on intuitions. For example, experimental philosophers argue that intuitions about things like reference are culturally variable. If this is so, then it seems either we have to say facts about reference are also culturally variable, or arbitrarily assert that one particular culture's intuitions are the ones to be trusted.
- We suggested reasons to doubt the experimental philosophers' claims: they tested for the wrong thing and used an inappropriate method to get at speakers' intuitions. Moreover, even granting that their experiments were well formed, one could argue that there is one particular culture whose semantic intuitions are to be trusted—namely, those of experts in semantics and the philosophy of language more generally.
- We then went on to consider the claim which denies that intuitions are important for philosophy, even when some—such as Kripke—seem to claim they are. We presented arguments showing that a close reading of Kripke indicates he didn't appeal to intuitions, even when he uses the word 'intuition': what he calls 'intuition' doesn't have any of the features pro-intuition people take intuitions to have.

Comprehension Questions

1. Spell out in your own words exactly what intuitions are meant to be.
2. Think of a philosophical argument you like or encountered recently. Is it fair to say it relies on intuitions?
3. Do you share Kripke's intuitions about his cases?

(continued)

4. Think of other instances involving semantic and speaker reference, and spell out in your own words what the distinction amounts to.
5. Which reply to the experimental philosopher do you think is strongest? Why?

Exploratory Questions

6. Should expert intuitions be the ones we attend to in philosophy? Justify your response in a few sentences.
7. Can you think of a way of phrasing the question about the reference of 'Gödel' in Machery et al.'s study that avoids the worry about the distinction between semantic reference and speaker reference?
8. If not intuition-based, what is the methodology of philosophy? Think of other fields, such as mathematics, linguistics, or literary studies. What tools are used in those fields, and how do they relate to the tools used in philosophy?

Further Reading

The place to get started is Machery et al. 2004. For a slew of experiments in a similar vein, which attempt to get round some of the problems mentioned here and elsewhere, see Beebee and Undercoffer 2016. If you have a taste for it, there are many experiments you could read about: about 'most', about so-called donkey sentences, vague terms, epistemic modals, and more—see the references in Hansen 2015, \section five. That paper also serves as a good overview, covering a lot of the material here. For the speaker/semantic reference issue, see Ludwig 2007, Deutsch 2009, Ichikawa et al. 2012. The two recent monographs attacking the use of intuitions mentioned in the text, Cappelen 2013 and Deutsch 2015, also provide good overviews of the topic.

10

The End of Reference?

A natural way to think about the theories that we have surveyed in this book is as (sometimes) competing efforts to capture or describe a certain phenomenon: reference. On that picture, to theorize about reference is like theorizing about, say, human eyes. There's a certain kind of thing, eyes, and the various theories are right insofar as they correctly describe that kind of thing: as long as what the theory says is true about eyes, it is a good theory.

That's the optimistic picture of the debate over theories of reference. There's another, less optimistic, picture of the debate: the participants are *not* talking about the same thing. They are, instead, talking past each other. They are all using the term 'reference', but they mean different things by that term and so they are engaging in a merely *verbal dispute*. This final chapter explores this latter option. On this construal, philosophers who take themselves to be having *a substantive disagreement* about the nature of reference have (in many cases) been confused. They have, instead, been talking past one another. This, however, is a somewhat pessimistic note to leave things on, so we will end by showing that there's a way to resolve verbal disputes that can result in intellectual progress.

10.1 Background: Chalmers on Conceptual Pluralism, Verbal Disputes, and the Subscript Gambit

A good way to start thinking about these issues is within the framework outlined in David Chalmers' paper, 'Verbal disputes'. According to Chalmers, philosophers should endorse a form of *conceptual pluralism*. According to this view, 'there are multiple interesting concepts (corresponding to multiple interesting roles) in the vicinity of philosophical terms such as "semantic", "justified", "free", and not much of substance depends on which one goes with the term' (Chalmers 2011: 23). According to Chalmers, it might be that a term like 'free' denotes a particular concept, but even if it does, that's not particularly significant: there's a range of concepts in the vicinity of all (non-basic[1]) philosophical concepts:

> The model also leads to a sort of pluralism about the properties that these concepts pick out. For example, it naturally leads to semantic pluralism: there are many interesting sorts of quasi-semantic properties of expressions, playing different roles.   (Chalmers 2011: 23)

No one of these is privileged. Many of them are equally interesting and philosophically significant. So, Chalmers concludes, this view leads to a kind of philosophical pluralism. Here are some of Chalmers' illustrations:

> It leads to epistemic pluralism: there are many different epistemic relations, playing different roles. It leads to gene pluralism: there are many different things that deserve to be called 'genes', playing different roles. The same goes for confirmation pluralism, color pluralism, and so on.
> In fact, I am inclined to think that pluralism should be the default view for almost any philosophical concept. It may be that, as it happens, usage of a term such as 'gene' or 'confirmation' or whatever in our community is uniform enough that it has a single referent. But even so, there will be nearby possible communities, and probably numerous speakers within a community, who use the term in a different way, with equally interesting referents.   (Chalmers 2011: 23)

What happens to be picked out by a term like 'freedom' or 'reference' or 'knowledge' is arbitrary and relatively insignificant. But that doesn't mean the study of freedom or reference or knowledge is unimportant: there is an important constructive project here—the project of identifying all the relevant concepts in the vicinity and of seeing to what use they can be put.

Chalmers' view springs out of a deep skepticism about philosophy as it has been practiced throughout its history. Chalmers thinks that because we have not been aware of conceptual pluralism, and haven't engaged in the kind of conceptual engineering that he advocates (for more on conceptual engineering, see Cappelen (2018)), very many philosophical debates have been pointless wastes of time, because they have been verbal disputes. When we are not aware of conceptual pluralism, the following will often happen: one speaker will take, say, 'freedom' to express a

---

[1] Chalmers has a theory of basic (or what he calls 'bedrock') concepts—that will not concern us here.

property, P, and another speaker will take it to express property P*. They both continue to use the expression 'freedom' and that will give the appearance that they are disagreeing with each other. One will say: 'Freedom is F' and another will say 'Freedom is not F'. It looks like they are disagreeing. According to Chalmers, this form of pointless verbal dispute has characterized much of philosophy—and so much of philosophy is, he concludes, 'pointless'. The way to fix it is to engage in a form of conceptual engineering.

Here is what Chalmers suggests we do when we are faced with a dispute concerning a sentence, S, which might be a verbal, non-substantive dispute because the speakers mean different things by a term T:

- First: one bars the use (and the mention) of term T.
- Second: one tries to find a sentence S' in the newly restricted vocabulary such that the parties disagree non-verbally over S', and such that the disagreement over S' is part of the dispute over S.
- Third: if there is such an S', the dispute over S is not wholly verbal, or at least there is a substantive dispute in the vicinity.
- Fourth: if there is no such S' then the dispute over S is wholly verbal.

Here are three illustrations of the method at work. Consider first the question of whether O. J. Simpson is a murderer:

to adjudicate whether a dispute over whether O. J. Simpson is a murderer is verbal with respect to 'murderer', one may bar the use of the term. In this case, it is likely that will be various sentences S'... such that nonverbal dispute over S' is part of the original dispute: for example, did Simpson slash his wife's neck with a knife? If so, the original dispute is not wholly verbal.   (Chalmers 2011: 11–12)

Here is how we can use this to clarify the dispute over whether Pluto is a planet:

In the case of 'Pluto is a planet', one may bar the use of 'planet'. Here it may be hard to find any nonverbal dispute not involving the term 'planet' that is part of the original dispute. If there is no such dispute, then the dispute is verbal.
(Chalmers 2011:12)

In philosophy, Chalmers' advice is this: that when 'faced with a dispute that is potentially verbal with respect to a term *T*, one can simply ask the parties: can you state what you are disagreeing about without using (or mentioning) *T*?' (2011:15). So, for example, in the case of debates over free will, we should proceed as follows:

One party might say 'Freedom is the ability to do what one wants', while the other says 'Freedom is the ability to ultimately originate one's choices'. We can then introduce 'freedom$_1$' and 'freedom$_2$' for the two right-hand-sides here, and ask: do the parties differ over freedom$_1$ and freedom$_2$? Perhaps they will disagree over 'Freedom$_2$ is required for moral responsibility', or over 'Freedom$_1$ is what we truly value'. If so, this clarifies the debate. On the other hand, perhaps they will agree that freedom$_1$ conveys a certain watered-down moral responsibility, that freedom$_2$ would be really valuable but that freedom$_1$ is somewhat valuable, and so on. If so, this is a sign that the apparent disagreement over the nature of free will is merely verbal.   (Chalmers 2011: 16)

10.2 Chalmers' Strategy Applied to 'Reference'

Let's try to apply Chalmers' strategy to the central term in the debates we have surveyed in this book—'reference'. We have presented much of this debate as a debate over what reference *really* is. That way of putting it assumes that there's a unique relation that all these authors are trying to characterize—some do it right, and others get it wrong. But maybe Chalmers' analysis applies here: at least to a certain extent, these are verbal disputes. There are different relations in the neighborhood of what we talk about when we use 'reference' which are similar to a certain extent, but are different phenomena. To guard against verbal disputes in the philosophy of language, what we should do is break things down and do that by introducing new terms for the different relations. The experimental data from the previous chapter, if you are convinced by it, provides some additional motivation for this strategy: there seem to be many relations that different cultures have latched on to. Why think ours is the privileged one, or even that there is a privileged one? Maybe the right strategy is, as Chalmers suggests, to find a range of properties (or clusters of features) in this vicinity, and give them different names to ensure there's no danger of verbal disputes occurring. Then just talk about those clusters of features and stop worrying about the question: 'What is reference?'.

What would be the relevant properties 'in this vicinity'? Here are some possibilities drawn from the material in the first part of this book:

- Predicativists try to show that names don't refer. According to them, reference doesn't play a role in giving meaning of names. Note, however, that predicativists appeal to a property that's very similar to what we have called reference: naming plays an important role in the theory (see Section 7.5), and naming appeals to dubbings, involves rigidity, and causal chains. Names don't refer, they say, but for an object to be in the extension of 'Michael' is for it to be named Michael, and for an object to be named Michael, for the predicativist, requires pretty much what Kripke requires for a name to refer to Michael. So, even if names don't refer (in the Kripkean sense), it's something in the neighborhood. We could say that they 'refer$_1$'.

- Names, we said in the beginning, are non-descriptive—you don't need to know any properties of the named object in order to refer to it. Indexicals, we said, also refer. Note, however, that indexicals are not transparent in the following sense: you do need to know something about an object to refer to it with an indexical. In order to use 'I' to refer to yourself, for example, . . . you need to know that you are the speaker. That is to say, indexicals have a character which a speaker must know, and in this they differ from names. Indexicals also are not passed along in causal communicative chains in the way names are. So indexical reference is like name reference in some ways, but different in other ways. It's a property in the vicinity. So call that property 'reference$_2$'.

- In Chapter 3 we talked about reference to the non-existent, e.g. Sherlock Holmes. In these cases, the thing we have called 'reference' doesn't—arguably—relate an expression to an object that exists. There can still be something like Kripkean causal communicative chains, though: the name 'Sherlock Holmes' was introduced by Conan Doyle and then passed along, but this is not a chain that started with a dubbing. There is still something Kripkean going on here, but not of the standard kind. So while reference to the non-existent is like reference to everyday objects in some ways, it is also distinctive. Call this 'reference$_3$'.

- In Chapter 8 we talked about plural reference. This, again, is distinctive along many dimensions. In an important sense there is no reference to an object. There's reference to more than one object— to a plurality. Why not mark this as a special relation, similar in some ways to the other paradigms of reference, but also significantly distinctive? Call this 'reference$_4$'.

- In Chapter 6 we introduced the idea of arbitrary reference: a lecturer in a mathematics class begins an argument by saying 'Let "n" name an arbitrary number', and can then go on to use 'n' just as if it were any other name. We saw that such names have a general character: if one establishes that n has a certain property, one can thereby conclude that *all* numbers have that property. This distinguishes them from other referential devices, so let's say that rather than simply referring, such expressions 'refer$_5$'.

- We saw in Chapter 2 that many theorists have thought that strange things happen when names occur in belief contexts. In particular, expressions like 'Superman' and 'Clark Kent' cannot be substituted *salva veritate*: Lois Lane believes that Superman can fly is true, but Lois Lane does not believe that Clark Kent can fly. Let's give what we used to call 'reference in an opaque context' its own name: 'reference$_6$'.

- In Chapter 4 we saw that many philosophers are convinced by Perry's argument that certain kinds of reference have a special connection to agency. Let's give that relation, the relation that's specially related to agency, its own name: 'reference$_7$'.

- Rigidity has played an important role in recent discussions of what is called 'reference'. Since it's an important phenomenon in this domain, let's give it its own name—it already has the name 'rigidity', but if we wanted to we could call it 'reference$_8$' and say that any expression that is rigid 'refers$_8$'.

And so it goes. We now have a range of expressions: reference$_1$–reference$_n$. They denote different relationships that can hold between expressions (or uses of expressions) and aspects of the world. Or think of it like this: each subscripted 'reference' stands for a cluster of features—there's overlap between many of them, but there's no identity.

In response to this, it is natural to ask: What has been gained? We've got a bunch of new words, but what kind of progress is that? If all we have is a thicker dictionary, then there's no point to this exercise.

The central advantage is supposed to be this: we no longer care about the question: *which one is* **really** *reference*? (We have put that 'really' in bold to make clear that those who ask such questions think that they are **very deep and important questions**.) But the proponent of the Chalmers-inspired strategy says: No, I don't care about that. There is no **real** reference (and even if there is, it doesn't matter what it is). None of these relations is more entitled to the label 'reference' than any of the others. If we endorse that strategy, then what we used to call 'reference' has been abandoned as an object of study and instead we study a variety of phenomena, no one of which is reference. Reference is not something we theorize about anymore. It figures nowhere in our overall theory of language. Consider, for example, a predicativist saying: 'I have shown that names don't really refer!' The reply is: what you have shown, if you are right, is that names have certain features, F_1–F_n. If you are right, that's interesting, but it doesn't show that names don't really refer—that claim presupposes that there is another cluster of properties that's 'real' reference. That assumption is what we have let go of.

Here is an analogy: biologists used to care a lot about what life was. What are the conditions that need to be satisfied in order to be life? What, **really**, deep down, is life? It turned out to be a mess: there's a very complex and messy set of features: animals, plants, viruses, fungi, and other things are, in some sense, all alive, but it turned out to be impossible to find a set of features that all and only those instances of life shared. In the light of this, you might insist that one cluster of features is privileged: these features are what life **really** is. Biologists have, on the whole, given up on that way of thinking. They just talk about a bunch of features. Fungi have some of them, and animals others. The question of which ones are **really** alive is pointless. The suggestion here is that the question: 'What is it to really refer?' is like that—it should be abandoned. If we do that, then in a sense, it will mark the end of reference.

Central Points in Chapter 10

- Throughout this book we've been assuming that when people disagree about reference, there is some one thing they're both talking about. There is some one phenomenon in the world and, say, the Kripkeans are right and the descriptivists are wrong when they say that reference is rigid. But you can adopt a more pessimistic standpoint on the debate, and think that they're not actually disagreeing. You could think there's a range of reference-type relations: names exhibit one, descriptions another, predicates a third, and so on. Maybe the Kripkeans are right about name-reference, and the descriptivists right about descriptive-reference, but neither is right about reference simpliciter, because there's no such thing. Although they think they're in this big disagreement, they're mistaken.

- To make sense of this idea, we discussed David Chalmers' work on verbal disputes. Sometimes it can appear that two people are having a debate even though, in fact, they don't disagree about anything (at least anything relevant to the debate). If Ross kisses someone

(continued)

other than his girlfriend Rachel, who decided earlier in the day they shouldn't see each other for a while, he might say 'I didn't cheat: we were on a break', She might reply: 'You did cheat'. Although this looks like a dispute, there's a sense in which they're not disputing the underlying facts: both agree he kissed the other person. What they disagree about is the verbal question as to if that counts as 'cheating'. This, for Chalmers, is a verbal dispute.

- Chalmers argues that verbal disputes are endemic to philosophy. Consider the free will debate. Some (compatibilists) think that one does something freely provided one isn't compelled to do it, either by others or by, for example, addiction or brain injury. Others (determinists) think that freedom is more metaphysically heavyweight: one does something freely only if one's action isn't determined by some past state of the world over which one has no control in conjunction with the laws of nature. Although it may seem like they debate when, for example, they discuss whether my eating cake for breakfast was free (the one side saying that no one was holding a gun to my head, the other that the past state of the world in conjunction with the laws of nature meant I couldn't not eat the cake), they in fact need not really disagree. The compatibilists can agree that my action was metaphysically determined; the determinists can agree that it wasn't compelled by any agency outside my control. What they disagree about is what we should call 'free'.

- That can seem somewhat depressing. If philosophical debates are frequently verbal, doesn't that mean, in a sense, they're unimportant? What becomes of the big questions about freedom, morality, knowledge, and so on, that we care so much about? Chalmers argues verbal disputes don't impugn philosophy; rather, they support *conceptual pluralism*. Conceptual pluralism says that even if there isn't one 'freedom' concept, there are nevertheless two related concepts freedom$_{compatibilist}$ and freedom$_{determinist}$, each of which are themselves worth thinking about and studying. This move of getting rid of a concept and replacing it with related ones he calls the subscript gambit.

- We considered applying the subscript gambit to the puzzles about references we've studied in this book. Thus imagine predicativism were true, and names were predicates. Would that mean names don't refer? Well, on the one hand, we don't normally think of predicates as referring expressions. On the other hand, for the predicativist, names are very strange predicates–their metaseman-tics is the causal chain theory Kripke appealed to, which is a feature most people associate with reference. So the relation predicates bear to their bearers, for predicativism, is kind of like reference but kind of not like reference. So we can appeal to the subscript gambit, and call it reference$_1$. We showed the same thing can be said for many of the puzzles considered in this book. The end result is we get conceptual pluralism about reference.

Comprehension Questions
1. What is a verbal dispute?
2. Give some examples of verbal disputes from the news, TV, or your own experience.
3. Think of a core philosophical concept and spell out how concep-tual pluralism might apply to it.

Exploratory Questions

4. Is philosophy still a worthwhile enterprise if conceptual pluralism is widespread?
5. Do you think Chalmers is right that many philosophical debates are verbal?
6. Try to spell out precisely, using the distinction between a sentence and the proposition expressed by it, the conditions under which a given debate is verbal, and provide an illustration.

Further Reading
The notion of a verbal dispute pops up in several different areas of philosophy. Chalmers et al. 2009 contains several papers questioning whether fundamental questions in metaphysics are merely verbal disputes. Greco 2015 considers the question of whether epistemology may involve verbal disputes. Extended discussion about verbal dis-putes in the context of conceptual engineering can be found in Cappelen 2018, Chapter 17.

Bibliography

Ahmed, Arif (2007). *Saul Kripke*. Bloomsbury Academic.

Andow, James (2015). How distinctive is philosophers' intuition talk? *Metaphilosophy* 46 (4–5):515–38.

Bach, Kent (2004). Descriptions: Points of reference. In Marga Reimer and Anne Bezuidenhout (eds.), *Descriptions and Beyond*. Clarendon Press, 189–229.

Barcan Marcus, Ruth C. (1946). A functional calculus of first order based on strict implication. *Journal of Symbolic Logic* 11 (1):1–16.

Beebe, J. R. and Undercoffer, R. (2016). Individual and cross-cultural differences in semantic intuitions: New experimental findings. *Journal of Cognition and Culture* 16 (3–4):322–57.

Bengson, John (2013). Experimental attacks on intuitions and answers. *Philosophy and Phenomenological Research* 86 (3):495–532.

Bianchi, Andrea (ed.) (2015). *On Reference*. Oxford University Press.

Boghossian, Paul A. (1989). The rule-following considerations. *Mind* 98 (392): 507–49.

Boolos, George (1984). To be is to be a value of a variable (or to be some values of some variables). *Journal of Philosophy* 81 (8):430–49.

Braun, David M. (1998). Understanding belief reports. *Philosophical Review* 107 (4):555–95.

Braun, David (2005). Empty names, fictional names, mythical names. *Noûs* 39 (4):596–631.

Braun, David (2015). Indexicals. In Edward N. Zalta (ed.), *The Stanford Encyclopedia of Philosophy* (Spring 2015 Edition). Available at: http://plato.stanford.edu/archives/spr2015/entries/indexicals/

Breckenridge, Wylie and Magidor, Ofra (2012). Arbitrary reference. *Philosophical Studies* 158 (3):377–400.

Brock, Stuart (2002). Fictionalism about fictional characters. *Noûs* 36 (1):1–21.

Burge, Tyler (1973). Reference and proper names. *Journal of Philosophy* 70 (14):425–39.

Burge, Tyler (1979). Individualism and the mental. *Midwest Studies in Philosophy* 4 (1):73–122.

Burgess, Alexis and Sherman, Brett (eds.) (2014). *Metasemantics: New Essays on the Foundations of Meaning*. Oxford University Press.

Cappelen, Herman (2012). *Philosophy Without Intuitions*. Oxford University Press.

Cappelen, Herman (2018). *Fixing Language*. Oxford University Press.

Cappelen, Herman and Dever, Josh (2013). *The Inessential Indexical: On the Philosophical Insignificance of Perspective and the First Person*. Oxford University Press.

Cappelen, Herman and Dever, Josh (2016). *Context and Communication*. Oxford University Press.

Cappelen, Herman and Dever, Josh (draft). Action without the first person perspective. Available at: https://philpapers.org/archive/CAPAWT.pdf

Cappelen, Herman and Lepore, Ernie (2005). *Insensitive Semantics: A Defense of Semantic Minimalism and Speech Act Pluralism*. Blackwell Pub.

Castañeda, Hector-Neri (1967). Indicators and quasi-indicators. *American Philosophical Quarterly* 4 (2):85–100.

Chalmers, David J. (1996). *The Conscious Mind: In Search of a Fundamental Theory*. Oxford University Press.

Chalmers, David J. (2006). Two-dimensional semantics. In E. Lepore and B. Smith (eds.), *Oxford Handbook of the Philosophy of Language*. Oxford University Press, 274–607.

Chalmers, David J. (2011). Verbal disputes. *Philosophical Review* 120 (4):515–66.

Chalmers, David J. (2014). Intuitions in philosophy: a minimal defense. *Philosophical Studies* 171 (3):535–44.

Chalmers, David, Manley, David, and Wasserman, Ryan (2009). *Metametaphysics: New Essays on the Foundations of Ontology*. Oxford University Press.

Cotnoir, A. J. (2013). Composition as general identity. In Karen Bennett and Dean W. Zimmerman (eds.), *Oxford Studies in Metaphysics*, vol. 8. Oxford University Press, 294–322.

Crane, Tim (2013). *The Objects of Thought*. Oxford University Press.

Crimmins, Mark and Perry, John (1989). The prince and the phone booth: reporting puzzling beliefs. *Journal of Philosophy* 86 (12):685–711.

Davidson, Donald (1973). Radical interpretation. *Dialectica* 27 (1):314–28.

Deutsch, Max (2009). Experimental philosophy and the theory of reference. *Mind and Language* 24 (4):445–66.

Deutsch, Max (2015). *The Myth of the Intuitive*. MIT Press.

Devitt, Michael (2011). Experimental semantics. *Philosophy and Phenomenological Research* 82 (2):418–35.

Dorr, Cian (2010). Review of James Ladyman and Don Ross, *Every Thing Must Go: Metaphysics Naturalized*. *Notre Dame Philosophical Reviews* 2010 (6). Available at: http://ndpr.nd.edu/news/every-thing-must-go-metaphysics-naturalized/

Dorr, Cian and Hawthorne, John (2013). Naturalness. In Karen Bennett and Dean Zimmerman (eds.), *Oxford Studies in Metaphysics*, vol. 8. Oxford University Press 3–77.

Dummett, Michael (1973). *Frege: Philosophy of Language*. Duckworth.

Elbourne, Paul (2005). *Situations and Individuals*. MIT Press.

Evans, Gareth (1973). The causal theory of names. *Aristotelian Society Supplementary Volume* 47 (1):187–208.

Evans, Gareth (1982). *Varieties of Reference*. Oxford University Press.

Fara, Delia Graff (2001). Descriptions as predicates. *Philosophical Studies* 102 (1): 1–42.

Fara, Delia Graff (2015). Names are predicates. *Philosophical Review* 124 (1): 59–117.

Fine, Kit (1975). Vagueness, truth and logic. *Synthese* 30 (3–4):265–300.

Fine, Kit (1983). A defence of arbitrary objects. *Aristotelian Society Supplementary Volume* 57:55–89.

Fine, Kit (1985). *Reasoning with Arbitrary Objects*. Blackwell.

Fitch, G. W. (2004). *Saul Kripke*. Acumen.

Fodor, Jerry A. (1994). *The Elm and the Expert*. MIT Press.

Frege, Gottlob (1948). Sense and reference. *Philosophical Review* 57 (3):209–30.

Friend, Stacie (2007). Fictional characters. *Philosophy Compass* 2 (2):141–56.

García-Carpintero, Manuel and Torre, Stephan (eds.) (2016). *About Oneself: De Se Thought and Communication*. Oxford University Press.

Gettier, Edmund (1963). Is justified true belief knowledge? *Analysis* 23 (6):121–3.

Goodman, Nelson (1955). *Fact, Fiction, and Forecast*. Harvard University Press.

Greco, Daniel (2015). Verbal disputes in epistemology. *American Philosophical Quarterly* 52 (1):41–55.

Hansen, N. (2015). Experimental philosophy of language. In: *Oxford Handbooks Online*. Oxford University Press. doi: 10.1093/oxfordhb/9780199935314.013.53. Available at: http://centaur.reading.ac.uk/60327/

Haslanger, Sally (2012). *Resisting Reality: Social Construction and Social Critique*. Oxford University Press.

Hintikka, Jaakko (1999). The emperor's new intuitions. *Journal of Philosophy* 96 (3):127–47.

Ichikawa, Jonathan, Maitra, Ishani, and Weatherson, Brian (2012). In defense of a Kripkean dogma. *Philosophy and Phenomenological Research* 85 (1):56–68.

Jackman, Henry (1999). We live forwards but understand backwards: linguistic practices and future behavior. *Pacific Philosophical Quarterly* 80 (2):157–77.

Jackman, Henry (2005). Temporal externalism, deference, and our ordinary linguistic practice. *Pacific Philosophical Quarterly* 86 (3):365–80.

Jeshion, Robin (2015). Referentialism and predicativism about proper names. *Erkenntnis* 80 (S2):363–404.

Kaplan, David (1977/1989). Demonstratives. In Joseph Almog, John Perry, and Howard Wettstein (eds.), *Themes from Kaplan*. Oxford University Press, 481–563.

Kaplan, David (1989). Afterthoughts. In Joseph Almog, John Perry, and Howard Wettstein (eds.), *Themes from Kaplan*. Oxford University Press, 565–614.

Kearns, Stephen and Magidor, Ofra (2012). Semantic sovereignty. *Philosophy and Phenomenological Research* 85 (2):322–50.

King, Jeffrey C. (1991). Instantial terms, anaphora and arbitrary objects. *Philosophical Studies* 61 (3):239–65.

Kripke, Saul A. (1977). Speaker's reference and semantic reference. In Peter A. French, Theodore E. Uehling Jr, and Howard K. Wettstein (eds.), *Studies in the Philosophy of Language*. University of Minnesota Press, 255–96.

Kripke, Saul A. (1979/2011). A puzzle about belief. In A. Margalit (ed.), *Meaning and Use*. Reidel 239–83. Reprinted in Kripke, Saul A. (2011) *Philosophical Troubles: Collected Papers Volume 1*. Oxford University Press, 125–61.

Kripke, Saul A. (1980). *Naming and Necessity*. Harvard University Press.

Kripke, Saul A. (1982). *Wittgenstein on Rules and Private Language*. Harvard University Press.

Kripke, Saul A. (2013). *Reference and Existence: The John Locke Lectures*. Oxford University Press.

Lance, Mark N. and O'Leary-Hawthorne, John (1997). *The Grammar of Meaning*. Cambridge University Press.

Leckie, Gail (2013). The double life of names. *Philosophical Studies* 165 (3):1139–60.

Lewis, David (1970). How to define theoretical terms. *Journal of Philosophy* 67 (13):427–46.

Lewis, David (1978). Truth in fiction. *American Philosophical Quarterly* 15 (1):37–46.

Lewis, David (1979). Attitudes de dicto and de se. *Philosophical Review* 88 (4):513–43.

Lewis, David (1983). New work for a theory of universals. *Australasian Journal of Philosophy* 61 (4):343–77.

Lewis, David (1984). Putnam's paradox. *Australasian Journal of Philosophy* 62 (3):221–36.

Lewis, David (1993). Many, but almost one. In Keith Campbell, John Bacon, and Lloyd Reinhardt (eds.), *Ontology, Causality, and Mind: Essays on the Philosophy of D. M. Armstrong*. Cambridge University Press, 23–38.

Lewis, Karen (2013). Speaker's reference and anaphoric pronouns. *Philosophical Perspectives: Philosophy of Language* 27 (1):404–37.

Link, Godehard (1983). The logical analysis of plurals and mass terms: A lattice-theoretic approach. In P. Portner and B. H. Partee (eds.), *Formal Semantics—the Essential Readings*. Blackwell, 127–47.

Linnebo, Øystein (2014) Plural quantification. In Edward N. Zalta (ed.), *The Stanford Encyclopedia of Philosophy* (Fall 2014 Edition). Available at: http://plato.stanford.edu/archives/fall2014/entries/plural-quant/

Ludlow, Peter (2014). *Living Words: Meaning Underdetermination and the Dynamic Lexicon*. Oxford University Press.

Ludwig, Kirk (2007). The epistemology of thought experiments: first person versus third person approaches. In Peter A. French and Howard K. Wettstein (eds.), *Midwest Studies in Philosophy*. Blackwell Pub., 128–59.

Machery, Edouard (2012). Expertise and intuitions about reference. *THEORIA. Revista de Teoría, Historia y Fundamentos de la Ciencia* 27 (1): 37–54.

Machery, Edouard, Deutsch, Max, Mallon, Ron, Nichols, Shaun, Sytsma, Justin, and Stich, Stephen (2010). Semantic intuitions: reply to Lam. *Cognition* 117 (3):363–6.

Machery, Edouard, Mallon, Ron, Nichols, Shaun, and Stich, Stephen P. (2004). Semantics, cross-cultural style. *Cognition* 92 (3):1–12.

Machery, Edouard, Sytsma, Justin, and Deutsch, Max (2015). Speaker's reference and cross-cultural semantics. In A. Bianchi (ed.), *On Reference*. Oxford University Press, 62–77.

Magidor, Ofra (2015). The myth of the de se. *Philosophical Perspectives* 29 (1):249–83.

Matushansky, Ora (2008). On the linguistic complexity of proper names. *Linguistics and Philosophy* 31 (5):573–627.

McGinn, Colin (1983). *The Subjective View: Secondary Qualities and Indexical Thoughts*. Clarendon Press.

McKay, Thomas and Nelson, Michael (2014). Propositional attitude reports. In Edward N. Zalta (ed.), *The Stanford Encyclopedia of Philosophy* (Spring 2014 Edition). Available at: http://plato.stanford.edu/archives/spr2014/entries/prop-attitude-reports/

McKeever, Matthew (2016). Against Type E. PhD thesis, University of St Andrews.

Millikan, Ruth Garrett (1990). The myth of the essential indexical. *Noûs* 24 (5):723–34.

Moltmann, Friederike (1997). *Parts and Wholes in Semantics*. Oxford University Press.

Moltmann, Friederike (2012). Plural reference and reference to a plurality. linguistic facts and semantic analyses. In Massimiliano Carrara, Alexandra Arapinis, and Friederike Moltmann (eds.), *Unity and Plurality: Logic, Philosophy, and Semantics*. Oxford University Press, 93–120.

Nado, Jennifer (2014). Philosophical expertise. *Philosophy Compass* 9 (9):631–41.

Ninan, Dilip (2010). De se attitudes: ascription and communication. *Philosophy Compass* 5 (7):551–67.

Ninan, Dilip (2016). What is the problem of de se attitudes? In Manuel García-Carpintero and Stephan Torre (eds.), *About Oneself: De Se Thought and Communication*. Oxford University Press, 86–120.

Oliver, Alex and Smiley, Timothy (2013). *Plural Logic*. Oxford University Press.

Owens, David (2011). Deliberation and the first person. In Anthony E. Hatzimoysis (ed.), *Self-Knowledge*. Oxford University Press, 261–78.

Perry, John (1977). Frege on demonstratives. *Philosophical Review* 86 (4):474–97.

Perry, John (1979). The problem of the essential indexical. *Noûs* 13 (1):3–21.

Perry, John (1998). Myself and 'I'. In Marcelo Stamm (ed.), *Philosophie in Synthetischer Absicht*. Klett-Cotta, 83–103.

Plunkett, David (2015). Which concepts should we use?: Metalinguistic negotiations and the methodology of philosophy. *Inquiry* 58 (7–8):828–74.

Putnam, Hilary (1975). The meaning of 'meaning'. *Minnesota Studies in the Philosophy of Science* 7:131–93.

Quine, W. V. (1960). *Word and Object*. MIT Press.

Rayo, Agustín (2006). Beyond Plurals. In Agustín Rayo and Gabriel Uzquiano (eds.), *Absolute Generality*. Oxford University Press, 220–54.

Rayo, Agustín (2007). Plurals. *Philosophy Compass* 2:411–27.

Rami, Dolf (2015). The multiple uses of proper nouns. *Erkenntnis* 80 (S2):405–32.

Rumfitt, Ian (2005). Plural terms: Another variety of reference? In José Luis Bermúdez (ed.), *Thought, Reference, and Experience: Themes from the Philosophy of Gareth Evans*. Clarendon Press, 84–123.

Russell, Bertrand (1912). *The Problems of Philosophy*. H. Holt Pages.

Sainsbury, Mark (2005). *Reference Without Referents*. Clarendon Press.

Salmon, Nathan U. (1986). *Frege's Puzzle*. Ridgeview.

Salmon, Nathan (1991). The pragmatic fallacy. *Philosophical Studies* 63 (1):83–97.

Salmon, Nathan U. (2005). *Reference and Essence*. Prometheus Books.

Saul, Jennifer M. (1997). Substitution and simple sentences. *Analysis* 57 (2):102–8.

Saul, Jennifer M. (1998). The pragmatics of attitude ascription. *Philosophical Studies* 92 (3):363–89.

Schein, Barry (2006). Plurals. In Ernest Lepore and Barry Smith (eds.), *The Oxford Handbook of Philosophy of Language*. Oxford University Press, 716–67.

Schoubye, Anders J. (2017). Type-ambiguous names. *Mind* 126 (503):715–67.

Schwarzschild, Roger (1996). *Pluralities*. Springer.

Schwitzgebel, Eric and Cushman, Fiery (2012). Expertise in moral reasoning? Order effects on moral judgment in professional philosophers and non-philosophers. *Mind and Language* 27 (2):135–53.

Schwitzgebel, Eric and Cushman, Fiery (2015). Philosophers' biased judgments persist despite training, expertise and reflection. *Cognition* 141:127–37.

Sider, Theodore (2011). *Writing the Book of the World*. Oxford University Press.

Sloat, Clarence (1969). Proper nouns in English. *Language* 45: 26–30.

Soames, Scott (2002). *Beyond Rigidity: The Unfinished Semantic Agenda of Naming and Necessity.* Oxford University Press.

Soames, Scott (2003). *Philosophical Analysis in the Twentieth Century, Vol. 2: The Age of Meaning.* Princeton University Press.

Soames, Scott (2005). *Reference and Description: The Case Against Two-Dimensionalism.* Princeton University Press.

Soames, Scott (2010). *Philosophy of Language.* Princeton University Press.

Sorensen, Roy (2016). Vagueness. In Edward N. Zalta (ed.), *The Stanford Encyclopedia of Philosophy* (Winter 2016 Edition). Available at: https://plato.stanford.edu/archives/win2016/entries/vagueness/

Stich, Stephen (1996). *Deconstructing the Mind.* Oxford University Press.

Stoneham, Tom (2003). Temporal externalism. *Philosophical Papers* 32 (1):97–107.

Textor, Markus (2010). *Routledge Philosophy Guidebook to Frege on Sense and Reference.* Routledge.

Velleman, J. David (2015). *Foundations for Moral Relativism.* OpenBook Publishers (second expanded edition).

Weatherson, Brian (2003). What good are counterexamples? *Philosophical Studies* 115 (1):1–31.

Weinberg, Jonathan M., Gonnerman, Cha, Buckner, Cameron, and Alexander, Joshua (2010). Are philosophers expert intuiters? *Philosophical Psychology* 23 (3):331–55.

Williamson, Timothy (2007). *The Philosophy of Philosophy.* Blackwell.

Williamson, Timothy (2010). Necessitism, contingentism, and plural quantification. *Mind* 119 (475):657–748.

Williamson, Timothy (2013). *Modal Logic as Metaphysics.* Oxford University Press.

Index